KU-284-923

Introduction: The Female Tradition

Long before the present-day women's movement led to a re-evaluation of the goals of feminism in the nineteenth century, there had been those who felt <u>reluctant to measure women's needs by men's achievements.</u> Were women, asked Eleanor Rathbone in the thirties, "to behave for ever like a little girl running behind her big brother and calling out, 'Me too'?"[1] That her own "new feminism" came, in time, to be dismissed by newer feminists serves to show how complex and elusive is the goal of sexual equality; or, perhaps, of any equality. For it is not only the women's banner that has been inscribed with the words "me too" in the long column of social advance; and women have not been the only group who, as they attained a wished-for goal, have found the gap between themselves and those in front of them as great as ever.

Education was one of the goals glimpsed from a distance in the nineteenth century. The fight for girls' secondary and higher education originated in the 1860s when Emily Davies discovered the force of persistent and articulate cries of "me too"; insisting, first, that girls should be allowed to take the same examinations as boys, then that they should have schools like boys' schools and finally, colleges like men's colleges. The work of Miss Davies and other pioneers achieved results. The late nineteenth century saw what one contemporary hailed as a "renaissance" of girls' education. From being a rather daring venture, the girls' high school became commonplace. Women were admitted to universities; not, it is true, to the most prestigious, but even Oxford and Cambridge, in a fashion, learnt to accommodate women's colleges.[2] By and large, by the twentieth century, the impression was that the battle had been won.

This impression seems to have survived into the years beyond the Second World War. There were, of course, always individual women who felt insulted to emerge from the Tripos with only the "title" of a degree. There were those who, from their own experience, knew that many fewer scholarships and grants were available to girls than to boys; indeed, that authorities across the board offered girls inferior provision. But all this amounted mainly to a feeling that there would have to be a lot of catching up.

In the period since the war, girls, it seems, have had a chance to

I

catch up; so have children from the working classes. Yet between both and the head of the column there remains a formidable gap, the sight of which inspires suspicion in feminist as in socialist observers. "Men have bowed to the pressure of women," writes Dale Spender, "and have opened up many institutions and subjects to women, but men remain decidedly in control of the institutions and the subjects." So, while women have had some success in gaining entry to education, it is entry to *men's* education and "serves to reinforce male supremacy and control in our society".[3]

Whether or not we endorse the view that women have no education of their own, it is beyond question that, historically, what they fought for was access to men's. Emily Davies, in particular, continually resisted any idea of specially constituted women's courses leading to women's qualifications which, she knew, would be regarded as worthless. The choice which faced her and other pioneers was between driving girls through hoops which chanced to be the hoops set up for men (regardless of their intrinsic value) and accepting "feminine" variants which, as they were feminine, had no status. To choose the former, like Miss Davies at Girton, or like many a high school headmistress putting in her girls for the Cambridge Locals, did not solve all problems, however. Nowadays, historians of education note how the pioneers deferred to the precepts of a double conformity, re-defining, rather than rejecting, the Victorian feminine ideal.[4] At Girton or at Lady Margaret Hall or any of the early women's colleges, great importance attached to decorum, and young ladies were constrained to be ladylike whilst tackling everything required of young men. High school teachers of the new order still purveyed the social necessity of marriage and other values of a hidden curriculum. It is noted, too, that in the new institutions "women were likely to be presented with images of male authority" since the very success of these ventures depended on the patronage of men. Women barely figure on their governing bodies, and in fact the Council of Maria Grey's enterprise, the Girls' Public Day School Company, was dominated and chaired by men from its inception to the 1960s.[5]

At this point, it is tempting to ask what else could be expected, given the period, and how would Dale Spender or any other feminist set about defining women's education, so that we may know what we are aiming at? The answer seems to be, that in a society shot right through with patriarchal values, "it is easier said than done . . . to suggest that women's interests and experience should influence the

Wom

I. M. MARSH COLLEGE
LIBRARY
Acc. No. 57000
Class No. 796.07 FLE

G

LIVERPOOL POLYTECHNIC LIBRARY

3 1111 00155 1389

Fletcher, S
Women first: the female tradition in Eng
M M 796.07 FLE 1984

Women First

The Female Tradition in
English Physical Education 1880–1980

Sheila Fletcher

LIBRARY
LIVERPOOL POLYTECHNIC I.M. MARSH CAMPUS
BARKHILL ROAD, LIVERPOOL, 17.

THE ATHLONE PRESS
London & Dover, New Hampshire

First published 1984 by The Athlone Press Ltd
44 Bedford Row, London WC1R 4LY
51 Washington St, Dover, New Hampshire

© Sheila Fletcher 1984

British Library Cataloguing in Publication Data
Fletcher, Sheila
  Women first: the female tradition in
  English physical education 1880–1980.
  1. Physical education and training—England—
  History
  I. Title
  613.7'0942   GV201
  ISBN 0–485–11248–5
  ISBN 0–485–12046–1 Pbk

Library of Congress Catalog Card No 84–70367
Cataloguing in Duplication Data applied for

*All rights reserved. No part of this publication may be reproduced, stored in a retrieval
system, or transmitted in any form or by any means, electronic, mechanical,
photocopying or otherwise, without prior permission in writing from the publisher.*

Typeset by Inforum Ltd, Portsmouth.
Printed in Great Britain by Nene Litho, Earls Barton, Northants.
Bound by Woolnough Bookbinding, Wellingborough, Northants.

Contents

To my sister, Anne
and to my daughters
Meg, Emma and Katharine

Acknowledgements

My warmest thanks for support with this study must be given to the Old Students of Bedford College of Physical Education, without whose help it could not have been written. For this and the assistance of two former Principals, Eileen Alexander and Pat Bowen-West, as for the generous and lively interest of all who gave up time to be interviewed, I am most grateful. A matter for sadness is that Freda Holroyd and Margaret Rosewarne-Jenkins, who both greatly helped me to understand my theme, should have died before the book came out.

I am indebted to many others: to Gillian Sutherland for advice and encouragement, to Margaret Claydon, Irene Glaister and Janet Weaver for help with research, to Trevor May for photographic assistance, Felicity Hunt for critical discussion, Barbara Fletcher for lateral thinking and Robert Green for help in innumerable ways. I acknowledge gratefully the generous support given over several years by Erica Burgon, who has been a mainstay of the enterprise.

For permission to use illustrations from their collections I would like to thank the following: Thames Polytechnic, 1 and cover illustration; Michael Bunney Esq., 2; the Headmistress of Bedford High School, 4; the Physical Education Association of Great Britain and Northern Ireland, 5, 6, 10, 19, 20; Bedford Physical Education Old Students' Association, all other illustrations.

S.F.

Illustrations

Acknowledge permission to reproduce to Bedford Physical Education Old Students' Association, with the following exceptions:

Cover illustration and No. 1   Thames Polytechnic

No. 2   Michael Bunney Esq.

No. 4   The Headmistress of Bedford High School

Nos 5, 6, 10, 19, 20   The Physical Education Association of Great Britain and Northern Ireland curriculum".[6] In real life, there is nothing to match Virginia Woolf's poetic fancy which created a women's college free from the destructive values of education as defined by men.

> Let it be built on lines of its own . . . not of carved stone and stained glass, but of some cheap, easily combustible material which does not hoard dust and perpetuate traditions . . . Next, what should be taught in the new college? Not the arts of dominating other people; not the arts of ruling, of killing, of acquiring land and capital . . . It should explore the ways in which mind and body can be made to co-operate . . . it would be a place where society was free; not parcelled out into the miserable distinctions of rich and poor, of clever and stupid.[7]

Real-life proposals to adapt education to the "nature" of women have mostly come, though, from those who take masculine values as the norm. From the eugenists of the late nineteenth century to Sir John Newsom in the mid-twentieth, their cry has been that the norm must be adapted to take account of femininity, by laying on cookery in girls' schools, for instance. Nor have such views been confined to men. Among the headmistresses who succeeded the earliest "me too" generation, were several who felt that the assimilation of girls' to boys' schooling had gone too far. Best-known, perhaps, was Sara Burstall, a Cambridge-educated mathematician, who pushed the domestic arts very hard at Manchester High School in the early twentieth century.

While Miss Burstall and other headmistresses strove to achieve the right balance for girls between the academic and domestic side, the "masculine" and "feminine" parts of the curriculum, a new subject had established itself which cannot easily be assigned to either. This new subject was Swedish gymnastics, which from the later nineteenth century took a strong hold in the emerging high schools. It was in no sense "borrowed" from boys: so far as physical education was concerned, the English public school, then and long after, was obsessed with English team games. On the other hand, gymnastics does not happily fit into the "feminine" tradition either. It is true that, long before the high schools, callisthenic exercises had their place in the somewhat genteel curriculum thought appropriate to young ladies. But those who introduced Swedish gymnastics to English schoolgirls at the end of the century no more identified with callisthenics than the gym mistress of the 1930s did with the Women's League of Health and Beauty. The new gymnastics originated in the work of a man, Per

Henrik Ling, and was taken up in Sweden by both men and women, through the Royal Central Gymnastics Institute which he founded in Stockholm in 1814. Ling's achievement was to ground gymnastics on anatomy and physiology, thereby opening up the remedial and educational possibilities of exercise. Though some of his followers came to England, no attempt to import his methods succeeded here till, in 1878, the London School Board decided to appoint a Swedish woman gymnastics teacher to introduce them to the elementary schools.

This appointment, and still more another, of the woman later known as Madame Bergman-Österberg, may be regarded as the crucial factor in launching a new career for women. For Madame Österberg, in no time at all, had turned her back upon the elementary schools and the School Board, and started a college for the purpose of training gymnastic teachers for the new high schools for middle-class girls. At a time when women were trying very hard to make their way into men's professions, she created one specially for them. In a matter of a decade or so, through her own commitment, force of personality and flair for capturing favourable winds, she managed to ensure that Swedish gymnastics took its place in the curriculum of girls' schools side by side with such venerable borrowings from the masculine tradition as Latin, and from the feminine as cookery and art.

Madame Österberg has her place in histories of physical education, and though she would probably think it cramped (in the best-known, she gets something like a quarter of the space which is given to public school games)[8] even she might have to admit that there is a great deal else to be covered. It is not the founder, however, who is sold short, but the phenomenon she created. For what she started really took off. In the context of a growing market, two of her students launched their own colleges, and by the outbreak of the First World War, there was a tight little specialist empire – or commonwealth, rather – of six institutions: Dartford, which Madame Österberg had founded, Anstey and Bedford, founded by her pupils, with Chelsea, Liverpool and Dunfermline, of varied origin, but all, by this time, wholly committed to the gospel of Ling. Further, by means of the Ling Association (their promptly-formed professional body) the gymnasts ensured that their new profession was recruited as strictly as a medieval guild.

It was a women's guild. Men were not excluded, but for many years they were effectively shut out by their lack of appropriate training, for there were no colleges of physical training in England for men before

4

the 1930s. Men appeared, therefore, on the periphery of the sphere of influence the women created, a sphere extending well beyond the confines of the specialist women's colleges, and surviving, essentially intact, into the years beyond the Second World War. While it lasted, this was virtually a world in which all sources of power and standards of excellence pertained to women. The atmosphere of Anstey College in the thirties has been likened to that of a family, "and Miss Squire was the mother *and there was no father*".[9] What other worlds so lacked father-figures? Not the women's colleges at universities, for they remained everywhere offshore islands against a land mass of masculinity. Not it seems, the high schools and grammar schools for girls, with their male patronage and male governors. By comparison with everything else in the history of women's education, gymnastics was notably, if not uniquely, promoted, institutionalised and authorised by women. In that sense, it seems to form the nucleus of what could be described as a female tradition.

The distinctive quality of this tradition should not be submerged in the broader context of women's eruption into popular sport in the eighties and nineties, which is often held to demonstrate a growing tendency to emulate men. Is it not likely, asks a modern writer, A.D. Munrow, "that it was psychologically necessary for women and girls to take part in activities already known and practised by men?"[10] He was thinking of hockey, cycling, swimming and cricket, which women took up from the 1870s, and in this he was probably right. Not only did the women follow the men, but the new public schools for girls, lacking any obvious female model, drew heavily upon the boys' tradition. When it came to games there was a "me too" element. But far too little attention has been paid to the way in which Madame Österberg deliberately harnessed this phenomenon to her own ends. Those ends were, simply, to train young women to become what she sometimes called the "health mistress" in schools. The heart of their training was Swedish gymnastics, which was what she knew and believed in. But, as we shall see, she was perceptive enough to combine Ling's system with English team games. The picture of her as an alien on the hockey field, urging her students to kick the ball, is entertaining,[11] but those girls were being trained as specialist teachers of gymnastics *and* games – a kind of specialist who had no parallel in schools for boys, where games were normally run by the pupils with help from any master who was able and interested.

Games formed part, then, of that female tradition which this book sets out to explore, but, arguably, not the most central part, despite their great popularity with schoolgirls and with students of physical training. It was a tradition which stemmed, essentially, from Madame Österberg's promotion of gymnastics, and which developed through the training institutions created by herself and other women for that purpose. It was a tradition substantially unchallenged by men until after the Second World War, and even then it seemed to gain momentum for a time by moving ideologically away from Ling to the perceptions of Rudolf Laban, from formal gymnastics to Movement and Dance.

When Munrow wrote, in the 1970s, this female tradition was almost history. He was able to admire what the women had achieved in creating a specialist profession while regretting that, through "historical accident", they had worked for so long in isolation that by then it was proving hard to put the men's and women's viewpoints together. "There are now many signs of a unified profession." But he felt that the process of assimilation had advanced more slowly here than elsewhere; in the universities, for example. If this were true it would not be surprising, since assimilation in the universities has never meant more than adding women to the tradition established by men. The other way round, assimilation often seems to look like a takeover bid, as, for instance, with the male incursion into personnel management, housing property management, infant teaching, nursing, all of them professions established by women in the nineteenth century.

This takeover element has not been lacking in the field of physical education. Certainly the rising influence of men appears as both a cause and a manifestation of the way in which women have lost their headstart. But it has not been a simple process. The changing social base of secondary education (with the spread of comprehensive and mixed schooling), the public control and re-making of the colleges, the academic "jacking up" of the subject in successive bids for external validation, are all factors which, since the last war, have dissipated the female tradition. This is a study of its making and breaking, based, for the most part, on exploration of the history of one college, Bedford, which, as it remained for most of its existence in the hands of its founder, exemplifies the process with exceptional continuity. It is also an attempt to explore the experience of education controlled by women, albeit in a context far removed from anything envisaged by feminists today. Where education is controlled by men, women, Dale

6

Spender says, "do not learn much about the value and strength of women".[12] What did they learn of such qualities in the world of the specialist physical training college? Should we, for instance, expect to find here evidence of that "double conformity" which has been so marked in women's education? Before we come to such things we need to consider the roots of the tradition in the nineteenth century.

I

The Nineteenth Century

There is some difference between a boy and a girl, as there is
between . . . English heart of oak and delicate spun glass.
Charles Kingsley, 1869[1]

Boys and Girls

A society inclined, as was Victorian England, to maximise the difference between the sexes, will naturally interpret this not only in legal
and economic but in physical terms, especially if it is also disposed to
maximise the difference between rich and poor and so can afford, for
its upper classes, indulgence in an ideal of feminine weakness. The
experience of Victorian women, therefore, relative to the experience
of men, was circumscribed not only by such disabilities as inferior
property rights, disenfranchisement and poor education, but by
corsets and a hundred other things best described in negative terms:
not having their legs free, not swimming naked, not riding astride, not
participating in really vigorous games or gymnastics.

The history of team games speaks for itself. It is well known that
organised sport developed in England from the eighteenth century
out of traditional country pastimes, and no one who has read of those
fearsome encounters in which whole villages were engaged, or is
acquainted with the rustic idyll in the opening chapter of *Tom Brown's
Schooldays* can doubt that tradition's absolute virility. What the
Victorians added to it was the development of cricket and football as
part of the educational process appropriate to the ruling class. Public
school games acquired a mystique in character-forming and the training of leaders at a time when, with the expansion of Empire, leaders
were very much in demand. Cricket, as Tom Brown pointed out, was
more than a game; it was an institution.

'Yes,' said Arthur, 'the birthright of British boys old and young, as
habeas corpus and trial by jury are of British men.'[2]

Should *Tom Brown* be blamed for the cult of athleticism which
developed in the public schools? Many of them came to be obsessed

with games. Already in the sixties the Clarendon Commission found that at Eton over twenty hours a week were devoted by boys to cricket practice if they hoped for a place in the team. A few years later Wilkie Collins, sickened by so much glorification of "the mere physical qualities which an Englishman shares with the savage and the brute", presented as the villain of *Man and Wife* a man corrupted by physical prowess. His book did little to stem the tide, and, most likely, for everyone who read it, a hundred thrilled to Newbolt's evocation of the playing field and the field of battle:

There's a breathless hush in the Close tonight
Ten to make and the match to win –
A bumping pitch and a blinding light,
An hour to play and the last man in.
And it's not for the sake of a ribboned coat,
Or the selfish hope of a season's fame
But his captain's hand on his shoulder smote –
Play up! Play up! and play the game.

The sand of the desert is sodden and red –
Red with the wreck of a square that broke –
The Gatling's jammed and the Colonel dead,
And the regiment blind with dust and smoke,
The river of death has brimmed his banks
And England's far and Honour a name,
But the voice of a schoolboy rallies the ranks;
Play up! Play up! and play the game.

If we turn from indigenous games to gymnastics, imported into England in the early nineteenth century, women are scarcely less excluded. The gymnastic revival in Europe, it is true, owed a great deal to the ideas of Rousseau, and its pioneer, the German Guts Muths, was concerned with education, and not only for boys. But if the movement began in education, it developed mainly in the context of war. The gymnastics of Nachtegall in Copenhagen and of Ling in Stockholm attracted royal backing as an outlet for patriotic feeling and a means towards military preparedness in the uncertain Europe of Napoleon. In England, too, it was the military authorities who concerned themselves in this field, appointing a Swiss officer, Clias, in 1822 to organize gymnastics at Sandhurst, Woolwich, Greenwich and Chelsea. Clias was a disciple of Guts Muths but approached his subject from a military standpoint. His barrack-square commands are a sharp reminder that his system is designed for men; indeed, we see these muscular youths vaulting through his textbook, stripped for action. Some ten years later, in 1834, the same young men disport themselves in Donald Walker's *Manly Exercises*, swimming, climbing, leaping, running. It is another world from the wands and dumb-bells Walker thought appropriate for ladies. Archibald Maclaren, whose gymnasium in Oxford gained such fame that he was asked, in the sixties, to reorganize physical training in the Army, conceived of it in broad educational terms, well beyond the concept of military drill; but not beyond the concept of sex. The human being whose harmonious development he strives to promote is undoubtedly male, with faults that are the outcome of the way men live. He is conscious of schoolboys "growing to one side" because of lack of exercise and men at university ruining their health with excessive study; of "massive, powerful men from the farm, the quarry, the forge, the warehouse, and the wharf; and slight, half-formed, half-fed youths from the factory, the shop counter, the desk".[3] "The Battle of Life requires for combatant the *whole* man, not a part," he writes. One does not feel he could have said, "the whole woman".

If we wonder what girls were doing while boys were playing games and taking manly exercise, the answer, for the prosperous classes at least, is that a girl had to learn to be a lady. It would be hard to exaggerate the force of the ideal of the lady in the nineteenth century. Its psychological and sexual implications, its central role in the emerging class structure of an industrial society are topics which have been extensively investigated.[4] Its physical impact comes home to us sharply when we are forced to feel the contrast between physical freedom and gentility. "I was free to wander where I pleased about the park and woods, to row the boat . . . or ride my pony on . . . the sea-shore," wrote Frances Power Cobbe of her childhood in Ireland.[5] At sixteen, though, she was taken to Brighton to spend a year in a finishing school, exchanging this freedom for "dismal walks . . . parading the esplanade and neighbouring terraces" along with other girls and a governess, whose duty was "to utilise these brief hours of bodily exercise by hearing us repeat our French, Italian or German verbs, according to her own nationality".[6] Elizabeth Wordsworth, later Principal of the first women's college at Oxford, also left a home in the country for a school in Brighton and "crocodile" walks. "A good deal of my readiness to encourage games in later years, at Lady

Margaret Hall, is traceable," she wrote, "to my Brighton experiences."[7]

A girl not quite ladylike must learn to be so. The best-selling
novelist, Charlotte M. Yonge, created as the heroine of *The Daisy
Chain* a tomboyish schoolgirl, Ethel May (appeasing, perhaps, some
spirit of her own youth which may have been more chafed than she
admitted by exercising "three times round the gravel walk which
bounded what grandmamma called the premises".)[8] The hem of
Ethel's skirt is always muddy and liable to be caught in briars; elated,
she jumps three puddles in succession; she charges round the house
and knocks things over. It will not do. We are left in no doubt that
these small faults are actually big ones, since they proceed from a lack
of that restraint which is inseparable from true womanhood. Ethel's
physical exuberance reflects a mental exuberance which must be
subdued and the reader is invited to admire her because, in the end,
she subdues herself.

"Is it," asked Herbert Spencer in the sixties, "that the constitution
of a girl differs so entirely from that of a boy as to not need these active
exercises? Is it that a girl has none of the promptings to vociferous play
by which boys are impelled?" The question had been brought to his
notice by the striking contrast between two schools which existed in
his part of London. One was for boys: here the large garden had been
turned into an open space to make room for games and gymnastic
apparatus. Shouts and laughter as the boys rushed out to play were
audible to Spencer at frequent intervals.

> How unlike the picture offered by the "Establishment for Young
> Ladies!" Until the fact was pointed out, we actually did not know
> we had a girls' school as close to us as the school for boys. The
> garden, equally large with the other, affords no sign whatever of
> any provision for juvenile recreation; but is entirely laid out with
> prim grass-plots, gravel walks, shrubs and flowers, after the usual
> suburban style. During five months we have not once had our
> attention drawn to the premises by a shout or a laugh. Occasionally
> girls may be observed sauntering along the paths with their lesson-
> books in their hands, or else walking arm-in-arm. Once, indeed, we
> saw one chase another round the garden; but, with this exception,
> nothing like vigorous exertion has been visible.[9]

"Why this astonishing difference?" he inquires; and proceeds to offer
the answer: girls are conditioned to be ladylike. If Spencer had lived in

Camden Town he might have been heartened to catch a glimpse of girls on the see-saw which stood in the garden of the North London Collegiate School.[10] This was, of course, no typical "Young Ladies' Establishment". Its pioneer headmistress, Frances Buss, as she explained to the Taunton Commission in 1865, believed very strongly that mental exertion and bodily exercise should go together. But even Miss Buss, when it came to exercise for older pupils, had to fall back in the 1860s on the conventional "callisthenios".[11]

There is a world of meaning in the Oxford Dictionary's definition of callisthenics as "Gymnastic exercises suitable for girls". The Greek roots of the word mean "beautiful strength", which in itself, apparently, commended it to ladies for whom "training naked" (the roots of "gymnastics") showed that *that* could hardly be suitable,[12] Callisthenics, the dictionary says, is "a term of young ladies' boarding schools", describing forms of physical exercise which aim to develop the beauty of the figure and to promote a graceful carriage. Rhythmical movements with wooden rings and light wands were accompanied on the piano, and often directed by military men. Captain Chiosso, employed by Miss Buss in the mid-century, is typical of many; though, fittingly, the Quaker girls at Ackworth at this time were drilled by a civilian, the school tailor. There was no single callisthenic system. In some schools it was merely dancing and deportment; in others, an attempt was made to follow a scheme which claimed to be based upon physiology, such as the musical gymnastics devised by the American doctor, Dio Lewis. Miss Buss, who adopted Dr Lewis's system, found it excellent.

> Easy, graceful and not too fatiguing, gently calling every part of the body into play, by bright spirited music which cultivates rhythm of movement.[13]

These rhythmical movements, performed indoors, could become excessively boring, however. Designed, as one male educationist noted, to give the pupils a better style of walking, "they do not supply the vigour and joyousness which belongs to the free and healthy play of boys".[14] Frances Power Cobbe would have agreed with that. "Beside the dancing," she recalled,

> we had "callisthenic" lessons every week from a "Capitaine" Somebody, who put us through manifold exercises with poles and

dumb-bells. How much better a few good country scrambles would have been than all these callisthenics it is needless to say.[15]

Girls' schools were so private in the nineteenth century that what went on in them comes to us mainly through such anecdotes as hers; with one exception: the Taunton Commission, appointed in 1864 to inquire into the old grammar schools of England, investigated some girls' schools as well. The country was divided up into districts and for each one an Assistant Commissioner made his report, not only on the grammar schools but on such girls' schools as were willing to admit him. The result, across the board, was a severe indictment of the incompetence and triviality of most of what passed for girls' education. While the main concern was with academic standards, more than one report directed attention to the depressing lack of opportunity for girls to let off steam in vigorous sport. "If the professors of callisthenics would devise some games which would do for girls what cricket and football do for boys they would render a public service," wrote one of the ablest men, Joshua Fitch.[16] "Girls suffer very much from the want of good games," James Bryce concluded. "A girl of sixteen looks upon the skipping rope and similar diversions very much as a boy of sixteen looks upon marbles." At day schools he found no "genuine hearty play", while "a boarding school has to fall back upon the dreary two and two walk along the dusty highway or the dull suburban street."[17] "In girls' schools there is usually a garden . . . but not usually a playground in the strict sense of the word," observed another, adding that girls "do not seem for the most part to have many outdoor games."[18] The physical deficiencies of girls' education were stressed most forcibly in the report of Daniel Fearon, an Assistant Commissioner not too far removed in years from his own schooldays under a headmaster who had brought to Marlborough the great Dr Arnold's philosophy of organised games. "Boys," wrote Fearon,

> have in their schools this great advantage over girls, that when they come out from class they can generally fall to some game in which they take the keenest interest and become so absorbed that they forget their lessons . . . Boys who are engaged in cricket, football, rowing, fives . . . during the intervals between school hours, not only have their bodies well-exercised, but also have their minds diverted . . . into a totally different channel.

Girls, he went on, had no such opportunity.

> The out-door exercises which they get are not generally such as to thoroughly divert their minds whilst exercising their bodies; and consequently many girls . . . cannot prevent their minds from running on their tasks.

Walking, croquet, and the mixture of games known as *les grâces* were all that was offered.

> Most of these games are too desultory and require too little organization to afford any real diversion to the players' minds; while croquet, which is no doubt a game of some skill and much interest, is not a healthy game, because it necessitates much lounging and standing still, and a good deal of stooping.[19]

Fearon's report was based on an inspection of schools in London. He concluded by urging that country schools which had spare ground should provide their pupils with games "which shall be sufficiently violent to exercise thoroughly their bodies and sufficiently difficult to thoroughly divert their minds".

But schools in the country were no better. Croquet, archery, hoops and swings provided recreation at the twenty schools in Yorkshire for which returns were analysed by Fitch.[20] In one instance the girls played cricket but this was at a school with sixty-five pupils and no less than ten acres of ground. Most young ladies' establishments were cramped and took very small numbers; over half on his list had less than thirty pupils, while six were so small they could not have fielded two cricket teams.

It was one thing, however, to feel the lack of feminine games that were "sufficiently violent" and quite another to say what should be done. The Assistant Commissioners were enlightened men, all in varying degrees committed to the idea of raising up girls' education and confident that girls could take on Latin and other things regarded as essential for boys. But on the point of games they had little to suggest. Fearon, who was exceedingly conscious of the limitations of indoor exercise, ended nonetheless by advising for girls' schools the musical gymnastics of Dio Lewis. What were the alternatives? Hockey at this time was in that intermediate condition between a country sport and a formal game; lawn tennis had not yet been invented; and football, even Miss Lawrence of Roedean, thirty years later, was quick to dismiss as "for many reasons quite unsuited to girls".[21] Cricket might have done. Though female cricketers were not so much in vogue as in the eighteenth century they were not unheard-of, and girls played at home. "Lovely. We played cricket with the boys in the morning", Lucy Lyttelton noted in her diary on a summer's day in 1854.[22] Cricket at school, however, had different connotations. Serious team games and all they represented could not easily have been grafted at this time onto even the most forward-looking girls' school. "The independent republican spirit of boys' schools," wrote Miss Beale in 1866, "should not be fostered in those for girls."[23] Girls, she explained, should early be accustomed to feel the duty of submission to restrictions, and Cheltenham in these years reflected her view that "the vigorous exercise which boys get from cricket must be supplied in the case of girls by walking and callisthenic exercises".[24]

When the Taunton Commissioners published their report in 1868 it revealed so plainly the general decrepitude of the grammar schools that there was widespread backing for reform. An Act was passed appointing Endowed Schools Commissioners with power to reorganise the old foundations and, among other things, to take from them endowment, where it could be spared, to start grammar schools for girls. In practice this was easier said than done. The gross defects of girls' private education had been exposed in the Taunton Report but, not unnaturally, diversion of endowment was strongly resisted by the governors of boys' schools and any assignment made to girls usually had to be prised away. The reforming impetus was strong, however. The Endowed Schools Commissioners were resolute men, even feminist; and though before long the impetus slackened when the work was taken over by the Charity Commission, the Endowed Schools Act had netted for girls more than ninety schools by the turn of the century.[25] Over the same period some thirty-five high schools sprang from the initiative of Maria Grey, who in 1872 was responsible for launching the Girls' Public Day School Company. If by 1900 it is possible to speak, then, of a *system* of secondary education for girls, in the sense of schools of acknowledged quality sharing common aims, these were its main components, loosely, informally held together through the Head Mistresses' Association formed by Miss Buss in 1874. With them, but not of them, were the new girls' public schools, the Rugbys of the movement: St Leonard's School, St Andrews, founded in 1877; Roedean, established in 1885, Wycombe Abbey in 1898. In another constellation were the new women's colleges started in the seventies at Oxford and Cambridge. It was an era which inspired one contemporary to write of a "renaissance" in girls' education.[26] In more mundane terms, the period created a complex of middle-class institutions without which Madame Bergman-Österberg's crusade for girls' physical education would have had no base.

Madame Österberg and the London School Board

It was not, in fact, the base from which she started. Her decision to concentrate on training teachers of physical education for the prosperous classes followed work in a very different stratum of society. As Miss Bergman she had been appointed in 1881 by the London School Board to superintend the physical education of girls and infants at schools in the metropolis. Her qualification was that she had trained at the Royal Central Gymnastics Institute founded in Stockholm in 1814 to promote the system of Per Henrik Ling.

Ling had developed his work in a context far removed from the London Board Schools. He was a patriot, eager to restore his country's pride after military defeats in the early years of the nineteenth century. Ling was very far, though, from confining himself to the military aspect of gymnastics, which was only one of the four categories into which he classified the subject. The others were medical (or remedial), educational, and aesthetic. His study of anatomy and physiology had convinced him of the therapeutic value of exercises based on scientific principles. His aim was to promote the harmonious development of the whole body through a system which progressed in its demands upon strength and skill, and included simple, free-standing exercises as well as work with apparatus. Long before Miss Bergman attended as a student, the Royal Central Gymnastics Institute had become a kind of temple to Ling; but in England, though one or two medical men employed his remedial exercises, Ling's gymnastics were scarcely known. In 1860 Edwin Chadwick, the public health reformer, commended them strongly as a means of counteracting the physical restrictiveness of girls' education – so harmful, he said, that

> in Sweden a special system of school gymnastics for females, formed by a celebrated medical professor of the name of Ling, has been long introduced . . . In England, mothers of the middle and higher classes take their daughters into the towns to receive dancing lessons. In Sweden, mothers of the same class take their daughters into Stockholm to receive gymnastic training . . .[27]

However, the gymnastic fashion of the day (and gymnastic clubs, some catering for women, were becoming popular in England) favoured not the Swedish but the German system, based, at some remove, on the work of Guts Muths. And the German approach, which gave prominence to skill on the parallel bar, the rings and trapeze, to dumb-bell exercises and figure marching, was a far cry from Ling's therapeutic bias (dismissed by Maclaren of the Oxford Gymnasium as "suitable to the invalid only").[28] The most dedicated publicist of Ling's work in England was Mathias Roth, a Hungarian doctor, who urged its educational merits for over twenty years from the 1850s before he succeeded in capturing the interest of the London School Board. In retrospect, it is easy to see that for most of that time he was casting seed upon particularly stony ground. The Education Department had abandoned the enterprising spirit of its formative years. Keeping down expenditure through the Revised Code had become a preoccupation which not even public interest in military efficiency following the Crimean War could overcome. In 1862 a proposal of Lord Elcho that elementary schoolchildren should be given drill to fit them for "possible Military Service" was rejected on the score of expense.[29]

Dr Roth persevered meanwhile in his solitary campaign to enlighten the government.[30] Undeterred by the indifferent reception of an earlier pamphlet addressed to Lord Granville, in 1870 he published "A plea for the compulsory teaching of the elements of physical education in our National Elementary Schools". It achieved nothing. That military drill (for boys) was admitted the following year as a grant-earning subject was hardly an achievement in the eyes of one committed to the ideals of Ling. How far it fell short can be seen from Roth's address in 1875 to the Social Science Association. The subject of his paper was "School Hygiene and Scientific Physical Education". Physical *education* is the phrase he uses and it is what he means (not physical training). But few, he admits, for all his efforts, have taken up Physical Education "in its true meaning". The teacher in this field needs to have a knowledge "of the structure and functions of the various organs of the human body . . . of hygiene and the sanitary laws [and] of the free exercises of Ling'. Thirty years before the nation was alerted to the wretched physique of Boer War recruits, Dr Roth produced figures to demonstrate the large-scale rejection of recruits for the army. The battle for good health must begin in the schools. "The teacher must be for every individual what the Officer of Health is for the parish."[31]

Only one, it seems, of her Majesty's Inspectors showed any interest in Roth's crusade, and there is no doubt that the missionary spirit regarding elementary education at this time resided, not among inspectors and officials administering the 1870 Act, but among members of the larger School Boards which were elected under its provisions. Of these, the London School Board was pre-eminent – for its size, the scale of its problems, the distinction and commitment of its membership. Very early on the Board had instructed a curriculum sub-committee, chaired by Huxley, that means should be provided in the schools for "physical training, exercise and drill".[32] Later, it encouraged the teaching of swimming, fitted school playgrounds with apparatus, and in some cases even made arrangments to keep them open out of school hours. The way in which the Board was persuaded to attend to the physical education of girls is an apt illustration of the use women made of one of the earliest civil rights granted them: the right to vote for, and to sit on School Boards. Mrs Alice Westlake, who represented Marylebone, certainly never achieved the renown of Margaret McMillan on the Bradford School Board, or of the first women elected in London: Elizabeth Garrett and Emily Davies. However, it was she who transformed a situation in which the physical well-being of girls in London elementary schools was virtually ignored. Boys had the drill sergeant, hired from the Army. Girls, she found – and she took a committee into slum schools to see for themselves – had something called "desk drill", "rather a means of securing proper discipline than . . . physical exercise"; or, in a few schools, they stood upon the benches in the classroom and did arm movements.[33]

Mrs Westlake was convinced by Dr Roth of the therapeutic value of Ling's system and he came before her committee to describe it, together with Miss Löfving, a gymnast from Stockholm. The upshot was that on the recommendation of this sub-committee Miss Löfving was appointed by the London School Board as "Superintendent of Physical Education in Girls' Schools".[34] From 1879 until 1881 she lectured, demonstrated and examined teachers in gymnastics, anatomy and physiology, urging her case with the vigour natural to an exponent of the Swedish tradition, of which women had long been part. "Women need health as well as men", Ling had stated, and regular women's courses were organised at the Central Institute from 1862. "Surely the sound development of . . . girls is not less important than that of boys," urged Miss Löfving, adding that in England it almost seemed to be left to chance. "There are many girls' schools where the children have no kind of exercise whatever, not even time for play."[35] She would have liked to see in England a college on the lines of the Swedish Institute; in fact, it was a question of doing what was possible with the indifferent facilities to hand. Just before she left she had the satisfaction of royal patronage at a display of Swedish exercises by Board School girls. The children came from all parts of the metropolis "and their appearance broadly illustrated the great contrasts of London life. The children from suburban schools were clean and neat; those from Drury Lane and the Seven Dials, some only six or seven years of age, wore the worn-out boots and stockings of women."[36] Though they came together from different schools for the first time they performed superbly. As *The Times* noted, in an hour and a half "not one stepped off with the wrong foot". The work was much applauded, and at the end Miss Löfving was presented to Princess Louise.

Mrs Westlake and her supporters had to contend with some resistance from the economy party on the School Board in their efforts to replace Miss Löfving with another expert from Sweden but, in the event, the appointment was made in December 1881 of Martina Bergman – later Madame Österberg. The work went on. Three nights a week, from 7.0p.m. to 8.30p.m., Miss Bergman gave classes to women teachers. One mistress from each school was required to attend; most were unaccustomed to vigorous exercise but they qualified in increasing numbers for the certificate issued by the School Board to those who passed the end-of-course examination.[37] When Miss Bergman arrived she had found eighty teachers trained in physical education; when she left the post six years later over 700 had received the certificate, and Ling was known in almost every Board School, slowly but surely, as she said, replacing "the many irrational exercises hitherto practised". Where the work was done well, "the stiff unnatural carriage of the 'old' schoolgirl disappears, her awkward, noisy way of marching gives way to easy, good walking and, above all, her body develops normally and gracefully". There was still the problem of the cramped positions which teachers allowed, or caused children to assume. "It is not rare to see children . . . twisted into the most unnatural contortions. The position of folded arms in front of the chest or on the back (the position most common during reading lessons) is a very injurious one from a physical point of view."

Out of doors, she thought, much more could be done with "the spacious, airy playgrounds". She looked to a future when outdoor games would be played as generally by girls as by boys. But "children need a leader in their games [and] the girls' playground will never be of real benefit until the mistresses themselves become interested and skilful players of 'fives' and 'lawn tennis' ".[38]

Fives and lawn tennis were a long remove from the experience of most Board School children and Ling's free-standing gymnastics (in the classroom) may appear a cut-price offer today. "There never has been a more efficient system of exercising many bodies in limited space and limited time," says A.D. Munrow.[39] And that is true. For free-standing work, as Madame Österberg explained, "we do not need apparatus or a large floor space . . . The exercises can be done in any schoolroom as long as there are not more than two children in each desk."[40] If her phrase "free exercises" seems a misnomer, when half the children stood on the seats and half on the floor between the desks, it must be remembered that in her view, and the view of everyone committed to Ling, this "free" work was the essence of the system. The necessary physiological progression was provided for at this stage, and apparatus work was supplementary. Madame Österberg was most emphatic, when she appeared before the Cross Commission, that though apparatus work had to be omitted, "The most important part, and the one which really develops the child best, is not omitted. The part which we practise with the children is the fundamental and the most necessary part."[41] She, too, spoke of physical "education". If the Government saw the deficiencies of drill "and enforced a real educational system, the system . . . should be the best there is to be got". The London School Board had set the right example in introducing Ling's Swedish system "which is the most scientific of all".[42]

She was an admirable publicist. In her early days in London she held Open Practices, to which both parents and teachers were invited. In June 1883 her girls stole the show at a display of drill and exercises before the Prince and Princess of Wales at Knighton Park, the residence of Edward Buxton, who was chairman of the London School Board. A hundred little girls, between four and seven, from Islington, Limehouse, the Borough, Bermondsey, Poplar and Ratcliff performed the motions "by which the neck and spine, the joints and every muscle . . . were brought into active and harmonious exercise, the lungs being exercised by singing and counting". The motley costume of the children was contained by their all wearing white caps

with red ribbons, and the style and discipline with which they exercised inspired the Prince to call it "a remarkable sight" and to
compliment the London School Board on doing work that was so
badly needed, "considering the localities from which those children
come".[43]

In May and June of 1884 a class of forty girls directed by Miss
Bergman performed at the International Health Exhibition and won
the Exhibition's Gold Medal for their work. The same year, girls and
boys (for the Swedish system was being tried with boys now) gave a
display in a Swedish gymnasium constructed in a Board School. The
girls, "in blue serge tunics and knickerbockers, with light blue sashes
round their waists", climbed ropes, performed on the horizontal bar
and earned applause for swarming up a climbing frame and slipping in
and out of it "with great ease and grace".[44] The close of Miss
Bergman's career with the School Board saw an impressive gymnastic
display at the Crystal Palace in 1887.

Madame Bergman-Österberg, as she was known from her marriage
the previous year, resigned in October 1887 in order to be able to
devote herself to the private physical training college which she had
already started. When her Hampstead Gymnasium launched four
students in 1885 on a full-time course in physical education, England
for the first time had its counterpart, however modest, to the Institute
in Sweden. And Madame Österberg had what no one who knew her
could have doubted she would have to have: a place of her own. As its
minutes show, the School Board's sub-committee got across her now
and then. Differences arose when they felt she went ahead without
seeking approval, employed her assistants on private work, and so
on.[45] In Hampstead she was "totally undisturbed by committee resolutions, untrammelled by inspection, and never interfered with . . .
she had the great advantage of being left alone . . . the whole work
being carried out as she thought".[46]

More than that, though: she had a vision, but it was not the vision of
Roth. Roth spoke strongly about sickly children, children of inferior
stature and physique, with chest complaints and spinal deformities,
for whom the teacher must be Officer of Health. Madame Österberg
was more realistic about what teachers could hope to achieve. When
the Cross Commissioners raised with her the question of gymnastics
for underfed children she allowed that little could be done. "If they
are starving I think it is better for them not to have any exercises."[47]
The *Woman's Herald* in 1891 chose to enthuse about her work for "the

poorest and the most neglected of London children", but by then she had given up the slums. It was not there that her vision could be realised. Madame Österberg, like others in her day who were eager to improve the race, felt bound to pin her hopes on the prosperous classes. The goals of physical education she defined as "*individual* and *race perfection*", to be attained by "the maximum of *health*, through increased organic development and activity; by the maximum of *beauty*, by harmonious development of the human form, and by increased *moral consciousness* through a more perfect . . . balance between the physical, intellectual and moral faculties. These qualities, transmitted by inheritance, will perfect the race". And Woman, in her view, was "the first factor" in race regeneration.[48] But not any sort of woman. "Let me air a grievance. I have got a fatal reputation in this country for being able "to make a woman out of any girl" . . . Now this is what I can not do. I can not make bricks without straw, or rather, not the kind of bricks I should like to make for England . . . Give me therefore the best of your womanhood . . . it will not be too good for my profession."[49]

To one of her students she recalled the reasons for her parting from the School Board: these were simply that the foundations of a healthy womanhood could never have been laid in the working classes.

> The physique of this class was so lowered and impaired by neglect and by bad conditions of housing, food and clothing, that unless the conditions could be changed, no radical improvement could be effected.

Feeling this, then, she had decided "that the secondary schools must be attacked and the foundations laid for an invigorated womanhood in classes which enjoyed happier conditions".[50] "Is it not rather funny that you here in England think that what is good for the poor cannot be good for the rich?" asked Madame Österberg, adding that this view had not impeded her for long. "I built the College and Gymnasium in 1885 and since then have been steadily working to improve the physical development of women in the upper and middle classes."[51] Here was the beginning of what was to evolve as a female tradition, and its earliest exponents were greatly admired by the writer for *Woman's Herald* who interviewed Madame in 1891.

> The sight of these strong, healthy, well-developed and happy girls, in full enjoyment of all that makes life beautiful, struck me very

forcibly, when compared with the ordinary stunted woman forced by unfortunate circumstances to struggle for existence.[52]

2

Too Good to Fail

"How do you account, Madame Bergman-Österberg," I asked, "for the signal success with which you have carried out this college plan, something quite new to us in England, you know?"

"I never for one minute doubted that I should succeed. The idea of training the body as carefully as we do the mind is too good to fail."
Woman's Herald, 20 June 1891

The overweening confidence of Madame Bergman-Österberg stands out, even at a century's remove. Did Emily Davies ever claim that Girton was an idea "too good to fail"? Did Miss Buss aver that "never for one minute" had she doubted that she would succeed? On the contrary, she doubted many times; and while it is true that the clock had moved on a little since those early pioneering days, one wonders whether Madame Österberg's buoyancy may not have owed something to imperfect perception of the deep conservatism of a culture which, after all, was not her own. Did she, for instance, when she spoke of training bodies "as carefully as we do the mind", understand how new and precarious was the idea of training the mind – the *female* mind – in England at this time; how superfluous it seemed still, not only at many a Cambridge high table, but up and down the country, to many a governor of many an English grammar school?[1] As for training bodies, was she aware of the anxiety currently expressed by medical men about women and athletics, anxiety shared by more than one of the small band of medical *women*? In an article entitled "Woman as an Athlete" Arabella Kenealy L.R.C.P. set out the imaginary case of "Clara":

A year ago Clara could not walk more than two miles without tiring; now [since taking up athletics] she can play tennis or hockey, or can bicycle all day without feeling it.

But at what cost! Clara has sacrificed the elusive aura of womanliness. Though still good-looking, "the haze, the elusiveness, the subtle suggestion of the face are gone". Indeed, she is acquiring a "bicycle face", that is, "the face of muscular tension". Formerly, we learn, she

25

had "an air of gliding rather than of striding from one place to another". Her voice is louder now, her tones are assertive and she is often out on her bicycle when she should be helping Tom with his lessons or sewing a new ribbon in Rosy's hat. Worst of all, Clara's athletic pursuits will jeopardize her future offspring. "For Nature knows what are the faculties whence this new muscle-energy is born. She knows it is the birthright of the babies Clara and her sister athletes are squandering."[2]

There are eugenic overtones here which we must return to, but Dr Kenealy's views on the squandering of maternal energy were not unusual at a time when it was thought that people had only so much energy to spend: if more were spent one way there was less to spend another. "Nature is a strict accountant," Spencer had written in 1861, "and if you demand of her in one direction more than she is prepared to lay out, she balances the account by making a deduction elsewhere."[3] His warning was repeated by Henry Maudsley, professor of medical jurisprudence, who in 1874 touched off a long controversy with his article "Sex in Mind and in Education". What concerned Maudsley was expenditure of energy through the demands of higher education. Girls took part in the intellectual race "at a cost to their strength and health", he said, and could be disabled "for the adequate performance of the natural functions of their sex".[4] In 1886 Dr William Withers Moore took female education as the theme of his address to the British Medical Association, giving his view that the educated woman, if not unsexed, would be "more or less sexless", and the human race would lose those who should have been its sons. "Bacon, for want of a mother, will not be born."[5]

To a medical profession already disturbed at the idea of Girton and the high schools, the growing enthusiasm for sport among women brought no comfort, and particular anxiety focused on the hazards of adolescence. Miss Creak, headmistress of the newly-founded King Edward VI School for Girls in Birmingham, would not allow hockey in the 1880s since her doctor advised that there was "great danger of girls getting permanent injury in vital parts if they indulged in such a rough and dangerous game".[6] A well-padded corset for female cricketers was recommended in an article in *The Lancet* in 1885, since "a severe blow on the breast might lead to serious consequences in fully developed women by excitation of any latent tendency to cancer, and in young girls by arresting development of the mammary gland".[7] Madame Österberg, then, embarked on her enterprise at a time when medical opinion was ambivalent about strenuous physical exercise for women; and this ambivalence, as in the case of Dr Kenealy, often reflected a concern with eugenics. Eugenics was an important strand in the complex of beliefs lumped together under the label "Social Darwinism", which took as their starting point the notion that a struggle for the survival of the fittest took place among human beings as among animals and plants. The word "eugenics" was coined in 1883 by Francis Galton, Charles Darwin's cousin, to describe sciences for the management of human heredity in the interests of improving the stock. The late nineteenth and early twentieth century saw a rising and ever more complex debate on "the quality of the race" and "national efficiency" which touched at many points on the role of women, and from which there emerged a whole range of pre-scriptions, many of them issued in the name of eugenics. Public receptiveness to such ideas was ensured in Edwardian Britain by the humiliations of the Boer War and by growing awareness of German rivalry in both economic and military terms. Social Darwinism did not constitute a coherent body of doctrine, however. "National effi-ciency" was called in aid by a wide range of experts and laymen, and in support of such diverse proposals as the introduction of cookery in girls' schools and sterilisation of the unfit.[8] Arabella Kenealy was only one of a number of doctors to make a contribution. In reply to feminist criticism of her article on "Clara", she came back with another in which she contrasted the beautiful children born to "An intensely womanly woman" of her acquaintance with "the puny sickliness, the spectacled, knock-kneed physiques" of the offspring of "a handsome muscular person, who is adept with her tennis racquet and a zealous cyclist". "The muscular reformer," she averred, "sees as woman's highest goal her capacity for doing things that men do, whereas her true value lies in her capacity for doing things men cannot do."[9]

This true value appertained especially to middle-class girls (that is, the category from which Madame Österberg drew her students), for a main strand in eugenist anxiety was that the poor would out-breed the middle classes. In this context, more than one doctor saw hockey as, potentially, a threat to the race. Dr Mary Scharlieb's view in 1911 was that

> Doctors and schoolmistresses observe that excessive devotion to athletics and gymnastics tends to produce what may perhaps be called the "neuter" type of girl . . . Her figure, instead of develop-

ing to full feminine grace, remains childish . . . she is flat-chested, with a badly-developed bust, her hips are narrow and in too many instances there is a corresponding failure in function.[10]

A few years earlier, another woman doctor had warned against "making physical health and strength the principal aim of our national well-being . . . There is a danger of making a fetish of exercise, and this is becoming increasingly marked amongst women".[11] "The pendulum has probably swung too far in the direction of over-exertion," wrote the headmistress of Manchester High School.[12]

There is no sign that such anxieties impaired the confidence of Madame Österberg. She was ready to admit that games, overdone, "may produce weakness instead of strength, bad habits instead of good ones . . . the same may be said about bicycling and swimming".[13] On the other hand, she was emphatic that properly regulated physical exercise was "the best training for motherhood".[14]

> The real aim of gymnastics is health. Taken in time they prevent bad habits, they correct bad posture and are conducive to correct movement. They are the necessary accompaniment of methodical games, to counteract one-sided development.[15]

Certain, it seems, that she had got the balance right, Madame Österberg was proud to associate herself with "the invaluable anthropological researches and anthropometrical experiments of Dr Francis Galton".[16] She measured the height, weight, lung capacity and muscular strength of her students regularly and sent them for sessions at Galton's laboratory in the South Kensington Museum. She certainly identified with public concern following the report in 1904 of the Interdepartmental Committee on Physical Deterioration, and offered Ling in the fight against decline in a nation which she seems to have backed to the hilt. "We mourn him not in black but remember him in Red, White and Blue" was the inscription which met her students on the death of King Edward, over a portrait she had draped in the Colours;[17] and she spoke readily of race regeneration.

> I try to train my girls to help raise their own sex, and so to accelerate the progress of the race; for unless the women are strong, healthy, pure, and true, how can the race progress?[18]

Her view of such progress did not depend, though, on preserving "Clara" from physical rigour. The course of training which she offered (and which became standard in the specialist colleges) could be called gruelling. Students were kept at it, with their gymnastics, their anatomy, physiology and hygiene, their demonstration lessons, games, remedial work and silent study, from the early morning cold bath till they went to bed. They were subjected to rigorous discipline. They were specifically taught to *command*. How could what Dr Kenealy regarded as the essential quality of Woman, "a species of aura, magnetic charm . . . a womanly potency imparting rest . . . without [which] woman is as incomplete as is a flower without perfume",[19] survive this?

Madame Österberg was herself inclined to talk of girls as if they were flowers. Her "English flowers" was the phrase she used, when in Sweden, referring to her students. To the Women's International Congress she began, "There may be those among you who, like myself, have watched the growth of girls and flowers". "For our educators," she affirmed elsewhere, "we want the flower of the race".[20] This romantic imagery was at variance, though, with her hard-hitting line on women's professions. She set out to create a new female profession, that of the specialist in physical education, and was exceedingly proud to have done so. Looking back, towards the end of her life, she recalled that as the result of her efforts, "A new profession, adequately remunerated, was thus created for woman, *one of the few which she herself has initiated.*"[21] As the *Woman's Herald* correspondent recorded, Madame Österberg was

> a sound Liberal and naturally thinks that women should have a vote. She is a warm supporter of her own sex and hopes to see all professions and trades open to women equally with men. She maintains that woman's *economical independence* will be of the very greatest importance in the question of her general emancipation.[22]

Feminist ideals did not always go well with the ideals of the eugenists, for there was at least the prospect of a clash between Woman's self-fulfilment and the progress of the race. None of this seems to have troubled Madame Österberg. While she took no active part in the English movement for female suffrage (apart from small donations to women's societies), she gave substantially to the Swedish movement and bequeathed a fund to help Swedish women "who devote themselves to study or the professions".[23] The different, and potentially conflicting, elements in her thinking appear in one obituary, which records that she regarded her college "as part of the movement for securing women's economic independence"; and also that "she was a true believer in Herbert Spencer's 'fine animal' ".[24]

The Modern Girl

The college Madame Österberg opened in Hampstead, though never large, was very successful. By the early nineties there were twenty students and a second property had been acquired to house a medical gymnasium. Working for the School Board, she had realised the publicity value of Open Practices; she welcomed attention in the press, and tributes to her work appeared in the *Lancet*, the *Pall Mall Gazette* and the *Weekly Illustrated*, as well as in journals appealing to women. By such means, the interested public heard more of Ling's system "of which Madame Bergman-Österberg is the successful representative in our country", and something of her students' regime. According to the *Woman's Herald*,

> They all worked with a will and under one will . . . I saw them plunge, dive, swim . . . in the splendid swimming baths, situated opposite the college . . . I paid a visit to the cricket and lawn tennis grounds, ten minutes by rail out in the country . . . I advise all those interested in woman's physical advancement to visit Madame Bergman-Österberg.[25]

In 1895, faced with the prospect of Hampstead torn apart to accommodate the railway line to the Great Central terminus which was to be built in Marylebone, Madame Österberg decided to move out of London. She purchased Kingsfield at Dartford Heath, a house with fourteen acres of grounds, and the college transferred there that autumn.[26] "Clara" could hardly have expected better than the gymnasium the ballroom provided, the playing fields, tennis courts and cycle track laid out, and the river bathing. Linking as she always did body and mind, Madame Österberg, amid all the labour of establishing a new institution whilst continuing to supervise the old one, did not forget to enlarge her students' outlook by bringing them in contact whenever possible with speakers who would talk about art or travel, by arranging concerts and filling Kingsfield with reproductions of Greek antiquities and Italian painting. As for the course, the two-year training in gymnastics, games, remedial work, physiology, anatomy and teaching skills, all conducted under strict discipline, proved as attractive in Dartford as in London. Despite the high fees more girls applied than Madame Österberg was willing to admit. "I am obliged to pick and choose," she told the International Congress of Women in 1899.

> To do otherwise would be to risk, even at this late date, the failure of my life's work . . . My girls are destined to become pioneers in all that relates to hygiene and a more rational method of life for the sex . . . I need women with brains and character. None other will do.[27]

And she told the students, "It does not matter how good you are, you will never be good enough for the profession you have chosen."[28] It was a missionary profession, after all: purging the girls' schools of the clubs and dumb-bells of the German system which was then in possession; offering Ling's scientific movement for unscientific musical drill; offering themselves, with two years' training, for the dancing mistress and the drill sergeant, both of whom were "equally ignorant of the laws which govern the human body".[29] For Madame Österberg, banishing the sergeant seemed to be not only a duty to Ling, but also in some measure a duty to women. "Let us once for all discard man as a physical trainer of woman," she said,

> let us send the drill sergeant right-about-face to his awkward squad. This work we women do better, as our very success in training depends upon our having felt like women, able to calculate the possibilities of our sex, knowing our weakness and our strength.[30]

She set herself, then, the double task "to train the teachers and create a demand for them".[31] By her account it was simple enough. Girton and Newnham made use of her services, as did Whitelands and Maria Grey and other training colleges and various schools. By degrees, when she had blazed the trail, she sent her own students into these jobs, "persuading Head Mistresses of the advantage of having a teacher who would give her entire care and attention to the one school".[32] Leeds High School was apparently the first to appoint a full-time gymnastics teacher. Others followed, "and thus the attached, or resident, gymnastic teacher . . . came into being".[33]

Of course, her own commitment underlay her success, but circumstances were favourable to her. Despite some medical foreboding, there probably could not have been a better time to sell physical education to the middle classes. This was the era, from the 1870s, when they took to their bicycles and roller skates, when they invented a new game, lawn tennis, organised old ones such as hockey,

contrived League Football and county cricket and built the first swimming baths on the rates. Considerations of costume, propriety and
physical risk impeded women. Nonetheless, by the 1880s they were
most definitely on the move. "Let our women remain women instead of
entering into this insane physical rivalry with men", implored the
Birmingham Daily Mail in 1881. But by the end of the decade,
Birmingham women were not only veterans of gymnastic classes but
had swimming clubs of their own, with their own instructors and gala
nights: they were playing competitive tennis and undertaking cycling
trials.[34] The athletic proficiency of English ladies awakened "frequent
admiration among foreigners", according to an account of women's
competitions at the Portsmouth Swimming Club in 1887;[35] while, in
the nineties, "Clara" and her friends provided many photographic
subjects for the new illustrated journal *Black and White*: "The Lady
Footballers at Crouch End", "The Ladies' Archery Championship at
Huntingdon", "The Ladies' Golf Championship at Hoylake", and so
on. In 1884, the year before Madame Österberg opened her college in
Hampstead, the first women's singles were played at Wimbledon. In
1895, the year she moved to Dartford, the All England Women's
Hockey Association was formed.

More significantly for her venture, these were years in which there
emerged a powerful cult of team games in girls' schools. The leaders
were the new public schools for girls, St Leonard's, Roedean and
Wycombe Abbey, but games took hold too in the range of day schools
springing from the late-Victorian "renaissance". Among the many
borrowings from the male tradition, team games are conspicuous,
although, it seems, they came in through the back door, launched
initially through the efforts of "the college women", those enthu-
siastic younger teachers who had played at Girton and the other
women's colleges. In no time, though, the ethic took root, and games
were promoted in the leading girls' schools with something like the
fervour of Marlborough or Rugby. When we read what those notable
headmistresses, Miss Dove and Miss Lawrence, wrote about games at
Wycombe Abbey and Roedean in the nineties, there is a strong sense
of having been here before: captains and vice-captains are choosing
teams, arranging fixtures, awarding colours; there is the familiar
attitude to slackers ("It is a great object to be kept in view to make the
games obligatory on all, as otherwise those very individuals whose
characters most need the discipline they afford, will evade them")[36]
and the broad appeal to *esprit de corps* or "the principles of corporate

life". Games, writes Miss Dove,

> provide a splendid field for the development of powers of organisa-
> tion, of good temper under trying circumstances, courage and
> determination to play up and do your best, even in a losing game,
> rapidity of thought and action, judgment and self-reliance, and,
> above all things, unselfishness . . . learning to sink individual
> differences in the effort of loyally working with others for the
> common good . . .[37]

Games foster the qualities "that conduce to the supremacy of our
country in so many quarters of the globe". If games were only
exercise, writes Miss Lawrence, other agencies might replace them,
"but considered as a means of training the character they stand alone.
For cricket, "that splendid national game", she claims much more:

> It is the game of Englishmen all the world over, and the interest it
> inspires lasts quite into old age. It is a strong social bond between
> the mother country and the colonies, between class and class, and
> race and race. It is impossible to limit the interest of the game to one
> institution or set of people. A boy or girl who plays cricket enters a
> world larger than his or her own narrow sphere, and is induced to
> care for impersonal ends beyond the immediate circle of the home
> or school.[38]

This looking "beyond the immediate circle" had a particular significance for girls. The whole approach of the two headmistresses is
redolent of the 'civic' values and 'public' spirit of the new girls'
schools, in contrast to the domestic values of the family-like school of
earlier days.[39] Girls must free themselves, writes Miss Lawrence,
from "the vices bred by a restricted life".[40] Even more than boys they
need to be taught to look outside themselves to the common good.
Women are often unselfish, writes Miss Dove, in relation to their
husbands and children, "but this personal devotion is quite com-
patible with what I may call family selfishness and they may be . . .
quite incapable of realising any interest whatever that is not bounded
by the four walls of their home". Where men acquired the corporate
virtues not only at school but in every walk of life, few girls were able
yet to enter professions. "It remains therefore for the school to teach
them almost all they will ever have the opportunity of acquiring of the
power of working with others," and there was no better means of
doing so than through experience of organised team games such as

cricket, hockey and lacrosse.[41] It had been a struggle in the early days. At first Roedean stood alone, said Miss Lawrence. "We had to explain our position to hostile critics, and to encounter much opposition from the parents of our girls, and we felt that we were carrying on a crusade." But at the time she wrote (in 1898), games had been taken up by almost every girls' school. "A wave of change" had moved public opinion.[42]

It can be sensed to this day in school histories. That erstwhile pioneer, Queen's College, Harley Street, which kept its curtseying and callisthenics up to the First World War, stands out quaintly in an era when so many hockey fields were being rented, so many girls' school clubs were being formed for the major team games (not excluding football)[43] and so many elevens were setting out in their long skirts, blouses and lettered caps for the exhilarating experience of a match away from home. The *Girls' Own Paper*, by the 1890s, was talking like Miss Lawrence about the courage and good temper to be acquired in any game "which necessitates combination among the players".[44] Miss Buss's successor at the North London Collegiate, reporting to her governors in 1898, called lack of a playing field "the one respect in which we are behind the times".[45] Miss Beale, at Cheltenham, who feared at first a sacrifice of womanliness (even down to the use of slang which might arise in the heat of the game) yielded to persuasion in 1891. A field was rented, and with unpeeled ash sticks the girls at Cheltenham took to hockey. They played informally at first, guided by those who had been coached by their brothers, but fairly soon the whole panoply of house games, colours and fixture lists appeared.[46]

It was on the crest of this "wave of change" that Madame Österbeg moved to Dartford where her students, instead of journeying by train to their cricket and tennis ground at Neasden, had spacious playing fields on the spot. How quick she was to respond to the market is shown by the way in which she introduced hockey in the first year of the new college, by supporting the initiative of some of her students who had played the game at their respective schools.[47] The Canadian winter game, lacrosse, which appeared at St Leonard's in 1890, also reached Dartford via a student. It is worth remembering that the major team games, as they came at first into the schools for girls, followed the public school tradition: that is, they were run by the girls themselves and coached by mistresses who also played. None of this was a matter for specialists until Madame Österberg made it so.[48]

Wholly unused to the English system, she nonetheless perceived very quickly that games and gymnastics could be combined to form the basis of the new profession. Time and again she took pains to stress that they were essentially complementary. Games had "wonderful value as adjuncts to the more systematic physical training".[49] English games and Swedish gymnastics formed "a safe and rational basis for Physical Education".[50] She paid tribute to Miss Lawrence and Miss Dove as the first headmistresses to realise "the enormous influence of out-of-door games". "To combine these games with Swedish gymnastics and thus create a perfect training system for the English girls, became, henceforth the one great aim of Madame Bergman-Österberg's work in England."[51] When we hear that "players must act quickly, do the right thing at the right moment, think of others but trust to themselves", we might be listening to Miss Lawrence of Roedean.

The only game that originated with Madame Österberg's college was netball, and this was actually the students' adaptation of basket ball, shown them by American visitors. Netball had particular merit in the eyes of the Swedish gymnast in that unlike hockey, cricket or tennis, "it is not one-sided, both arms are used and the body is held in a more upright position".[52] The overriding aim, after all, was health, from which it followed that all activity must take account of the Laws of Health. Madame Österberg, like Roth, never tired of insisting that Physical Education, properly defined, implied understanding of the sanitary laws.

> If every mother and every teacher had a rational understanding of the value of physical exercise, based on anatomical and physiological laws; if to this was added a practical knowledge of personal hygiene, a long step would be taken to solve some of our present difficulties and problems.[53]

Her students were turned out not only as gymnasts but as crusaders in this cause; and here again she had the good fortune to cultivate ground that was already prepared. Years before the opening of the Hampstead college, the Laws of Health, as a girls' school subject, had been pioneered by Miss Buss, who in 1865 told the Taunton Commission that "lessons on the structure of the human body, with applications to health" had been introduced at the North London Collegiate School. Following that, the Endowed Schools Commissioners saw to it that the Laws of Health were a standard element in schools for *girls* established under the Endowed Schools Act.[54] What better lead-in for the "mistress of health", imbued with the therapeutic gospel of Ling, than this scattering of the seeds of physiology and hygiene through girls' grammar schools all over the country?

By 1900 Madame Österberg's students had more than established their reputation.

> They go literally everywhere. Some are snapped up by the great American colleges where Ling is already known, and they simply have to carry forward . . . a work that others have begun. Others find work ready to hand among their own kith and kin. Wheresoever, in fact, the physical status of womankind is capable of being raised, there are to be found one or more of the teachers whom Madame Österberg has trained. They consistitute collectively the "little leaven" that, in time, so many people think will leaven the whole lump.[55]

The list of posts held by Madame Österberg's students reads, by the First World War, like a roll call of Girls Public Day School Company foundations, grammar schools, boarding schools, well-known and lesser-known, almost all the product of the past forty years. Already one can see, setting this alongside the list of schools from which students are drawn, the circular movement which was to characterise the world of women's physical education: Dartford students are appointed to Roedean; Roedean's pupils are sent to Dartford.[56] There are other, more glamorous indications of success: the students' performance in 1900 at the International Congress of Physical Education in Paris; the attendance at Dartford of distinguished visitors, including the Prime Minister, Campbell Bannerman. But this two-way traffic between schools and college is the plain endorsement in the market place of an idea "too good to fail". The reputation of her college drew visitors even from the Mecca of gymnastics in Stockholm. More remarkably, the British Navy set up a Swedish gymnastics school in Portsmouth. "My conception of what gymnastics is, and what it can accomplish, has been totally revolutionised," wrote Commander Grenfell to Madame Österberg after watching her students perform.[57] When he left the Navy to teach at Eton, Grenfell introduced the Swedish system. One of his successors, Commander Coote, later took Swedish Gymnastics to Harrow. Another, Roper, developed it at Bedales where the founder-headmaster, J.H. Badley, was already convinced that Madame Österberg's methods were "the best for boys, no less than for girls".[58]

Ling had triumphed. By the end of her career, the German system had been bested in the schools; so much so, that there were even teachers, trained for two years in "some other system", now retraining in the methods of Ling.[59] The climate of opinion was changed, of course, from what it had been when she first came to London. The shocking fact that during the Boer War many thousands willing to enlist had had to be rejected on medical grounds led to England's "physical deterioration" being made the subject of government inquiry.[60] Means were recommended to grapple with the problem at the very start of life, through creches and clinics, improved milk supplies and infant feeding. Education authorities were empowered to provide school meals for underfed children. School medical inspection was introduced and in 1907 a medical department was established at the Board of Education under the charge of a doctor, George Newman. It was Newman, looking back thirty years later, who saw Madame Österberg as the precursor of that new understanding of health which marked the new century. She was, in his words, "the morning star of a reformation".[61]

Two Nations

The morning star, though, fades with the dawn. And while fading is not a word to use of Madame Österberg, she does not seem to have taken a main part in the reformation as it developed. A contrast can be drawn between her early days with the London School Board, from the fulness of which she gave important evidence in 1887 before the Cross Commission on Elementary Education, and her commitment, once her college was established, to training young women as a kind of crack corps to teach gymnastics in the secondary schools. When Newman, then, recalls her enthusiasm at the time school medicals were introduced, we must remember that by 1907 she had little contact with the children who needed them. Her students, of course, did teaching practice in the local elementary schools. They took gym classes in the Dartford Drill Hall and promising children came out of school hours to attend a gymnastics club at the college. Apart from this, though, as we have seen, all the thrust was towards secondary education. And when, at the beginning of the twentieth century, the Swedish system in the *elementary* schools came under challenge, it was not Madame Österberg who led the forces that repelled the attack.

Even in London, where Swedish drill was still extolled at the end of the century, it had never caught on for boys. London in any case was hardly typical. Outside London and the forward-looking cities of the north and midlands, were hundreds of School Boards and thousands of schools untouched by Ling. If they had drill it was military drill. The military tradition was by no means dead. The Cross Commission, though it gave its blessing to the Swedish system Madame Österberg described, recommended military drill for boys. And in 1902 as the Boer War ended, the Board of Education issued a manual on physical training based on methods used in the Army. Elementary schools were advised to use drill sergeants trained on the Army Gymnastics Course and were even referred to a War Office handbook, *Infantry Training 1902*. A former Inspector of Army Gymnasia was appointed by the Board to promote the drilling. Teachers as well as pupils were expected to attend the drill sergeant; even elderly schoolmistresses found themselves dragooned in this way. In her School Board days, no doubt Madame Österberg would have been loudest in the outcry against this. Now resistance came from the Ling Association (a professional body, formed by her students, which she declined connection with), the N.U.T. and its former president, the M.P., T.J. Macnamara.[62]

The question was eventually re-examined and again Ling triumphed; in 1909 a new, Swedish-based *Syllabus* was drawn up for use in the elementary schools. With George Newman at the Board of Education came the appointment of a team of inspectors highly sympathetic to all that Madame Österberg had for so long striven to achieve and, in turn, deriving support from the standards she established in girls' schools. There is a sense, though, in which these standards tended to re-define rather than modify the gap between middle-class and working-class schooling. For one thing, there was the question of teachers. Madame Österberg had always been eager that the Swedish system should be known in colleges which turned out teachers for the elementary schools and had herself introduced it at Whitelands. By 1905 the Ling Association could claim a dozen colleges had taken it up[63] and four years later physical education was made compulsory in all training colleges. What they offered, however, could hardly compare with the specialist course at Dartford, not one hour of which was deemed superfluous to the high demands of the profession. The Ling Association from time to time debated the problem of training elementary school teachers. The Board of Education in 1909 started vacation courses for them. But there remained two worlds: in one of which, a single gym tunic had sometimes to be passed round among all members of a group.[64]

Games, the native element so skilfully combined by Madame Österberg with Swedish gymnastics for the perfecting of English girlhood, were yet more distant from the experience of children in the elementary schools. The playing field, and all that it stood for, was quite another thing from the Board School playground; and while the new games mistress passed on to schoolgirls a modicum, at least, of Tom Brown's inheritance, it could not be passed on to ordinary children, for each of whom government regulations required open space of only thirty square feet. "Open space" was not "playing space" but space unoccupied by buildings, and in those years, with the new concern for fitness, attention was more than once drawn to its inadequacy. "It has been suggested, and probably with truth", wrote one school inspector in 1904, "that the recent marked gain in physique of our upper-class women upon the men is due to their lately acquired freedom to use their limbs on the tennis, hockey and golf grounds."[65] The same man had been shocked to see elementary school children "pour violently into the playground" at break, "make a brief bear-garden of it" and then rush indoors. As the English character had been largely formed in public school playgrounds he hoped to see it "similarly moulded in the playgrounds . . . in the people's schools". A Departmental Committee on Playgrounds in 1912 also pointed to the contrast between facilities for children of different classes. It was, of course, one of the many distinctions between elementary and secondary schooling, distinctions not invented by the new games mistress when she introduced her girls to hockey any more than by the new classics mistress taking them for Latin. The fact was that girls were entering into the education of the privileged classes just as people were becoming more aware of the needs of the under-privileged. While Manchester children, in the words of one witness before the Committee on Physical Deterioration, were said to be "losing the instinct of play", middle-class schoolgirls were gaining it.

It was for them that the Dartford college had been called into existence, and it was in response to the demand they created that two of Madame Österberg's students started colleges of their own. Rhoda Anstey and Margaret Stansfeld had both been trained by her in Hampstead. They had learnt the Swedish system at the fountainhead. Less directly, they had learnt, no doubt, that this was work which could be extended. In 1897, two years after training, Miss Anstey established a clinic in the midlands to undertake remedial care. To this she soon added the first few students who wished to specialise in gymnastics; she bought a skeleton, appointed staff, and by 1899 the gospel of Ling, the great tradition of the Swedish Institute, was being proclaimed not only from Dartford but from Halesowen. In 1903 the third English college in the Ling tradition was opened at Bedford by Margaret Stansfeld. Madame Österberg's army of Swedish gymnasts, "small, as yet, but growing", had the means to new recruits.

It cannot be said that she was pleased about it. Those who have been entrusted with the gospel do not always want it spread by others and the evidence is that Madame Österberg reacted to the founding of Anstey and Bedford much as Marie Stopes reacted some years later to competition in another field: she was furious. While she lived, however, the Dartford college maintained its primacy. She died, aged sixty-six, in 1915 and not without a sense of occasion, as became her. As the *Journal of Education* noted,

> There was a striking dramatic completeness in the passing of Madame Bergman-Österberg. On July 28 she completed thirty years of service as head and pioneer of the movement for training women as teachers of Ling's Swedish system. On the following day she breathed her last.[66]

By the time she died there were no fewer than six colleges training girls to teach Swedish gymnastics. Three of them (Dartford, Anstey and Bedford) had been founded by herself or her students. One, Dunfermline, (which the Carnegie Trust had established in 1905) was directed by one of her students; while two which had at first been more eclectic (Chelsea College, launched in 1898, as part of the South Western Polytechnic, and the Liverpool college, which Irene Marsh had established in 1900) had by now gone over to Ling. Queen Alexandra House, which up to the First War clung to its "British" gymnastic system, was forced by pressure of its own old students in the post-war years to go over to Ling;[67] and Nonington, founded in 1938, offered a course which was broadly Swedish. Right into the middle of the century, therefore, up to and even past the Second World War, there survived, in a form she would have recognised, all that Madame Österberg had in mind when she conjured up the idea that was "too good to fail". This survival we must now explore, first of all noting that not only the strength but the isolation of the female tradition can be traced right back to its founder.

"Although in such a real sense a public benefactor," one contemporary wrote of Madame Österberg, "she was never a public worker."

> Her domination within the college being complete, she took no part
> in the organisation and development of the profession of gymnastic
> teaching outside it, and was little in touch with general educational
> matters.[68]

We have seen that she did not engage in the fight to keep the elementary schools "Swedish". As for her concept of the new profession, not only did she lack the breadth of view to welcome efforts by women she had trained to establish colleges of their own, but she resisted very stubbornly all attempts by her own old students to involve her in launching a professional body. In 1899 they formed the Ling Association, to band together trained gymnastic teachers; but she would have none of it, refused to be its president, and instead formed the Bergman-Österberg Union which was confined to those trained at Dartford, arguing that the other group admitted people whom she did not consider properly trained.[69] Partly, this reflects personal pride (on a scale which did not afflict her successors); partly, an inward-turned professional pride, an isolating factor which this female tradition never succeeded in shaking off.

As it turned out, she judged rather badly. The Ling Association was highly effective in projecting the values she believed in into an era well beyond her own. The arrangements she made to secure the stability of her own college did not work out;[70] and the continuity which she aspired to was, in fact, achieved by her pupil, Margaret Stansfeld, at Bedford College, the founding of which in 1903 she had certainly resented. Through the medium of developments at Bedford we now follow the idea that was "too good to fail".

3

Ling in the Ascendant

In A Huge Bonnet She Ate Little Jam Rolls
(Bedford students' mnemonic for gymnastic table)

As perhaps happens with a first generation, the founders of the colleges were far more diverse than the institutions they created. While Madame Österberg, Miss Anstey and Miss Stansfeld were from the very first apprenticed to Ling, others were converted: Miss Wilkie of Chelsea trained at Stempel's (German) Gymnasium in London; Miss Marsh of Liverpool trained at Southport with the Alexanders, who at that time did not offer the Swedish system. In origin, too, they were a mixed bunch: Madame Österberg, from Sweden; Miss Wilke, "a poor girl from Bavaria" (who became Wilkie in 1914); Miss Marsh, the daughter of a Liverpool merchant; Miss Anstey, the country woman from Devon, and Miss Stansfeld, who is rather hard to place (despite the fact that she lived long enough to carry on what Madame Österberg had started right into the middle of the twentieth century). She died, aged ninety-one, in 1951, having actively governed her college in Bedford until 1945 and remained close to it even in retirement. There is thus no shortage of people who knew her, but no one seems to know about her early life. A Victorian history of the Stansfeld family may be consulted in the British Museum, but it throws more light upon the parks and manors of those branches resident in Yorkshire than on Church Street, Edmonton, where Margaret Stansfeld was born on 10 March, 1860.[1] Registering the birth, her father, James Stansfeld, gave his occupation as "master baker". How prosperous he was it is impossible to say; but it seems he died young, and left a large family. And we may infer that they had to struggle from the fact that Margaret and an elder sister took a step uncommon in the middle classes: they became pupil teachers in a Board School. In those days the career of a Board School teacher was scarcely within the limited range of occupations open to a lady. In the event, things took a different course. Madame Österberg descended upon London, starting her classes in 1881. Margaret Stansfeld went to them, gave up her school work and became such an able exponent of Ling that when the

Hampstead college opened in 1885, she was one of the instructors.

To a girl with her physical vitality (and at eighty she could still show how a rope should be climbed) gymnastics must have been a revelation. To a nature so thoroughly disposed to self-discipline, Ling's ideal of ordered excellence must have made an immediate appeal. We do not know what she thought of Madame Österberg. Austere and quite undemonstrative herself, it seems unlikely that the show of emotion, the rather theatrical turn of phrase that came so naturally to her teacher could have been other than distasteful to her. "Send me girls with heart to understand woman's physical difficulties; send them with brain to understand me and my plans . . . send them, above all, with will and enthusiasm to serve and help woman . . . however she needs helping."[2] That was not Miss Stansfeld, at any age. Still less could she ever have defined her task, before an audience, as "moulding and shaping . . . the most beautiful and plastic material in the world – the human body." Did she think of it as beautiful? Even that is not easy to discern. She had a tendency, in old age anyway, to destroy the poetry of beautiful movement by some all-too-audible banality: "That girl should wear a brassiere!"[3]

While she worked for Madame Österberg Miss Stansfeld taught gymnastics in a number of girls' schools of the new order: Shrewsbury High School, the latest achievement of the Girls' Public Day School Company; Dame Alice Owen's Girls' School in Islington and the new High School for girls in Bedford, both of them very recently established with endowment under the Endowed Schools Act. These were the missionary days of the eighties, before the bicycle corrupted "Clara", before Madame Österberg with flaming sword drove the drill sergeant out of the girls' schools, before Roedean really got going and team games caught on. At Bedford, when she went there, the girls had hitherto been drilled by a sergeant and played their own kind of hockey in the playground with a string ball and walking sticks.[4]

In 1888 she left Madame Österberg's and gave more time to the Bedford girls. The high school was expanding, its demands increased, and though she cut down her work elsewhere, she had a multiplicity of other commitments. As she told Madame Österberg in 1898,

I teach in one other school in Bedford and in the Kindergarten Training College. In Cambridge I have several schools for a weekly lesson, a small class in the Newnham Gymnasium for the children of the university professors, and the Cambridge Teachers' College.

In London for many years I have been teaching physiology and gymnastics at the Froebel Institute.[5]

Now in her late thirties, she looked back with pleasure on what had been achieved, at Bedford especially.

I wonder whether you will remember what the girls were like when you saw them in '88? If so, you will realise what uphill work it was at first. But now ten years of steady work has naturally had its effect, and I think they compare favourably in carriage and physique with any schools I have seen. Gymnastics are very popular in the school, and I believe the girls enjoy their lessons.[6]

They did, if not without a touch of fear. "She was very alert and commanding and we were all afraid of her."[7] For some, the twenty-minute class was a highlight. For her, it was one of eight twenty-minute slots following end-on through the morning, four days weekly. And in every slot she drew from each girl what an admiring inspector called "tense work", work "that appeared to touch the extreme limit of requirement".[8] Like all teachers of Swedish gymnastics she struggled, too, with dress. The custom had been for girls to drill in their ordinary clothes, tightly whale-boned "in a suit of armour that clasped us . . . in all sorts of agonising places",[9] and parents at Bedford, as at Roedean and Cheltenham, needed some persuading to allow their daughters the short blue serge dress Miss Stansfeld required. Commanding as she was, there were still two families in 1898 who would not fall into line.

These two families my utmost powers have failed to persuade to get costumes. These exceptions are my failures, and I must confess to nursing somewhat of a feeling of resentment against them, though, poor children, it is not their fault . . . they would be only too glad not to be singular.[10]

The claims of Bedford High School and the rest did not absorb her energies entirely; like Madame Österberg and Miss Anstey, she took patients for remedial treatment. But there seems never to have been any doubt that her commitment was to teaching and in 1903 she took the critical step: buying a house to start a college.

Thirty years earlier Emily Davies had settled on Hitchin for her women's college because it was well-placed between Cambridge and London. A similar claim could be made for Bedford and over the years it was common enough for visiting lecturers to come over from Homerton, or from London, to Miss Stansfeld's students. In this case, though, there were other factors: not only the base she had established in the High School but the existence of several elementary schools and the Froebel College for teaching practice. Dartford and Anstey certainly suffered from being ill-sited in this respect; indeed, in 1907 Anstey moved to Erdington, chiefly to gain easier access to schools.

It was still a dashing thing in 1903 for girls to think of going to college at all, and Miss Stansfeld made it plain at the outset to the thirteen who came to her in Lansdowne Road that their work and behaviour would be very important, "for on us depended the future of the College".[11] As to their work, "life was largely a matter of all work and very little play; lectures in the mornings, games in the afternoon and study in the evenings filled our days".[12] As to their behaviour, some at least thought themselves "*very very* young" in retrospect, "and the 'Adventure' was really very Victorian, not a glimpse of Edward VII anywhere".[13] Thus, they had accepted as a matter of course the rules about putting on a hat and long skirt to step from one college house to another. "In our day legs were indecent things to show, and when coming from No.29 to 37, we had to put a skirt on. Our trouble was: Shall I put the skirt on over my tunic and spoil the pleats, or do I put it under my tunic and look a sight?"[14] They practised teaching in elementary schools where the children had never seen a tunic before and one girl found, in her first teaching post, that she had to fight to get the pupils into tunics because the headmistress was averse to seeing "the sickening twist of the female knee".[15]

"Those were good days; full of work . . . lots of it."[16] Because they were so few there was the feeling of a family, enlivened though by "that spice of pioneering which gave the whole thing a particular importance for us".[17] Forty years on, the pioneers saw themselves in the quaint style of another age: in long skirts and boaters cycling into town ("I have a snapshot of some of us just off for a cycle ride . . . wearing our long skirts"),[18] in gym tunics that reached to the knee, white blouses and yellow silk ties, thick blue woollen knickers, black woollen stockings ("None of these garments were taken off either for gymnastics or dancing").[19] Those bright stars who played hockey for the County wore stiff starched collars and their skirts were actually six or seven inches above the ground ("Those we wore for going outside college were down to our ankles").[20] The pioneers remembered being taught to swim suspended from a pole in that part of the Ouse that was used in those days as the Town Baths. They remembered Rogers, the cricket coach ("Pitch it on the daisy!"), "Mr Perkins", the skeleton, Monsieur Bertrand, the fencing master, and the Swedish gymnast, Miss Lindelöf, who said, "If you not can do it, it is better to don't."[21] For the first Set, with only thirteen students, team games had to be helped by outsiders: they played hockey with the Bedford Ladies' Club, and lacrosse with the Bedford High School.

Ling and Molly Evans

Forty years on, the first Set of students could remember feeling a sense of intrusion when another house was taken in 1904 for the nine students of the next generation. The powerful ethos of the family-like college, which survived this expansion and a good many more, will be examined in the next chapter. Here we are especially concerned with training; and the experience of training in these early days is evoked not only in reminiscence but in student textbooks and notes. Molly Evans, who was one of the "intruders" who joined the college in 1904, kept hers to the end of a long life.

Opening Nils Posse's authoritative volume, *The Special Kinesiology of Educational Gymnastics*, she would at once have come across the statement: "No one today can *invent* a system of physical education; he can merely repeat long-proven truths and add more detail to the knowledge already defined by science."[22] Baron Posse saw the Swedish system as the framework of all possible systems in the future. That another half century proved him wrong is not to say that human anatomy changed but that society changed its attitudes. Molly Evans had no worries of this kind. She was presented with the Ark of the Covenant, "the only system whose details have been elucidated by and derived from mechanics, anatomy, physiology and psychology, and whose theory has survived the scrutiny of scientists all over the world".[23]

What did it amount to in practical terms? Posse's book runs to nearly 400 pages of methodical explanation. The basis of Ling's system, as he makes clear, lies in progression; and progression relates not only to the growing strength of the child but to the scientific sequence of each lesson as it proceeds from introductory exercises to general movements, thence to special movements and back to the comparative tranquillity of respiratory exercises at the close. "This sequence, table, or 'day's order,' is *the* characteristic of Swedish gymnastics – its very kernel," Posse explains.[24] Girls who had learnt Swedish gymnastics at school (and several of the early students at Bedford had been taught by Miss Stansfeld at Bedford High School) would have found such words described something familiar; but that in itself could only have brought them to the brink of understanding what they now had to grapple with. The simple idea of progression, for instance, ramifies alarmingly. In any one movement, progression could be made by combining several motions, by changing from oscillatory to statical action, by changing the rhythm, by decreasing the base, by increasing the lever of the weight or the muscular resistance, by changing the velocity, or by changing from excentric to concentric activity. "For instance", Molly Evans would have learned, "yd. *d* stoop st. 2 A elev. is at first begun from Str. stoop st. pos."[25] If at this point she felt she had gone mad, she could look up the index of gymnastic shorthand with its 130 abbreviations to assist her in the construction of tables. "The nomenclature may at first seem odd," Posse admits, "but the teacher will soon become familiar with it and find it a great help."[26] Thus, *hor.* for horizontal, *hlf.* for half and *st.* for standing; so that *hor. hlf. st.* means "one leg raised backward to horizontal position in a line with the body, which inclines forward; the supporting leg is bent".[27] In the main part of the book, with many diagrams, the movements of the Swedish system are described. The Appendix classifies the vast battalion of over a thousand exercises – all the arch-flexions, heaving movements, balance movements, movements of the shoulder blade, abdominal exercises, lateral trunk movements, leaping and respiratory exercises. Posse also gives examples of tables appropriate to the needs of men, women and children.

Evidently undaunted by all this, Molly Evans, when nearly ninety, recalled her college work as "intensely interesting".[28] Her own theory notebook is a miniature Posse, opening with the confident declaration that gymnastics is "a system of postures und movements in harmony with the needs of the body and having bodily perfection for aim". In a conventional schoolgirl's hand she lists the three parts of a gymnastic movement, its five fundamental positions and ten groups of likely faults. From that she advances through the hierarchy of exercise, from the arch-flexions to that point of conclusion where, she says, respiratory movement is essential "at the end before the class is dismissed". In another notebook she has composed nearly sixty tables

in the gymnast's shorthand, each embodying movements appropriate
to the various parts of the body, but always in the sequence which the
system ordained and which Bedford students fixed in their minds by
using the mnemonic at the head of this chapter.[29]

The theory of gymnastics had to be backed by studies in anatomy
and physiology, subjects which required intensive cramming, as
Molly Evans' diagrams and notes bear witness. Her textbooks here
were *Gray's Anatomy* (which she recalled as "a fascinating book"), a
Physiology for Beginners and a *Manual of Human Physiology* (both of
these at about the level which would be introductory for medical
students). Clearly this was not Tripos stuff; but neither was it that
"travesty of Science" introduced at about this time at King's College
for Women in London. The "Home Science" course there, where
students engaged in domestic tasks in a "kitchen laboratory", was a
product of the anti blue-stocking trend.[30] The domestic science
mistress trained in this way came into the girls' grammar schools and
high schools at about the same time as the gym mistress. They were
both non-graduates; the "hands and feet people".[31] For all that, there
was this difference between them: that one had followed a course of
training which sought as its great aim to elevate housework, the other,
a course which sought to elevate the race.

> The aim of Swedish Educational Gymnastics is to exert a very
> serious influence upon the working . . . of the body precisely as the
> study of say, logic or geometry does upon . . . the mind.[32]

The *seriousness* of the Swedish system comes over strongly in remedial
work. Here Molly Evans was supplied with the *Hand-book* of Dr
Anders Wide, the current director of the Orthopedic Gymnastic
Institute in Stockholm. Its frontispiece photograph shows apparatus
in the imposing setting of the Institute, all presided over by a bust of
Ling, whose medical gymnastics had been developed there since its
inception in 1827. Dr Wide's *Hand-book* and Molly Evans' notes treat
of spinal curvatures (kyphosis, lordosis, scoliosis), foot deformities
(talipes varus, equinus, calcaneus, valgus, cavus), knock-knee (genu-
valgum) and dislocations. Neuralgia and other nervous diseases,
including St Vitus Dance, are there, as are anaemia and constipation,
emphysema and heart disease. Sometimes Molly Evans is constrained
to admit that "GYMNASTS can do *absolutely nothing*." But, more
commonly, therapeutic massage may be expected to bring some relief
and she outlines the appropriate treatment, offering here and there,

among the Latinisms, brief glimpses of Edwardian Britain. Rickets is common among children, she writes, "especially those of the poorer classes as is seen from the numerous cases brought for treatment to the hospitals". "Young bakers who work many hours in a hot enervating atmosphere" and young brick-layers may suffer from knock-knee. In her notes on the spine she castigates stays, "which when worn by growing girls hinder the full development of the dorsal muscles".

Remedial work was Ling at its most "womanly", an aspect of the system very close to nursing and the fullest expression of that therapeutic principle which had led Maclaren of the Oxford Gymnasium to dismiss Swedish free-standing exercises as only suitable for invalids. Regular provision for medical inspection, with a follow-up in remedial treatment, was a common feature of girls' schools by this time, but did not always mean the school took Swedish gymnastics. At the North London Collegiate, for instance, which had pioneered medical inspection, an eclectic system of gymnastics was used (with a German bias) in preference to Ling; and Sara Burstall, who went from the North London to become headmistress of Manchester High School, was one of that minority of headmistresses who, in the early twentieth century, thought the Swedish system "not sufficiently feminine" and preferred exercises done to music, "since these throw much less strain on the high nerve centres". What these headmistresses sought for girls was "an education suited to their needs as women".[33] The "feminine" ideal is not far below the surface in the arguments of both sides in this controversy. While Swedish gymnastics claimed to be "serious", calling for "as much attention, effort and expenditure of . . . energy" as mathematics,[34] this was very far from a recommendation in the eyes of those who felt that the German system was more restful and graceful for girls. With recreation seen, as it seems to have been, as a concession to femininity, the Swedish system appeared unfeminine in that it scorned such palliatives.

> No one asks that a lesson in Euclid shall be first and foremost recreative but that it shall exercise the pupil's logical faculties, develop his thinking powers, and train him to have their full control. Just so the Swedish system trains the body.[35]

Both sides claimed the development of *muscle* as a fault in the other, and here again, it is assumed that muscle is masculine. Of the anti-Ling headmistresses it was said, "Their aim for girls is not the development of muscle";[36] but others insisted that the German system was "far too severe for women",[37] and likely to do harm through apparatus work on parallel bars, rings and trapezes which brought excessive muscular development. One girl who applied for the course at Bedford and who had worked on parallel bars was told by Miss Stansfeld, "You're deformed, but I'll take you!"[38] Devotees of Ling alleged of the "Germans" that "their apparatus was invented first, and the human body produces exercises to suit it".[39]

Molly Evans, then, was pledged to a system which was seen as too masculine for girls by some girls' schools (though by most boys' schools as too feminine for boys), and which offered her a range of images, from the "womanly" practice of remedial work to the "manly" practice of command. *Commanding* was a technique which had to be learnt, and Posse underlined its importance. "A lesson is best led by commands from the teacher, the class being arranged in ranks, military fashion."[40] Molly Evans noted two kinds of commands: the "preparatory" and the "executory". Sometimes, said Posse, there was also the "cautionary". "For instance: '*Without moving the shoulders* (cautionary), *head backward* (preparatory) – *bend*! (executory).' " "Every lesson should begin with the command '*Attention*!' " Then, "To start the class, command '*Class, forward – march*!' " The class then marches, left foot forward, right foot following, "with a speed of a hundred and fourteen to a hundred and sixteen steps a minute", and the length of each step two feet and a half. "We formed up in pairs and marched twice round the gymnasium," one of the first Set at Bedford recalled, "starting with a firm stamp and paying particular attention to carriage; we came up the middle, numbered and divided."[41] Among the most vivid of her recollections was "the thrill of that first *well-marked* step as our gymnastic lesson started".

The gymnastic lesson was always in the morning, when they also had anatomy, physiology, gymnastic theory and teaching practice. There was no question of allocating weeks, let alone a term, to work in schools; teaching had its slot in the ordinary timetable, and students had to rush from the gymnasium or lecture room onto their bicycles and into Bedford. They went to the High School and the Modern School for Girls. They also went to the elementary schools. "Then you *did* feel a pioneer, then your training showed up, and your personality! Those miraculous people who could keep order in a class of large, unruly boys . . . Those large classes of keen-to-bursting small girls!"[42] One student found when she went to take a class that the headmaster sat there, flicking with his cane the legs of children who misbehaved.[43] Another – the live wire of the first Set, who "used slang when slang was not used and 'made-up' when make-up was not countenanced" could entrance a large class of tiresome boys "by racing up and down the wall bars like a monkey, eating nuts out of the palm of her hand".[44]

After teaching came the dash back to college, for more lectures, or lunch, perhaps. Every afternoon was spent on the games field, playing hockey, netball or lacrosse in winter, cricket and tennis in the summer months. After tea, there were more lectures (as there were on Saturday mornings; matches were on Saturday afternoons). At some time in the week came Miss Moon from London, with her accompanist, to teach them dancing, Monsieur Bertrand, the fencing master, and Miss Frederiksson, or later Miss Lindelöf, to take them for remedial gymnastics. There was also First Aid to be fitted in, and elocution lessons, to help them *command*. The pages and pages of Molly Evans' notes had to be written in the private study period every evening before she went to bed. There was no other opportunity. "I always fell asleep when I should have worked," said a near contemporary;[45] and so, perhaps, did she.

The Ling Association

What the "over-pressure" lobby would have made of Molly Evans' day we can but guess.[46] It does not seem to have attracted their attention. The arduous regime of the specialist colleges (for there was nothing to choose between them) set firmly in its mould in these pre-war years, under the aegis of the Ling Association.

Madame Österberg, it will be remembered, would have no part in this professional body formed in 1899 by her own old students, and turned them down when they asked her to be president. As one of them recalled, "She had never envisaged a professional association operating on democratic lines as a separate thing from her college."[47] Other names were canvassed, including Miss Stansfeld's. She was not in fact president till 1910 but played a key role from the beginning. Much of the Association's early work concerned the definition of professional standards. Membership at first was confined to gymnasts trained by Madame Österberg, or in Stockholm. Students of Miss Anstey's college were admitted in 1900, provided they had had a year's teaching experience; and in 1902 Miss Stansfeld went, with others, to inspect the work at Anstey before it was decided that students trained there could be admitted unconditionally.[48] In 1904 the Ling Association established its Gymnastic Teachers' Diploma. Madame Österberg, again, would have nothing to do with it, but in the next two years the training at Bournemouth,[49] Bedford and Dunfermline was inspected and recognised for examination. In these years the Association acted as guardian of the purity of Swedish gymnastics. When Irene Marsh first applied for membership for her college in Liverpool she was turned down for using musical drill.[50] No heresy of this kind ever contaminated Dartford, Anstey or Miss Stansfeld's college. The enterprising Miss Wilkie of Chelsea, whose work had started out in the German tradition, ventured to run an experimental class in which doctors, teachers and others interested tried Swedish exercises with music and without, contrasting their experience with the German system.[51] But in 1907 she went over to Ling.

The triumph of Ling was assured, moreover, by a change in government attitudes. As we have seen, in 1902 the Board of Education had issued a manual on physical training for the elementary schools largely inspired by a War Office handbook. The Ling Association objected strongly, and drew up a memorial, "Women teachers for Women", which gained some 1400 signatures from doctors, teachers and people of standing.[52] Others protested to their M.P.s, and letters to the press included one from Miss Stansfeld. Military drill, if bad for boys, was worse for girls, she said, pointing out that "in spite of all the good work women gymnastic teachers have done of late years, no women experts have been consulted".[53] Official attitudes were on the turn, however. Where the late-Victorian Education Department had for so long been deaf to the arguments of physical educationists such as Roth, policy-making in the early twentieth century passed to men who were intensely sympathetic. Robert Morant, who became Permanent Secretary of the Board of Education in 1903, saw the elementary schools as crucial in the battle to raise the standard of the nation's health. It was Morant who achieved the introduction of school medical inspection in 1907 and who brought in as the Board's Chief Medical Officer Dr George Newman, a crusader of the stamp of the great Victorian, Sir John Simon. Newman in his first year met the views of the Ling Association by his appointment of a *woman* inspector of physical instruction. The committee he set up to draft a new syllabus was chaired by a woman, Dr Janet Campbell, and had two women members, one of them Miss Rendel, the new inspector, who had trained at Chelsea and taught at Dunfermline, the other Miss Koetter from the L.C.C. It also included Commander Grenfell, the naval man converted to Ling by Madame Österberg, who had introduced Swedish gymnastics at Eton. Newman's committee set out to draft a syllabus which was to be "definitely Swedish in character"[54] and what they produced in 1909 was generally welcomed by the Ling Association. Miss Stansfeld, though, was among the purists who felt it tried too hard to be recreative. "While we all want children to enjoy their lessons, earnest work is in itself a pleasure, and it is an educational mistake, therefore, to strain after amusement."[55]

The triumph of Ling did not solve the problem of the elementary schools. Madame Österberg, it will be remembered, had come to the view that Board School children started from a base so pitifully low that the Swedish ideal could not be built upon it. In the ensuing quarter of a century much had been done for them, and more spoken of, but the base was still low, and the means to raise it continually exercised the profession. The promising developments of 1909 – the Swedish syllabus, and Parliamentary action to check the nation's "deplorable physical degeneration" by making physical training compulsory in schools and training colleges – inspired in the gymnasts the feeling that "it behoves us to do our level best to make our Association a power for good in the country".[56] They were dismayed by the inadequate training of the elementary teacher. A resolution of 1909 urges that a minimum of thirty-six hours per year should be devoted to physical instruction at the Training Centres for elementary teachers, "that all Training Centres engage the services of a fully trained and qualified expert . . . that the Authorities exert their power to insist on suitable costume and provide adequate floor space and changing accommodation". The number in a class should not exceed thirty, "since efficient individual work is most important for future teachers".[57] In 1911 the Association pleads that elementary teachers who showed special aptitude for physical instruction should have extra training.[58] In 1912 the Board of Education made hygiene and physical training additional optional subjects for teachers in elementary schools and a hygiene and physiology exam was introduced for the Teacher's Certificate. However, all this fell very far short of the training provided in a specialist college. There were indeed Two Nations at school. " 'Ands on your 'ips, down on your 'aunches, and when I say 'op, 'op!" commanded one teacher as a Bedford student arrived at her class.[59] Such commands were not to be found in Posse.

The Ling Association had problems nearer home, in that no way was found in these pre-war years of coming together with the Bergman-Österberg Union of Gymnastic Teachers. No way was found, either, of dealing with the men. The only male gymnasts qualified for membership were those very few, like Commander Grenfell, who had trained at the Institute in Stockholm. Ling had not made significant advances in the public schools and boys' grammar schools, while the government's policy, after the Boer War, of appointing drill sergeants for the elementary schools created a body of low-grade instructors who could not be assimilated to the new system. In 1908 a small men's section was introduced at the college in Dunfermline, and from 1908–12 a one-year men's course ran at the South Western Polytechnic, but apart from this there were no specialist men's courses comparable with the training at the women's colleges. What had developed was quite unusual: an important element of English education created and sustained by women.

It can be seen growing in professional consciousness in the period before the First War. The Ling Association occupied itself with salary and status as well as training. Miss Stansfeld was a member of the sub-committee which early drew up a scale of fees appropriate to gymnastic teaching.[60] It was she who started the Association's library and she took a main part in the holiday courses which did so much in these early years to create a sense of professional identity. They were held annually and offered gymnastics, games competitions between *alumnae* of the different colleges, lectures, visits to schools and clinics, and the pleasures of social intercourse. The programme of the first one, in 1900, included "a rousing gymnastic lesson" given by Miss Stansfeld, as well as her paper on "minor deformities of the Lower Extremity".[61] She was in great demand to take gymnastics, and to give papers on specialist themes. Thus, "The Results of School Life on the Child", from her pen, meant the postural defects caused by carrying heavy school bags. Broader and more controversial topics, such as "Mrs Butler's Social Purity Crusade", were presented by outside speakers or by Mrs Adair Impey, the member whose enterprise was also responsible for launching the gymnasts' professional journal. In 1908 the initial number of the *Journal of Scientific Physical Training* opens with Mrs Impey, as editor, defending the use of "scientific" in the title and making the case for a journal to represent the profession's "technical and scientific" interests at a time of increasing but inexpert commitment to physical training in the public sphere.

Under these public bodies we find people who have no knowledge of gymnastics, compiling syllabuses . . . we find Education Committees appointing "experts" as organisers of physical training in large districts . . . without the least conception of the extent or kind of effort . . . work in such virgin soil entails.[62]

Now is the time, she says, when the real experts must "enlarge the borders of [their] sympathy and . . . push forward those methods which have proved to be good in the educational service of the race".

The phrase sums up the profession's ideology, its moral basis. That bodily harmony had moral as well as physical significance was always stressed by Madame Österberg, who saw gymnastics as a means to achieve "increased *moral consciousness*" as well as health.[63] What this meant was scarcely defined; but for all that, as we shall see, "the educational service of the race" was a real commitment for several generations of women trained in Swedish gymnastics, and may even have formed part of the attraction, later, of the "Movement" concept which displaced Ling. However that may be, the idea of service in the late nineteenth and early twentieth century drew a growing number of middle-class ladies from the private into the public sphere, and in that sense the gymnasts were responding to the same call which led other women to sit on School Boards or undertake a professional involvement in philanthropy. Where Madame Österberg wrote of moral consciousness, Miss Stansfeld more commonly wrote of flat feet. But students left her having dwelt on the heights, possessed by a sense of moral value in their work which lasted a lifetime. The period, for women, as one said later, "was an era when you did hitch your wagon to a star".[64] Whether this star was what she showed them of the teacher "imbued with a wish to serve",[65] or of the subject as "a means to discover . . . and reinforce the goodness that is in all children",[66] or their own perception of her as remarkable, "in my whole life the person I owe most to",[67] is not clear and does not matter very much. It was a star which burned very brightly at Bedford in the early twentieth century.

4

Stanny's Stues

These years are still the years of my prime.
Muriel Spark, *The Prime of Miss Jean Brodie*

A booklet compiled in 1964 to mark the sixty-fifth anniversary of the founding of the Ling Association consists of profiles of the pioneers. "Unique and inspiring". We read of Madame Österberg. "Dominating . . . often intimidating". Her memory will live on. "Her intrepid spirit and brilliant, dynamic power will continue to inspire future generations of young women."[1] Those who wrote thus had themselves been inspired, but were no longer young. By the 1960s, it is doubtful if there were many young women familiar with the work of Madame Österberg, or with the style that she represented. Not only Ling, but the charismatic teacher had by now become obsolete. And, whatever forces were at work in education, none of them tended to sustain authority in the shape of deference to a single figure, the arbiter, focus and cynosure of all. The classic era of the Great Headmistress, or female head of a women's college, begun in the 1870s, had ended.

There is, perhaps, no better example of its force, while it lasted, than Bedford College. Miss Stansfeld, unlike Miss Beale in her day, did not actually sit upon a throne. Nor did her spiritual enthronement extend, as in some cases, to modes of address. She was not "Madame", like Madame Bergman-Österberg, or "Domina", like Miss Wilkie of Chelsea. But it would be difficult to overstate the college's dependence on her over forty years. The first Set of students dreaded Wednesday because on that day Miss Stansfeld went to London. Nothing seemed to go well without her and their spirits sank until the four-wheeled cab was heard coming back up the road at night.[2] These girls, unlike those earlier pioneers, Emily Davies' students at Hitchin, some of whom seem to have felt they were treated as "a mere cog in the wheel of her great scheme",[3] almost idolised their Principal – a mark of their unsophistication perhaps, or of the fact that Ling, with its tables and commands, lent itself to reliance on a leader. "She was just our Chief," wrote one, looking back.[4]

She was also a mother-figure – not at all in the style of Miss Anstey, who brought in children off the street to dance and sing in her "Pixie Class" and even adopted some of her own, but in the way of tending the student family. It was recalled how, on one occasion, hastening off to London, she heard a student sneeze, and how later a telegram arrived at college: "Get Freda hot – signed Cinnamon."[5] Returning, "she would come to our rooms and discuss the events of the day, help where help was needed, and perhaps clear up some misfortune which had befallen us".[6] It became customary after supper for them to join her in the drawing-room where "she would make us feel that this was indeed our home, talking to us, sometimes reading to us".[7] She was an excellent raconteur and for some "This was the most peaceful and precious time of the week."[8]

The ethos of the college did not really change from its beginnings in 1903, to 1945 when Miss Stansfeld retired. There were many other changes: increased numbers, enlarged facilities, extension of the course from two to three years;[9] but none of them, nor even the effect of two wars, greatly altered the "feel" of Bedford, which was essentially that of a family. It was, (and still is) a matter of pride that "College" had not lost "the family spirit in which [it] was originally conceived";[10] and "conceived", with its suggestion of conscious thought, is probably apt; for the family spirit, even at the start with only thirteen students, was at least as much a reflection of attitudes as it was of numbers. Emily Davies, who had started out with even fewer students, from the first rejected the family model. "My 'idea' of the College," she wrote, "is that of a society not a family."[11] But then, she was thinking of the colleges for men. The specialist colleges had no such prototype, and this may be one reason why, for all their professionalism and their commitment to such "public" ends as "the educational service of the race", they remained in many ways as private as the family-type girls' schools of an earlier day. In the 1930s, to an outsider, Anstey still seemed like "a large Victorian family" mothered by its Principal, while Bedford students, though ten times their original number, were well-nicknamed "Stanny's Stues".[12]

Undoubtedly, the family spirit was preserved by the fact that until the 1950s, the colleges were outside the public sector. Bedford started as Miss Stansfeld's property. In 1930 she formed a company with senior members of her staff, but effectively, for over forty years she was accountable to no one. This seems to place her more in line with the owner/headmistress of a private school than, say, with the heads of the new girls' grammar schools, all accountable to governing bodies. Her attitude to money, though ("Money is dross!" she is reputed to have told the students) would not have gone down with the owner/ headmistress. She drew a salary, and modest dividends from Bedford Physical Training College Ltd, while at the same time opening her own purse, like a kind mother, to help needy students, welcome back Old Students (members of the "family") and provide those little extras in Lansdowne Road which normal budgeting would not stretch to. Any thought of cosiness should be dismissed, though. Hers was the reserved, if not daunting, manner which marked so many of the new race of women in authority in education. She was the "just but beneficent ruler, commanding obedience to impersonal laws" and aiming, despite those sessions in the drawing-room, to cultivate her students' loyalty "to the impersonal standards she represented, not . . . to herself as an individual".[13]

It has been said of this new race of women that, on the whole, they presented their pupils with conservative images of women's work and lives.[14] As a group, the heads of the specialist colleges hardly bear this out. Madame Österberg, for instance, had not only the quality of foreignness, but was, more unusually, a married woman working; and, still more unusually, working in England, while her husband, Per Österberg, worked in Sweden. What did the students make of that?[15] Miss Wilkie was another colourful foreigner. Living with her parrot in the heart of Chelsea, she delighted in the milieu of art and folk dance and was a great friend of Cecil Sharp. She loved bright colours, and taught in scarlet (tunic, girdle, stockings and shoes). Her ordinary dress was also distinctive, sometimes with sleeves that were long and draping, embroidered yoke or Liberty stole. "A long string of amber . . . beads completed the picture, while a flowing cloak . . . was added for outdoor wear."[16] Miss Anstey, striding around in her *djibbah*, corsetless and sandalled, was regarded as a crank by many local people and by some of her students. She was vegetarian, passionately feminist, and so devoted to astrology and horoscopes that she was inclined to accept for training anyone born under Sagittarius.[17] Miss Stansfeld, well-groomed and of conservative demeanour, seems to fit the stereotype of female authority. But not entirely. It does not really fit that she professed no form of religion; and clearly this still puzzles some who recall her as a woman of exceptional moral stature. "She had a wonderful inward light", and yet was no Christian.[18] "She wasn't religious, but to me, she was the most religious person that I've ever met. She was a *good* woman."[19] It was not, then, with her, as with some other heads of colleges, that work was the channel for a Christian vocation.[20] Yet Swedish gymnastics seem to have provided the means of projecting the values she adhered to, and to this end she launched her students (who probably only thought they had come to play hockey) on a most arduous Pilgrim's Progress.

Students

Apart from the fact that as she grew older Miss Stansfeld did less teaching herself, the means whereby students perceived her standards, and gradually took them for their own, remained unaltered over the whole period. The first intimation came at the interview which in most cases preceded admission. Whether this occurred in the pioneer days of her middle age and "raven-black hair" or later, when she was grey and in her eighties, made no difference. "The strength and vitality in her face made anything else quite secondary."[21] Some girls were confident: "Coming from Cheltenham I don't think I doubted she'd accept me."[22] Most were very shy, and at least one mother came to Bedford as nervous as her daughter, though she was a crack shot with crocodiles.[23] Miss Stansfeld addressed herself mainly to the parents. With the would-be student her remarks took a form which Edwardian schoolgirls must have been used to and children as late as the 1940s still had to tolerate: personal comment, which, whatever the intention behind it, had the effect of cutting-down to size. "Is that a bought blouse or home-made?"[24] "Stand up, child!"[25] "Speak properly, now, – you sound as if you'd got a plum in your throat."[26] "Do remove your hat, I'm sure you're not used to wearing one."[27] Whatever they may have felt at the time, no one, looking back, admits to resentment. "She told me my feet were too big and they were flat, but did it so nicely," as one explains.[28]

The real cutting-down to size came later. Schoolgirls who had been "captain of everything" were, as one said, "brought down to ground level" before they had time to discard their school uniform.

On my blazer pocket in red letters were HC NC TC – Hockey Colours, Netball Colours, Tennis Colours. I get to Bedford; and up against girls who'd been coached with first rate staff – games coaches – I was nowhere. And I was pulled up time and time and time again, and humiliated and made to take a free hit again and again and again, and muffed it worse and worse and worse! It was very public, the humiliation.[29]

For their first term they were on probation. Those judged inadequate had to leave. "The minute a new student comes into the dining room, I know," Miss Stansfeld was wont to acknowledge, "whether I'm going to train her or not."[30] But *they* did not know. "You nearly died from anxiety."[31] For the whole term a sword of Damocles hung over all but the most phlegmatic. "Phyllis tells me she may have to go – she's only just come!" said the startled mother of a girl who later became Principal herself.[32] The number of entrants always shrank. "We started with thirty-five, finished with twenty."[33] "We came in, sixty; we went out, fifty."[34] "Six to ten students sacked after the first term."[35] This *salon des refusées*, over the years, included a girl who "talked broad Liverpuddlian", one who had a babyish-sounding voice, one with a stammer, and, very nearly, one who had not confessed to wearing glasses. "You know very well that I have a rule that I will not take students who wear spectacles!" And then, "You needn't come back after Christmas!"[36] This particular student, tougher than most, reckoned it was not an out-and-out rejection. She decided to come back; and nothing happened. "I think sometimes she said things to see what you were made of."[37] Possibly, for no thunderbolt descended on the head of another resilient girl, early accused of being very self-centred, who told Miss Stansfeld that with life so uncertain, nobody could be anything else.[38]

The Bedford day has already been described. Broadly, the pattern of devoting the morning to gymnastics, lectures and teaching practice, the afternoon to games and the evening to more lectures and private study, holds good throughout. It was a long working day, which sometimes began even before breakfast when junior students acted as "bodies" so that the seniors could practise massage; the tightly packed timetable involved a great deal of rush and the repeated changing of clothes. The hectic rush was not only a consequence of pedalling in and out of Bedford every day but of a curriculum so overloaded that in effect the teaching never let up; no moment offered when the student was able to take things at her own pace; the pace was determined by the prodigious quantity of work and the high standards set. In such respects the regime at Bedford was much the same as that at Dartford or Anstey. Any reader seeking to *feel* what it was like should turn from college histories to Josephine Tey, whose splendid novel *Miss Pym Disposes* supplies the experience vicariously. In real life it called for Spartan qualities. Students grew accustomed to sustained fatigue;[39] there were times when, for that reason alone, they were not reluctant to lie down on the plinth and submit to massage. They learnt to suffer pain – whether the agony of "junior leg", or of some chance blow in the gymnasium. "However much you hurt yourself you *never* showed it."[40] What most, though, found hardest to endure without flinching was the severe, if not ruthless criticism to which they were subjected incessantly. In the eyes of their various tutors it seemed as if they could never do well. They were never praised. Indeed, they went through a process, common enough in successful groups, of being pulled down to be built up again. Some would say the second stage never happened. Some did not wait to see if it would, and some, as we know, were turned out by Miss Stansfeld, as by Madame Österberg, for lack of ability or failing in other ways to match up to her unbelievably exacting requirements.

Behind all this was the question of standards. The aim was perfection. In their special field, students could come as close to it at Bedford as they would ever again in their lives – if they had it in them. If they had not . . . "Stan" was like Josephine Tey's Hermione, who saw her college as a bright gateway into the future for deserving youth. "If one or two found the gateway a hazard rather than an opening, then it was unfortunate, but no reflection on the builders of the gateway."[41] At Bedford, all that had been dinned into students in the name of discipline, integrity, achievement, came to the test for each individual eventually in the form of the "crit. class", a very public teaching demonstration in line with the tradition established in the elementary training colleges. In the presence of her own Set and most of the staff, the student gave a lesson in the college gymnasium to a class from one of the elementary schools, not generally children she had taught before. When it was over and the childen dismissed, each with an orange or a penny apiece, the girl stood forward to be torn to pieces by members of staff and such of her contemporaries as were called upon to offer a "crit." Even the most able seem not to have been praised beyond a curt "That's it!" from Miss Stansfeld. "It made you courageous through agony, really."[42] Some were not sufficiently courageous, and wept. The *publicity* of it comes up repeatedly as the real torture; as painful, almost, for girls who gave "crits" as for those who were "critted". Only an outsider with nothing to lose could afford the effrontery of one little boy who stuck his tongue out at the staff and yelled, "Got yer eye full?"[43]

The "crit. class" survived until the 1940s. During most of our period, therefore, it was both the climax of professional training and the most intimidating feature of a discipline which governed the students from breakfast to bedtime. The general impression is that students from day schools tended to resent the discipline most; and that these included some who also felt conscious of the college's social elitism, which was the consequence of high fees.[44] In the late thirties, one or two students received small grants from County Councils; and by the fifties, as we shall see, support, or lack of it, from such quarters had become crucial to the college's future. But, in effect, throughout the Stansfeld era, there was little hope of anything from public funds. Those whose parents could not find the fees scraped through somehow with help from relatives, or from such bodies as the Girls' Realm Guild, the Thomas Wall Trust and the Gentlewomen's Employment Association. Some were helped by Miss Stansfeld herself. But if not everyone found the fees easily, the great majority came from independent schools. The link with school was tremendously important. Time and again, it seems, girls chose Bedford (as they chose Dartford, Anstey or Chelsea) if they had been taught by someone who trained there. This applied to all kinds of schools, but in the boarding schools, with their large games staff, it could amount to a tradition.

> All St Swithin's staff were from Bedford. I did not even know that other colleges existed.[45]
>
> Students in the college . . . went back to the schools to become the staff who sent more students.[46]

Among the day schools, Miss Stansfeld's college had a special link with the Bedford High School (where she went on teaching to 1918 and where, till her retirement, she supplied the gym staff). Girls' Public Day School Trust schools were prominent as, among boarding schools, were Wycombe Abbey, St Leonard's and Cheltenham Ladies' College. Speaking of the twenties, one former student recalls that Cheltenham sent no fewer than eight or nine entrants in her year out of a total forty-two, and she remembers them as "*fearfully* confident!" "I can see ourselves now, waiting for the start of some lecture or other, and their voices ringing across that big lecture room: " 'Were you in Coll. One or Coll. Two?' " Her own school drew the sarcasm of the Vice-Principal.

"Where do you come from?"

"Henrietta Barnet."

"Dr Barnardo's, did you say?"[47]

Bedford was the most snobbish of the colleges, with less of a "social mix" than Dartford or Anstey and certainly less than the one in Chelsea (where it was possible for London girls to train economically by living at home), or the Liverpool college of Irene Marsh. Of Bedford as late as the 1940s one Old Student said, "I don't remember anybody without the right accent doing well."[48] While another, from a midland grammar school (who did well enough to be Principal later) was nonetheless conscious as a new entrant of "cloaked public school girls" forming a distinct group: less interested in teaching, she fancied, than her own kind, but "great games players."[49]

Games were the magnet which drew some girls into physical training.

> I adored hockey . . . and it came to the end of my time at school and I thought, "I'll never play hockey again. Well, all right, I'll go to college and then I can go on playing hockey!" I hadn't a clue I was going to be a teacher . . .[50]

> I thoroughly enjoyed games, dancing and gymnastics . . . The implications of teaching the young never entered into my head.[51]

> I was very keen on games, especially cricket.[52]

Or she might have said, especially hockey or lacrosse. Here were already the preferences and talents which carried some into the international class. "Always two or three in the English eleven," as one put it.[53] Out on the games field they were what Jean Brodie called "the crème de la crème".

It is very difficult, in retrospect, to judge their intellectual calibre. Over the whole period Miss Stansfeld was free to select students as she wished, and even after 1935, when the college course was recognised by London University for the award of the Diploma on Theory and Practice of Physical Education (for which School Certificate on entry was required), there were students who continued to qualify only for the College's own Diploma. Any impression, though, of hearty girls with very little brain would be wide of the mark. Apart from the evidence of later careers, the period throws up a number of instances of girls going into physical training as an alternative to university.[54] University, to the upper middle classes still meant mainly Oxford or

Cambridge, where places for women were hard to come by. To some parents, also, a college like Bedford, of the family type, seemed better for a daughter. "My mother wouldn't contemplate the university . . . didn't care for it for girls."[55] In whatever way they made the choice they seldom seem to have regretted it. With all its rigours, this was what they wanted. "I loved *moving*," as one of them said.[56]

"The energetic movement of girls should never be restrained as 'unrefined' or 'unladylike'," Molly Evans put in her notebook. Nonetheless, it is clear from the context that she is thinking chiefly of schoolgirls.[57] That questions of refinement could not be ignored when it came to the movement of *young ladies* is plain from the views of one observer in 1909, who concluded, on acquaintance with Anstey, "that it was possible for women to live a life of freedom and development *without losing one whit of their womanliness*".[58] Many people had a different reaction. Students of the Hampstead college were resigned to being called "those dreadful girls" by passers-by who saw them in "gym-suits" on the playing fields, "and to overhearing discussions of our character by men who don't know how troublesome skirts are and by women who don't know how delicious it is to be free of them".[59] Miss Stansfeld, as we saw, had problems with some parents at Bedford High School in 1898 when she wanted the girls to wear a short dress for gymnastics. By the time she came to establish her college, the "gym-slip" was no longer such an innovation. Yet it was still possible in 1910 for a young man solemnly to warn his fiancée, when he saw the picture of a Dartford girl playing hockey in her college tunic, "If there is any chance of your wearing kit like that, my foot comes down bang and you have no more hockey!"[60] This was the context in which Bedford students, in the early days, put skirts over tunics to step from one college house to another. And not only skirts: hats, gloves and coats were worn for that short distance, up to 1914. The only exception was Demonstration Day, when students were allowed in the road in tunics. "It seems today quite stupid," one of them recalled,

> but we must remember that Miss Stansfeld was always alive to the feelings of others; she was jealous for the good name of her College, and though always ahead of the times herself, she did not expect the neighbours to feel as she did, and she did her best not to offend them in any way.[61]

Many years earlier, Emily Davies had imposed on the pioneer students at Girton her own kind of double conformity: that is, they

were to behave like ladies, to the last detail, while omitting nothing of
the academic studies pursued by men. The prize (admission to the
University) must not be jeopardised by failure to wear gloves. In
contrast, the physical training specialists were independent of the
male establishment. They made their own rules and approved their
own courses.[62] On the other hand, the whole point of their training
was to win acceptance for their work in the schools, which meant
getting the support of middle-class parents. Miss Stansfeld, no more
than Emily Davies, could ignore the opinion of conventional society.

There is no sign that she wished to do so. College life, indoors as
well as out, combined the values of the gymnasium with those of the
drawing-room. At meals, for instance, it was expected that students
would eat heartily, and food was good. Stanny's Stues could never
have complained, like the girls at Hitchin, of puddings made with
dripping. "I would lay stress on food, and plenty of it," Madame
Österberg had declared, deploring the fact that girls were often taught
that it was unladylike to have large appetites.[63] At the same time, great
pains were taken with the *bienséances*, the social graces. Students in
Lansdowne Road were encouraged to acquire the art of small talk
through a system of "following" which survived well into the 1950s.
This meant that at meal times, you sat *tomorrow* where the girl who
came ahead of you in the alphabet was sitting *today*. Students thus
were obliged to change neighbours and, more important, were bound
eventually to have to make conversation to the staff. Table manners
also came under scrutiny. "There were large asparagus beds and
strawberry patches in the vegetable gardens, so the first summer
term, we were taught the use of finger bowls."[64]

That was the genial side of family discipline. The rest is often
recalled with incredulity, "I wonder what would happen nowadays if
students were told 'Everyone in bed by 9 o'clock tonight!' "[65] In 1904
it was accepted without question. Bedtime, in the forties, was still
enforced at 10.30p.m. by members of staff who would check if need
be to see that lights were out, just as earlier in the evening they might
check to see that students were working in their rooms. By that time it
was not so readily accepted. "They were sort of into everything," one
recalls, "you didn't have anything that they didn't know about or try
to interfere with . . . they just seemed to enter into everything you
did."[66] When cold baths before breakfast were the rule, steamy
bathroom windows were commented on.[67] The moral undertow of
petty discipline was seldom far below the surface. "I'm only telling

you this for your *mother*'s sake!" declared one tutor in the 1940s, hauling a student out of bed to tell her that she had left the landing light on. That is discipline in the style of the Victorian ladies' academy.[68] The impression is that, before the First War, the "schooly" atmosphere was taken for granted, and that even in the thirties some girls welcomed it. One loved Bedford because she loved school "and in a way it was a continuation of school".[69] Others recall it as "very enclosed",[70] "terribly restrictive",[71] but say that they enjoyed it. "You were put in a nunnery",[72] according to one view of the Bedford regime in the 1920s, while a student of the forties still labelled it "convent-like".[73] Going out with young men was out of the question, had there been time for such diversions, nor were men allowed to visit in college. "Miss Stansfeld guarded us like porcelain"[74] is a comment which could be applied throughout.

Were restrictions at Bedford exceptional? One student was convinced of it in 1938, when her first impression of Lansdowne Road was "Had gone to boarding school and lost all freedom. Not a bit like college life."[75] But what kind of college life had she expected? All colleges then were *in loco parentis* and women's colleges took this very seriously. In practice, the notion of parental authority was subject to a range of interpretation. At one end of the spectrum, the day-to-day life of women students at Oxford and Cambridge was by this time relatively free.[76] The ethos of teacher training was quite different, and can be traced back to the kind of discipline thought appropriate in the nineteenth century to students from comparatively humble homes. Though it had softened in the course of time, there were still colleges between the wars (especially those run by the churches) where all the trappings of school remained, including uniform, lights-out, prefects, and where every minute was accounted for. In a sense, Bedford and the like were hybrids, where students with the background and expectations of girls at Oxford were subjected to a discipline comparable with that of the general colleges. This was partly due to the nature of the work (vocational training cannot well be optional, and physical training, more than most, was conceived in terms of command and authority) and partly to that Victorian inheritance which survived so well in this particular milieu. Miss Stansfeld, living long into the twentieth century, and amazingly responsive, as we shall see, to developments in her profession, never lost the habit of keeping in leading-strings those who were designed to be leaders. It could have been said of her, as it was of Madame Österberg, that she believed in "woman's salvation through woman", yet that it was "a curious feature of one who assessed women's powers so highly that her college regime allowed nothing in the nature of self-government".[77] Even the Games Club at Lansdowne Road was simply "College" by another name, with Miss Stansfeld controlling it as president till she retired at the age of eighty-five. It was not till then that a student raised the question why, in fact, it should be called a "club" when membership was compulsory.[78] After that, student power lay dormant for well over another ten years.

The overall impression of the Stansfeld era is, for all that, one of happiness. Old Students may recount how the main fuse was pulled to enforce "light-outs" and then conclude, "It was a wonderful three years."[79] The oldest Old Students, those who were at Bedford before the First War, patently carried into old age their extraordinary sense of gratitude at being there, at having had the "privilege". Their comments recall that springtime of women's education at Hitchin when happiness, too, had very little to do with the exigencies of the regime, and a student, asked for her predominant feeling during the first term, answered, "Gladness".[80] As late as the twenties it could still be an experience for a girl of eighteen or nineteen to find that she could "work hard as a normal healthy person, with a clearly understood code of conduct".[81] Memories of hard work, "where one lived entirely in the present", of "striving and of achievement" and of "wholehearted enjoyment" return.[82] Students all remember that life was strict but they also remember its camaraderie, the pleasures of the games field and gymnasium, punts on the river, bicycle rides, picnics, or the play produced by their Set, which more than likely contained such characters as "Cerebella, a serving maid", or "Lady Patella, affianced to Sir Dynevor".[83] They remember buns from the Cadena cafe "with an almondy centre and thickly iced", practical jokes when they dressed the skeleton and sat it down in the examination room. And through it all runs the major experience of contact with Miss Stansfeld and what she stood for. "Our incredible good luck in being at College with Miss Stansfeld as Principal", is the first thought that comes to one student of the early twenties.[84] Another calls it "a very great privilege and unforgettable experience to have been under her influence. She prepared us for LIFE at its best."[85] Only in the earliest days at Bedford does one actually hear of a student whose conscience prompted her to take off her hat-band when she felt her work was below college standards;[86] but a kind of mental removing of the hat-band, even in later life, is not unknown among those formed in the Stansfeld era. They continue to be "Stanny's Stues" in subtler ways than were ever thought of by the schoolboys who devised that nick-name.

This is not surprising. For many of them, a lifelong relationship was only just beginning when their training ended with "the thrill of having the Badge pinned on one's new tunic and then exit through the *front* door of '37'!"[87] Senior Students almost invariably joined the Old Students' Association. This very powerful Victorian device for for-warding the interests of schools and colleges had soon been taken up by women. Former *alumnae* of Girton and Somerville, of Dartford, Anstey and a hundred high schools, were banded in this way by the twentieth century. Bedford followed suit in 1909 and from then on its Old Students' body was one of the most redoubtable media for transmitting its sense of identity. There was the background of a shared profession – and here its Old Students had much more in common than, say, the old students of Bedford College, London. There was professional refreshment and renewal through well-organised holiday courses – it is not by chance that the Association sprang, by popular demand, from one of the earliest. There was, above all, devotion to Miss Stansfeld, who, as one decade succeeded another, seemed to be immortal. If the college was her family, the Old Students formed her extended family – with less than a hundred members to begin with and more than a thousand by the time she retired. "Thank you all very much," she said then, "for giving me such a happy life."[88] And the *Reports* of the Association are very much like a family album, catching the bright spots: the Past vs. Present cricket match in 1911 when Mary Nield was chaired to her tea in honour of eight wickets for forty-one runs; the presentation in 1913 of a silver mug to the college's first "grandchild"; the "twenty-first birthday" in 1924 when the Association gave Miss Stansfeld a car to mark the college's majority. Members of the family came back *en masse* for the holiday course which ran every year till it became biennial in the 1920s. They looked around the old home, admired the changes ("so excited to see a beautiful new pavilion – oh, lucky Present and To Come!"[89] and went away longing for the next reunion. Some would spend a week-end at college occasionally, "to see how people were getting on", always sure of an affectionate welcome. "Come as often as you can, stay as long as you can and come without notice,"[90] Miss Stansfeld told them. The strength of family feeling at

Bedford proved something of an obstacle, as we shall see, after the Stansfeld era was gone. Meanwhile, successive generations of students were lapped in this warm, amniotic fluid.

Staff

For some of them, if one may extend the metaphor, the umbilical cord was never cut. They came back as members of staff. Over the whole period Miss Stansfeld effectively recruited her staff from among her Old Students. Obviously, this was not possible at first. The initial take-off in 1903 she had accomplished with the help of a colleague at the Bedford High School, Elizabeth Roberts, who joined her in the enterprise in Lansdowne Road and retired when she did, forty-two years later. Miss Roberts taught hygiene and anatomy and supervised the domestic arrangements. In those early days Miss Stansfeld herself took gymnastics, physiology, anatomy, massage; and teaching practice at the High School. In 1906 she was able to make the first two appointments of students she had trained and from then on the teaching staff was virtually indigenous.[91] ("Ought I to know that person?" she asked many years later, encountering in college, after her retirement, a member of staff who had trained at Dartford.)[92] In 1930 the tight little group was drawn still tighter as senior staff became shareholders in the private company, Bedford Physical Training College Ltd, which Miss Stansfeld formed that year to assure the college's future.[93]

To students in those days, the college staff "seemed like younger relations of hers",[94] and some she had indeed called to Lansdowne Road much as a matriarch might summon her children to the family hearth as need arose. It must be remembered that she chose the first posts taken by all students as they finished training. Headmistresses all over England consulted her, or came to Bedford to study the field. Job advertisements between the wars might specify "Bedford or Dartford-trained". They were, as the father of one girl put it, "the Oxford and Cambridge of P.T. colleges" and from the mid-twenties to mid-thirties it could be said that Bedford was "top".[95] When Miss Stansfeld had decided which post she should apply for, the student's completed application form was checked for errors by the college secretary and she appeared in the Principal's room in whatever she proposed to wear at the interview. Miss Stansfeld might object to her "vegetable silk stockings" or tell her to borrow a more suitable hat.

Advice and guidance did not finish there. After a year or two in this first job the young gym mistress might receive a letter suggesting she apply for a more senior post, or, in rare cases, come back to Bedford. This last was, effectively, a royal command. Freda Colwill, summoned in 1916 to become the college's first specialist in dancing, recalls how, after only two terms in her first post at the Maynard School, Exeter, she received an "explosive" letter from Miss Stansfeld, insisting that she come back on the staff. Naturally uncertain how to face her headmistress, she hesitated for a day or two. A second letter came, and she made up her mind. "It needed a bit of courage, really . . . I thought, well I must do it if Miss Stansfeld really wants me . . . I felt I owed her an enormous debt for what she'd given me at college." In any case, she was thrilled to be asked. It was "the greatest honour in the world".[96] By the end of the thirties Miss Stansfeld's magnetism did not pull in Old Students quite as promptly: at least, in one case the royal summons (this time by telephone) had to be followed by negotiation with the school's headmistress over the provision of a successor.[97] The outcome was the same, though – and not surprisingly: for most Old Students this was the accolade, and those who were chosen can still remember the nervous pleasure, on return, of entering by the *front* door of "thirty-seven".

In 1916 when Freda Colwill went back, Miss Stansfeld was already fifty-six but strenuously combining the running of the college with prodigious efforts in aid of the war, and especially for the soldiers billetted in Bedford. Some were quartered in the medical room and these received her especial care. Indeed, what struck Miss Colwill and others, was her great tenderness towards these men, her mothering of those in the college billet, treating their feet when they returned from a route march, helping to ease them when they were sick. In various ways, the war, while it lasted, broke the isolation of Lansdowne Road. The soldiers, the sewing bees in the gymnasium, the sandwich-cutting and concerts for the troops, the ferrying of porridge to the Corn Exchange ("I remember driving . . . in a 'growler' with Miss Stansfeld and . . . a large bowl of porridge [in] . . . the cab for the soldiers"),[98] brought the world in and the students out. Normally, apart from their work in the schools and an occasional gymnastic display, not only the students but the staff at Bedford dwelt in considerable isolation. Tutors were single, and all "lived in"; or all but one, for in 1932 there was one who refused to, and got away with it.[99] If students worked something like a forty-four-hour week (excluding matches and private study), tutors certainly worked no less. The teaching load was succeeded every day by supervisory duties in the various houses. There was no private life during term. Might she attend a May Ball? asked Miss Colwill. "Yes," said Miss Stansfeld, "if your work doesn't suffer."

Possibly her own reserve made Bedford more isolated than the other colleges. Miss Wilkie of Chelsea got her students to organise races for children in Battersea Park; Miss Marsh in Liverpool ran classes for working girls, and for the blind and the deaf and dumb. An important feature of life at Anstey was regular work with girls' clubs in Birmingham. Students taught there and the girls came to the college to watch gymnastic demonstrations, drink tea and be harangued by Miss Anstey on the link between gymnastics and good citizenship. "Very soon," she told them in 1911, "women would probably get the vote and they must prepare themselves to exercise it properly."[100] She was devoted to female suffrage and Anstey more than once gave hospitality to the Gymnastic Teachers' Suffrage Society.[101] In 1911 Miss Anstey led her staff and some of her students in the gymnasts' contingent of the great suffrage procession in London. There is no sign that Bedford took part. Miss Stansfeld is alleged to have favoured the cause but it is not easy to imagine her marching behind the gymnasts' blue and silver banner. Bedford's suffrage memories seem to be confined to attendance at a local meeting where dead rats were thrown through the window, and to a student play, "How We Won the Vote", in which the part of Mrs Pankhurst was played by Phyllis Spafford, a future Principal.[102]

"Miss Stansfeld's one main object in life was to get what she felt was best for her college";[103] and if she defined that more narrowly than some, her definition was superbly executed. First, she picked the talent from among the Old Students. Then she burnished it with extra training, never ceasing to seek what was new. What was new in the 1920s was Ruby Ginner's Revived Greek Dance and she sent Miss Colwill to the Ginner summer schools. By 1930, though, what was new was the Central European Dance inspired by Laban, and she sent Miss Colwill off to Vienna (and her successor, later, to Dresden) to study under a pupil of his. In her middle eighties, in the Second World War, she was still at it, despatching a young colleague for anatomy sessions at the Royal Free Hospital when the doodle bugs were at their height.

All this care and training achieved her aim of creating a pool of talent at Bedford; but it was a pool and not a flowing stream. There was no obvious further step for these able and committed women.[104] Highly honoured, perhaps, in their twenties, to be invited to join the Olympians, they moved into their thirties, forties, fifties – still, essentially, Stanny's Stues. The effects of this are a matter of conjecture (and will be something to consider later, in relation to the tutor who succeeded Miss Stansfeld); but it seems reasonable to assume that their special position over so many years, dominating in regard to the students, but dominated themselves by their leader, had something to do with the kind of behaviour characteristic of them as a group. They were, for instance, rather larger than life; inclined to be histrionic in their teaching. "They all had their images to put across."[105] (People remember Miss Petit's Irish curses, Miss Roberts demonstrating gravity with rice, Miss Wilkie, who began her lectures a hundred yards before she entered the room.) More to the point, they were habitually sarcastic. "They could be cutting." "Cruel, in a way." "You were all right at Bedford, really, if you were good at something and if you were buoyant. If you were weak, you had a very hard time."[106] Students were insulted as a matter of course. It was, somehow, part of the system; as it is, or was, the system in the army for the sergeant major to insult his men. "You can't have your tunic that length," said one tutor to a newcomer, "with legs like yours!"[107] "Bay-bee, Bay-bee!" sneered another, to a girl with a babyish voice.[108] When the "following" system in the dining room brought students beside some members of staff, they were petrified. "I just felt inadequate."[109] It is ironic, but not surprising, that some who remember suffering as students are themselves recalled as members of staff who laid about them with a bitter tongue. Fear was an element in the teaching; and when fear of performance met fear of a tutor, the chances were that the latter would win. One student, having failed to dive off the top board, was cycling back to college when she threw down her bicycle, ran back, and plunged in, fully dressed.[110]

In retrospect it is easy to see that tutors also were under pressure, driven to compete for the energy of students by a system which never let up; by their ideals, and, most of all, by the need to be worthy of their leader. "She inspired one, there's no other word for it."[111] It was not easy, all the same, to approach her on matters peripheral to college, and Freda Colwill in 1932 had to screw up her courage to go and tell Miss Stansfeld that she was engaged to be married. Whatever its prestige in the world outside, marriage meant, at Bedford, finding a replacement for an excellent and well-trained member of staff. So when Miss Colwill confessed her engagement, Miss Stansfeld's reply was, "We'll see who's going to follow you"; and the encounter passed in deciding which of the Old Students would be best to have trained. As for the training of the present students, Miss Stansfeld would certainly never have consoled them for poor results, like one early Oxford Principal, by telling them they were sure to get married.[112] She professed, in fact, to hope they would not; on the grounds that as married women they would devote themselves to one man only, insead of to many hundreds of pupils. There is no sign at all that she was anti-men;[113] only that she was entirely engrossed in "the educational service of the race"; which meant, in the training of gymnastic teachers.[114]

5

A Sacred Trust

The gymnastic mistress has so much influence that she should
regard it as a sacred trust.
Dr H. Crichton Miller 1921[1]

One does not deviate from Ling's principles if one keeps to the
spirit of his work.
The Leaflet, 1924

Bedford had produced its first hundred Old Students by 1911. Of the
two thirds employed then, well over half were teaching in schools.[2]
Twenty years later, in 1931, school teachers were seventy-eight per
cent of those employed; they were seventy-two per cent in 1945.
Other kinds of teaching appear in the records: Bedford contributed to
the growing number of county physical training organisers, lecturers
in general training colleges, university training departments, and
physical training colleges (notably their own). Some Old Students,
especially in the early days, carried on remedial work in private
practice, or ran their own dancing schools. Some worked in girls'
clubs. We find the occasional inspector of schools and the one or two
employed by industrial firms. A number applied their remedial skills
in the physiotherapy departments of hospitals (the two wars made
exceptional demands and the Almeric Paget Massage Corps drew a
dozen Bedford-trained gymnasts out of school teaching soon after it
was formed in 1914). In the 1930s the Ling Association and the
Central Council for Recreative Physical Training were directed by
Bedford women.[3]

School teaching, though, remained the staple. "We have now a
comprehensive system of physical training which forms an integral
part of public education," wrote the Board of Education's Chief
Medical Officer in 1921. And he went on to enlarge on the value of
games in girls' secondary schools. This was more than routine
endorsement. When Newman stated that too few girls, rather than too
many, were playing games, he had an eye to the controversy over the
effects of athletics on women which had broken out again at this time.
Feminism and Sex Extinction was the alarmist title of the book in which
Dr Kenealy once more enlarged on the baleful effects of competitive

games. She wrote of the "sterile glint" in the eyes of young women of strenuous pursuits, of hockey players "incapacitated for lactation" and "grim-visaged maidens of sinewy build, hard and rough and set as working women".

> All the subtler, vital and inspiring impulses of natural womanhood have been rudely smothered in tussles of big muscles, in sensational crazes for making hockey-goals, and similar crude aims, quite alien to natural girlhood.[4]

If her fears for the neutering of girls were now obsessive, and she was inclined to see in every hockey player "stigmata of abnormal Sex-transformation precisely similar in origin to male antlers in female-deer", it must be remembered that the losses of war had added a totally new dimension to anxiety about the falling birth rate. The year her book came out, 1920, the National Birth Rate Commission's report urged "the women of the Empire to save the Empire" by exerting themselves to reverse this trend.

Whether the gymnasts read Dr Kenealy, they undoubtedly read a letter in *The Lancet* in 1921 when a London headmistress took a very similar line. At one time, wrote Miss Cowdroy, she had encouraged girls to take up the work of the gym and games mistress, thinking it the ideal occupation. But, "the more I came in contact with women who had trained for it, the more I was disappointed with the effect of that training upon them". Girls who took up hockey and cricket seemed to deteriorate, she said. "They seemed more selfish, more concentrated upon material things and material advantages." As for the women trained as "physical experts", few in her experience avoided a breakdown. Like Dr Kenealy, she argued that athletics brought "hard muscles, a set jaw, flat chest . . . aggressive manner and . . . ungainly carriage". Athletic women also often suffered from nerves, heart trouble, rheumatism or "displacement of some kind". "Sometimes the monthly disability that should prove them women stops for long periods." Their marriages, she said, were often child-less. If they gave birth they had difficult confinements and produced children physically inferior to "the stalwart sons many a slight feminine woman produced in Victorian days". Their minds, too, were unhealthy. While affecting to despise men, they were yet "inordinately occupied with the discussion of sexual matters" and attracted the passion of neurotic girls. "Let it be recognised," she concluded, "that the present cult is a retrogression, and the young girl have placed before her the ideal of true womanhood".[5]

Miss Cowdroy's letter, lacking any evidence, or indeed any sense that evidence was needed, was warmly welcomed by a Harley Street doctor in the next issue of *The Lancet*. Dr Leslie Thorne Thorne (*sic*) had also seen women whose health was permanently damaged by athletics. "And even if they escape physical injury I find they have degenerated into beings of neutral sex who are unfitted for either the work of men or women."[6] The "sexless gymnast" reached the national press, a focus of complex anxieties about the appropriate role of women, and potentially as damaging to the movement for women's physical education as the Victorian "overstrain" argument had been to their academic training. "The indictments made against us have been numerous, sweeping and most deprecatory," wrote Mrs Adair Impey, pioneer founder of the *Journal of Scientific Physical Training*. They were also "insufficiently based on . . . facts", and the gymnasts, like the female academics of the eighties, set themselves to supply hard evidence.[7] In a letter to *The Lancet*, Dr Margaret Thackrah, the medical officer employed at Dartford, said she had come across temporary amenorrhea "in about 1.5 per cent of the students', and challenged the vague hints of sexual deviance.

> That such [abnormal] women do exist is certainly true, but to say that the condition is due to the practice of athletics seems to me to be making a very unfair assumption. The cause, so far as it is possible to apprehend it at all, is probably a very complex one, connected with the social conditions of the time, the excess of the female population over the male, and in particular the conditions, of necessity, prevailing in boarding schools and resident colleges, in which numbers of women live together without any male society whatever.[8]

Miss Stansfeld was among those who addressed the Medical Officers of Schools' Association on "Games for Girls" in 1921. Following Dr Alice Clow (who, from research into the menstrual experience of students, and girls at Cheltenham Ladies' College, argued that no harm came from games and gymnastics), Miss Stansfeld countered "the many vague statements" of the opposition with experience of Bedford. Student health there was excellent, she said, despite the fact that on entering college, girls began a life which, in her estimation, multiplied their physical work ten times. As to their experience of menstruation, in seven out of a hundred cases there had been temporary amenorrhea. Since many girls found their co-ordination suffered during their periods she did not allow any games or strenuous gymnastics in the first three days. She had inquired, by questionnaire, into the experience of pregnancy and childbirth among Old Students. Their response (of which she gave details) showed a very healthy state of affairs, while "the weight and general health of the babies left nothing to be desired".[9]

The "neat little snowball of accusations" thrown by Miss Cowdroy at sportswomen generally "and gymnastic teachers in particular" was held to have melted in the face of such evidence, and the games mistress was adjured not to fear "the sudden loss of her means of livelihood as a result of this outcrop of Victorian views".[10] The snowball had contained "some very hurtful stones", though, and the Ling Association proceeded to carry out a fertility study of married women gymnasts in the hope of settling the matter.[11] They took up the criticisms one by one, comparing marriage rate, age at marriage, mean fertility, nursing capacity, incidence of abortion and infant mortality among the gymnasts with data collected in 1914 (by the National Birth Rate Commission) for Girton women and their non-collegiate sisters. The results were less conclusive than they had hoped. The gymnasts came out with a slightly lower marriage rate and slightly fewer children than the other groups, (though there was the problem that this data related to the difficult wartime and post-war years, where the other was collected in 1914). Fewer gymnasts seemed to breast-feed their children. Mrs Impey had to admit that

> the poor figures in nursing power cannot be explained by the war and are the surprise of the investigation. They are entirely contrary to expectation formed from personal knowledge of a very wide group of friends. The good nursing mothers include two internationals and several territorial or county players.

The gymnasts, however, had the fewest sterile marriages and a very low rate of abortion and infant deaths. The onus of proof that they were decadent mothers "still rests," she declared, "with the anti-games people".[12]

The Gym Mistress

There is nothing to suggest that "the anti-games people" frightened any applicants away from Bedford (where, had they but known it, in

1921 the marriage rate among Old Students was apparently below the gymnastic average).[13] Another bonus for "the anti-games people" would have been the discovery that Bedford Old Students, for the years 1914–24, gave birth to considerably more girls than boys, thus, it seems, fulfilling yet another prophecy (and given its implications, by far the most insulting) to emanate from the opposition.[14] Miss Stansfeld seems to have had no trouble with recruitment. In 1919 the course had been extended from two to three years, and during the twenties the annual intake rose from forty to fifty students; among whom, probably, fewer were familiar with Arabella Kenealy than with Angela Brazil, whose schoolgirl stories now lent glamour to the hockey field. Not that games are everything, in her eyes; indeed, her plots depend very often on some singularity outside school, and even the big set pieces of school life include music festivals and craft competitions as well as tennis tournaments and cricket matches. She gives her readers, though, an exciting sense of the changes that were overtaking girls' schools; and team games, along with the gymnasium, laboratory, and the tentative discussion of careers, appear as emblems of that brave new world which was rising from its Victorian foundations in 1906, when her first book came out, and still under construction in the 1920s.

Angela Brazil's girls, it must be said, are so adept at captaining and coaching that we rarely see the games mistress, but when we do meet her she does not resemble the unsexed harridan presented by Miss Cowdroy.

> "Which is the nicest teacher of all?" asked Jean. "I think most of us like Miss Latimer best, the games mistress. She's very popular with everybody. You see, we always have such fun at gymnastics, and of course we love hockey and cricket."[15]

If Miss Latimer had trained at Bedford, Miss Stansfeld would have warned her against the dangers of attracting excessive popularity. "To expect crushes and *never* encourage them!" was her advice to third year students.[16] "Soppiness" they knew as a fact of life which, like many facts, might be distasteful, but which was greatly to be preferred to a precocious heterosexuality.

> I wish the girls of the working class had more games and we should have less slobbering along the road with young men every night, which seems to me so unwholesome and so decadent.[17]

78

Many would have endorsed this view expressed by Mrs Adair Impey. The Peter Pan world of schoolgirl fiction mirrors the long and sexless childhood which middle-class parents sought for their girls. "Was it not an argument in favour of games that they delayed maturity?" one woman asked, at a meeting held in 1922 in the thick of the "anti-games" debate. Mrs Adair Impey agreed with her.

> The girls who play games do not have time to powder their noses. It is not because they have no use for the opposite sex, but because they have not yet got to the stage of thinking about them, and I think that is an argument in favour of games.[18]

Middle-class schoolgirls, then, had crushes, while working girls were "slobbering along the road" with young men.

There seems no reason to doubt the impression that while any mistress might be adored, the gym and games mistress was adored more than others; at least, if she was young. Miss Latimer, one feels, did not yet face the problems of the ageing gymnast, was not yet the trim but somewhat scrawny figure, tunicked still but non-participant, bossy and austere, that some became.[19] On the contrary, Miss Latimer lives on, in the memory of thousands of middle-aged women, as one who walked like a prince among her colleagues, those provincial B.A.s and Oxford graduates not distinguished for their physical grace. If there was a New Woman, this was she. From the ordeals of Bedford and the rest she emerged with beautiful carriage and an air of confidence not bestowed by any university. Where else, in the ambivalent inter-war years, half of which had gone before women were admitted to adult suffrage, should schoolgirls have found a model which proclaimed so clearly, "I am a citizen of no mean city!"?

"They stood out; they were *quality*." In such terms runs one recollection of the 1930s.[20] It had seemed impressive, in that particular school, that the two gym mistresses, alone of all the staff, had their special base, the medical room. As to their subject, everything about them affirmed that "this was wonderful stuff!" They spoke proudly of Bedford College, and on their gym slips, "heavy, double-pleated", wore "that badge", the sign of their distinction, which had first been pinned on by Miss Stansfeld. "Their tunics were *quality* compared with ours. It was just like privates and officers."[21] The gym staff were officers in a way which did not apply to the classics mistress. They were leaders in the moral sense. When the head of a new physical training college tried to recall in the 1950s what was owed to such colleges as Bedford, she put the moral contribution very high.

> Thinking back to my own schooldays at the Clapham High School, I realise the confidence we had in the sense of justice and fair play of the Gymnastic Mistresses, who came to us then from Bedford Physical Training College. I can recall many incidents in our school life that impressed this upon us, and the enjoyment we had in trying to live up to the standards they put before us.[22]

The former gym mistress may put it more prosaically, but there is no doubt that she accepts that view. She will point out that, alone among her colleagues, she came across every girl in the school. This was partly through her ordinary teaching, whereby she had "an easier, more friendly contact with girls in changing rooms, journeying to matches";[23] partly through her medical work, (she was, in Madame Österberg's phrase, not only the "gymnastic" but the "health" mistress, and in this role had standing with parents long before parent-teacher bodies existed); and partly through the feats of organisation which she was called on to perform. "The old-fashioned games mistress, trained to command, was invaluable in any school."[24] She it was indeed who caused girls to move "in an orderly fashion from here to there", directed squads of them to carry chairs and, in general, handled the masses, whether for speech days and great occasions, or school lunch (a double sitting). To her at all times it was a duty "to set an example of orderliness . . . which I'm sure leads to a discipline in the mind",[25] and to concern herself with "general behaviour . . . response to discipline . . . pride in appearance."[26]

Command, discipline, orderliness: words so alien now to education make the gym mistress a natural candidate for any model of social control. To this she might well answer, "I am sure we believed we were teaching the *girls* rather than the subject."[27]; or, "Miss Stansfeld made us realise . . . that the children we taught would be affected more by what we were and how we taught than by what we taught and the techniques we used";[28] or, "I think they liked us and thought we were human. At least we knew every one of them . . . as people."[29] Part of her pride consists of seeing herself as "more human" than other teachers; but the old-fashioned gym mistress would not object either to being considered "a power in the land";[30] provided that by this was meant a power for *good*.

> Women must enter the religion of education prepared to work for
> the same purification of spirit, the same consecration of self as does
> the priest . . .

said the Principal of one training college in 1917.[31] A similar message,
from Miss Stansfeld, was characteristically brief and secular. "A true
teacher," she told her students, "must be imbued with a wish to
serve."[32] The wish to serve was their armour, then, against adulation
and the vanity of moments when, as one says, "it suddenly came over
me – the power of the eye – I could have done anything I wanted with
those girls!"[33] It could be armour, too, in circumstances unimagined
in college days: teaching African girls in Lagos ("When you said,
'Run round the room' they said, 'But the room is square!' ")[34] or
teaching in the Liverpool blitz:

> The girls struggled to school . . . from some distance . . . To gather
> them up and calm them down we begin with Folk Dancing in the
> Hall. I would play records and they would creep in and begin
> dancing the old favourites until we seemed in the right frame of
> mind . . .[35]

The ideals which launched the gymnastic profession came to full
flowering in the inter-war years. Students trained at Bedford during
that period "knew exactly where they were going".[36] They never
knew it like that after the war; partly because there were tremendous
changes, as we shall see, in the nature of the subject, and partly
because, as one writer put it (from the standpoint of the 1950s), "the
challenge has come to standards that were once taken for granted".[37]
In viewing the inter-war heyday, however, we cannot help noting that
despite the high standing which the games mistress had with the girls
and her acknowledged moral authority, she generally lagged behind
her colleagues in matters of pay and official status.

Miss Stansfeld's reported view, "Money is dross!" was scarcely the
view of the Ling Association (seen from the first, by some at least, as
the gymnasts' trade union) or of Madame Österberg, who boasted
repeatedly that her students could earn at least £100 a year. "Will you
let me start her in a school with £100 salary, non-resident (or £60
resident)?" she asked one father in 1896. "It would ripen her
character and make a splendid woman of her if you gave your *cheerful
consent* to her fulfilling her profession."[38] The figures Madame
Österberg cited were in line with the starting salaries offered then to

"graduates" from Girton and Newnham, and some £20 more than the average salary of women elementary school teachers.[39] To a girl who had never earned, it was wealth. Whether, as Madame Österberg claimed, it guaranteed her economic independence, depends on how that term is defined. As contemporary budgets show, the young high school mistress generally relied on free board and lodging at home in the holidays and would have lived close to the bone without it.[40] Her independence was never luxurious. "Do not try to save out of £100 a year at the expense of your health", wrote one observer, advising young teachers that "the one absolutely necessary indulgence for a high school mistress is a good holiday."[41] Judging by their letters to the Ling Association, gym teachers needed this as much as anyone, particularly as they grew older. But could they afford it? Up to 1914 their £100 salary seldom rose to more than £120 maximum.[42] Further, as a contemporary account of pay and prospects felt bound to indicate, their teaching life was shorter than that of their colleagues, "and there are no headmistress-ships to which to look forward". The only "plums" were posts in the Inspectorate, or as county organisers, and these were so few as scarcely to affect the question.[43]

By the First World War, the early euphoria on pay and prospects seems to have subsided. "No doubt, in the usual injustice of things appertaining to teaching, men will be better paid than women are, for doing the same work," was one comment in the *Journal* in 1909, in regard to a proposal to run a course for men at the South Western Polytechnic.[44] In 1913 the Ling Association circularised its members to find out how many were supporting dependants, since "in trying to get a higher rate of pay for women, it is usually urged as an objection that they have only to provide for themselves".[45] Teachers' complaints provide many indications that things had changed from a few years back when the trained gymnast "could say with pride that hers was one of the best-paid professions".[46] Some thought the market had become overstocked and that this was reflected in the readiness of applicants to accept less than £100 a year and in the readiness of headmistresses to require them to teach other things besides gymnastics. We have no means of knowing how many from Bedford sympathised with the teacher who wrote in 1913 that if things got worse "it will be necessary to combine and strike".[47]

Things did get worse: not only in the sense that the gym mistress, like other teachers, had to suffer, in the post-war recession, a five per cent "voluntary abatement" of salary, but that she found herself on the wrong side of the graduate/non-graduate gulf when the newly-instituted Burnham Committee made its recommendations in 1920. Public opinion, Madame Österberg had said, "had to be guided to acknowledge the trained gymnastic teacher as the equal . . . of any other trained teacher. Her salary was to be a fair equivalent for her work."[48] And in the fluid conditions of the 1890s she had broadly achieved this equality. The graduate distinction knocked it on the head. At a Ling conference in 1924, where Bedford representatives raised the question of the gymnastic teacher's outlook, it was suggested that she allowed herself "to feel inferior in the presence of graduates."[49] In fact, in this period her training was enhanced. The course at Bedford and the other colleges was extended to three years in 1919, and in 1922 the Chartered Society of Massage and Medical Gymnastics took over the examining of remedial work. Students thus were able to qualify not only as gymnasts but as physiotherapists. All this, unfortunately, was peripheral to the crucial matter of the Burnham Committee. The Committee's list of qualifications equivalent to a pass degree did not include the Ling Diploma, nor were the physical training colleges accepted as "recognised institutions" under the celebrated Section 7(e). When the question of recognition was discussed, the local authority representatives on the Committee "instanced in particular the low standard of attainment reached by the majority of entrants to the colleges", and though the Teachers' Panel disagreed, the outcome for the colleges was adverse.[50]

Through the inter-war years, therefore, questions relating to graduate status were constantly before the Ling Association and its members' wilder suggestions (such as that gymnasts should be pensioned off earlier than other teachers in view of the arduous nature of their work)[51] were discouraged, as likely to imperil the great end. Fortified, from 1918, by the long-delayed assimilation of members of the Bergman-Österberg Union, the Association was also involved in the movement to gain university recognition for the training which the colleges offered. In 1928 a committee, led by the Principal of Chelsea Polytechnic and including Miss Stansfeld, petitioned the Senate of the University of London to institute a Diploma in Physical Education. At present, as they pointed out, teachers gained diplomas from their own colleges, "and we consider it of the utmost importance that a Diploma shall be granted by some Central Authority to represent a definite standard of training . . . and to give the profession the dignity it deserves".[52] The London University Diploma in Theory and Practice of Physical Education was instituted in 1931 and gradually the colleges were inspected and recognised – Bedford in 1935.[53]

This was certainly a big step forward but it did not bring graduate status. In 1936 strong representations were made again to the Burnham Committee; the comprehensive nature of the training was stressed, and the comprehensive nature of the work in schools.

> These teachers are naturally referred to as "specialists" [but] this specialisation is . . . by no means narrow. Their responsibilities extend to the whole school and cover the physical education of each pupil in all its aspects.[54]

It would hardly have been politic to list all they covered; Guides, girls' clubs, lost property, school stationery, measuring for uniform, hygiene, First Aid. Bedford gymnasts, like the rest, found themselves involved, too, in general teaching: "For my first year I occasionally taught French . . . in a "free" period . . . because the headmistress . . . was seldom able to get to her lessons."[55] "Took a rather backward little first year class for Arithmetic, and also for English."[56] The games mistress, it might appear, was the rock on which the whole school rested, but throughout this period she had to be content to remain one of "the hands and feet people", as one put it, wearing her best hat on great occasions when her colleagues wore their gowns, and being paid twenty per cent less than they.[57]

Did she resent this? At one level, certainly. As Cicely Read, Vice-Principal of Bedford, who had helped to put the gymnasts' case to the Burnham Committee in 1936 pointed out on another occasion, gymnastic teachers spent a lot on their training.

> They are equally as efficient in their own subject as the specialists in History, Mathematics etc. . . . they put in equally as many hours of work yet are not included in equal terms of payment.[58]

At the school level, though, the gym and games mistress seems to have been remarkably tolerant, combining what might be called "masculine" authority and command in a female community with "feminine" acceptance of lower pay and a myriad of dogsbody jobs.[59] According to one who left Bedford in the twenties, "Questions of salary, status and hours of work just didn't come into the picture."[60] "I just accepted it," says another, "I never felt inferior."[61] But she adds, "I wasn't on the breadline," explaining that she had enough home backing to be able to wait until the end of term to receive her salary cheque (a point of consequence at a time when teachers faced the still-surviving gentility of being paid only at the end of term). Some schools made a half-termly advance. At Croydon High School it was £30 in 1932 and the new games mistress found to her amusement that for her alone this standard payment was more than would be due at the end of term. She does not remember resenting this.[62] "I honestly believe," writes another, of the thirties, "we never thought of differentials in those days."[63] This one certainly had no private means; indeed, with difficulty had financed her training. Launched in a job, her main view was, "I was lucky to be earning." The sentiment is echoed by many who began work in the inter-war years. At the College's Diamond Jubilee, in the affluent sixties, a distinguished Old Student tried to convey that it had seemed a privilege to get a job in 1926, and that the first instalment of her modest salary had spelt "unbelievable riches".[64]

To this industrious, responsible, and, one might say, womanly spirit, the professional *Journal* addressed itself in years when its readers faced salary cuts and "the shutting down of prospects". "A gymnast without a sense of vocation is a poor thing," it assured them, "and while salaries wax and wane those who have this precious gift can still put in their quota of work in raising the standard of national health, self-respect and conduct."[65] The ups and downs of the inter-war years did nothing to impair this sense of moral leadership. The gymnastic teacher's tireless concern for the national well-being, whether in her own small world, the high school, or in that other world, the elementary school, where missionary work was still more needed, runs through the debates of the Ling Association. Should the gym tunic be replaced by shorts? Even such a question had its ethical side. "When we are waging war on the tunic, I think we should go rather carefully," as one said, "because of difficulties in the elementary schools."

> Up to the moment I am still in favour of recommending [them] to adopt the tunic as their standard dress . . . It cuts down the number of garments the children wear – we get rid of their petticoats – they have something neat which they can wear in their homes, and the tunic takes a little of the character of our work into the home, and helps to gain the co-operation of parents, who are beginning to understand that the work nowadays is physical education and not just drill. Having got a tunic, knickers and blouse made in the

needlework lessons, then we say that now we will take off our tunics; this helps towards cleanliness; then we take off our stockings and so on.[66]

But the world of the elementary school was changing. "Secondary education for all" – on Labour's agenda from the early twenties – had achieved, by the time of the Hadow Report in 1926 a fair respectability. Central and "senior standard" schools and "higher tops" were proliferating. Hadow set the seal on a forward movement by pronouncing that all children should proceed at eleven to some form of secondary education. This must, of course, involve a higher standard of provision. "The elementary schools," as the Committee oted, "do not possess gymnasia or employ teachers expertly trained." They hoped, among other things, that, "where possible", the new "modern" schools would have their own playing fields. What was "possible" reflected the recession. Nonetheless, in the 1930s reorganisation did take place. Gymnasia were built and playing fields laid and the Board of Education set itself to top up the training of suitable senior school teachers with courses in physical education run by county organisers and other gymnasts who had trained in the specialist colleges.

In such ways the gospel spread further in the inter-war years. Loyalty ran high. The period had opened with English gymnasts sending subscriptions to a relief fund for the impoverished granddaughter of Ling, and it closed with them sending their brightest talent to the Swedish Lingiad in 1939. "We did pure Ling gymnastics there," recalls a Bedford member of the team, contrasting that with the "more progressive" work displayed by teams from other countries.[67] It is possible, though, that even she did not realise how impure "pure" Ling had become since the days of Madame Österberg.

Ling Under Challenge

"New Theories in Gymnastics" was the title of a paper read in 1921 to the Ling Association. Its author was a young woman, Cicely Read, one of Miss Stansfeld's early students recently appointed to the Bedford staff, and due in the fullness of time to succeed her. With the Principal, then over sixty, withdrawing from the active teaching of gymnastics, Cicely Read took charge in this field. Half Miss Stansfeld's age, and young enough to feel the sense of psychological release running through the gymnastic world at this time because the taboo on any departure from the holy principles of Ling had been broken, she spoke mainly of the work of Elli Björkstén, the Finnish pioneer of change. Others, later, paid tribute to the courage shown by Björkstén in breaking with a system which had ossified to such an extent that "the fear of spoiling Ling's creation prevented all development and killed all initiative".[68] Miss Read, in 1921, confined herself to analysing the Rhythmic Movements and Relaxation which Björkstén introduced. "Those engaged in physical training must . . . experiment with new methods to suit the altered conditions of life," she told her audience. They should not see gymnastics "merely as corrective . . . to bad habits of posture". As if even such judicious advice were too daring, she closed with an assurance that such theories were not "a reversal of the older Swedish system, based in the beginning on the work of P.H. Ling, but an amplification of it."[69]

The previous summer, in Holiday Week, Bedford Old Students had found their gymnastics taken by Miss Read "entirely on the new system of relaxed movements," and thought these most interesting, "even though many complained after them that they felt they had done no work."[70] Björkstén's approach was indeed "force-saving", by which was meant, as Miss Read explained, "not a diminution of effort, but a proper direction of energy along the best lines to produce work" since rhythmic movements took advantage of gravity "and of the elasticity of muscular tissue".[71]

To us, now, part of the interest arising from this change of direction must lie in its affinity with the broad educational trends of the period, especially in its attention to psychology. Molly Evans, in her generation, had learnt from Posse's *Kinesiology* that no one could *invent* a new system of gymnastics since a definitive scientific system had already been invented by Ling.[72] Björkstén drew attention to the limitations of the so-called scientific approach, with its impeccable anatomy and physiology and almost total disregard of the mind. Gymnasts, she said, subscribed to the ideal of harmony between body and soul, but were interested only in the body. Gymnastic teachers should study psychology. They should pay more attention to *joy* as a necessary factor of *physical* well-being. "Tense, restricted movements," she wrote, "have a . . . disastrous effect psychologically."

It is often very distressing to see a group of children . . . doing free-standing exercises in gymnastics with tense muscles and nerves, angular, wooden movements and hard expressions on their faces, telling of weariness and constraint and displaying stiffness and lifelessness in place of the keen delight they should be feeling in the use of their minds and bodies . . . Surely this state of affairs is a sufficiently serious indication to teachers that the methods and aims in gymnastic teaching are in need of reform.[73]

This new approach provoked enormous interest in England. In 1923 Cicely Read and her Swedish colleague on the Bedford staff produced a pamphlet translating one chapter of Björkstén's recently-published *Principles of Gymnastics for Women and Girls*. The whole work did not appear in English till the thirties but Björkstén's methods became well known through English-Scandinavian summer schools and were constantly under discussion in the literature of the Ling Association. Through it all we sense the pressure for change and the countervailing pressure of anxiety. "One does not deviate from Ling's principles if one keeps to the spirit of his work" seems to have been the fall-back position at the Ling conference in 1924.[74] But a member in the same year claims to identify a "growing revolt" against the principles of Ling, doubting whether the younger gymnasts remember much of the original system.[75] Some defend that system by denying that the idea of rhythm is anything new. "[We are] making a further and fuller use of it than we have done in the past."[76] Several take their stand on the importance of *posture* ("The physico-psychological expression of the harmonious working . . . of body and soul.").[77] "A plea for static Movements and against Music" is the title of one article of 1927, which opens: "The teaching of Physical Exercises is undergoing a revolution". Music indeed was revolutionary. Irene Marsh's college at Liverpool had been excluded from the Ling Association in the past because she used music. But Elli Björkstén took a different view. Music could be helpful towards attaining some of the aims of gymnastic teaching, it was a powerful agent psychologically. "The younger teachers," comes the view from the Ling Conference of 1927, "certainly have not the same fixed idea of the incompatibility of music and gymnastics which was held by teachers who were trained some years ago."[78] Back and forth the argument goes: "Music with gymnastics"; "Rhythm, Risks and Safeguards"; "Was Swedish Gymnastics dull?" Some contributors, as might be expected, debate the question in moral terms. The new approach may be psychological, one points out, but "it depends on the teacher if the

1. Madame
Bergman-Österberg
about 1890

2. The young Margaret Stansfeld   3. Miss Stansfeld in old age

4. Miss Stansfeld's class at the Bedford High School,
probably 1890s. Evidently all these girls had
been persuaded to wear gymnastic costume

The first college: Dartford, 1890s

5. Gymnasium with chandelier

6. Swedish exercises out-of-doors

The family style of the early colleges: Bedford

7. 37 Lansdowne Road   8. Students, 1906 (Molly Evans front left)

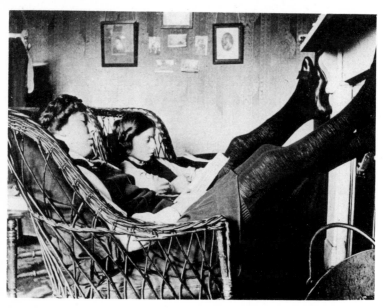

9. Study, 1915

SWEDISH EXERCISES.

Handbook of Free-Standing Gymnastics.

By E. ADAIR IMPEY.

The new Syllabus issued by the Board of Education is in accord-
ance with this book, which is especially arranged to suit the needs of
the ordinary Class Teacher, and consists of—

A.—Descriptions of 42 starting and final positions, illustrated
   by 70 photographs and drawings.

B.—Forty progressive lessons, about 400 exercises, covering the
   work of six standards, one complete lesson to a page, with
   commands, faults, etc.

C.—Ten infant lessons (about 100 exercises) **adopted in the
   Army Council Schools**, with the permission of the Author.

D.—A discussion of the values and effects of the different classes
   of movement (fuller than that in the official Syllabus).

E.—A short **Physiology of Exercise.**

Attention!

Price **3/6** of any Bookseller or

Messrs. SHERRATT & HUGHES, 33 Soho Square, London, W.

FOR MANY YEARS WE HAVE HELD LARGE CONTRACTS FOR THE SUPPLY OF

GYMNASIUM COSTUMES,

to the

Principal Ladies' Colleges and Schools, and Junior Student Centres under Provincial Committees.

Principals of Colleges and Schools are invited to write for Samples and Free Estimate.
N.B.—When writing please mention the name of this Magazine.

Navy Gymnasium Costume	10 6	Ribbed Woven Knickers	4 6
Also in Fine French Serge	14 11	Stronger Make	5/9 & 6 9
Tunic only	6 11	Navy Cloth Knickers	4 6
Fine French Serge Tunic	9 11	Navy French Serge Knickers	7 6
Knitted Sweaters	4 6	Golf Jerseys, all sizes, from	4 6
	Braid Girdles, 1 -		

N.B.—Our Gymnasium Costumes are the highest grade in quality and finish. Every
Costume is cut by experts to individual measurements, and made in our own modernly
equipped workrooms.

WILLIAM SMALL & SON,

School and College Outfitters,

106 PRINCES STREET, EDINBURGH.

Established 1852.

Games attracted many entrants to the colleges

11. Lacrosse, 1919 (note the square crease)

12. Tennis by numbers, 1920s

13. Lateral Trunk Movement: sideways flexions

14. Balance Movement

Greek Dance, 1930s

15.

16.

17. Modern Dance, late 1930s

18. Modern Educational Dance, 1960s

19. *The Leaflet*, December 1968

20. *The Leaflet*, January-February, 1969

21.

'Transference of weight'

22.

only goal given to the pupils is that of movement, suppleness and strength or if they at the same time be imbued with ethical qualities".[79] Another is fearful of corruption resulting from what are termed "rhythmic-plastic excesses".

With all the bandying of technical terms, what we are witnessing is a conflict which assailed the world of education generally. We can plot the slow retreat of the Victorians in the resolutions of the Ling Association. The view that "teachers tend to over-teach their classes and that children learn best by experiment and experience" was rejected in 1924. But by 1929 the tide had turned and members rejected a resolution "That the importance of disciplinary training tends to be neglected in modern methods of teaching gymnastics".[80] The extent to which change had in fact been assimilated by the late twenties is neatly summarised in a talk given by Cicely Read at a conference in 1929. In the old days, she said, the gymnastic teacher had kept fairly strictly to the sequence of the lesson as laid down in the text books of Ling and his followers. "All movements were executed to command . . . and no movements taken in continuous rhythm except such natural ones as marching, running, skipping." Team work in the gymnasium was practically unknown, while the use of music "was of course quite unheard-of". Looking back, it was easy, she thought, to see the faults of the old Swedish system, with its over-emphasis on posture. "One cannot deny . . . that in the hands of a weak teacher the lesson could be unutterably dull."[81]

Dullness had not always been regarded as a crime. "To gain good results in sciences, languages . . . many a hard lesson has to be learnt . . . So with body training," Madame Österberg had said. "The recreative element should not decide the choice of movements."[82] And in 1909 Miss Stansfeld had argued, appropos of the Board of Education's new syllabus, "It is an educational mistake to strain after amusement." Ten years later, the Board revised this syllabus, "straining" further to make the work enjoyable and recreative, and in 1933 they published a *Syllabus* which marked a much greater advance on this road. It has been pointed out that the change that had taken place in the presentation of a lesson is plain from the first sentence of the first exercise: "Running anywhere, at a signal stand still."[83] Indeed, the sample lessons as much as the photographs evoke the exuberance of young children "running after balls thrown by the teacher in all directions", "chasing a coloured braid held by the teacher as she runs about the playground", imitating horses, birds and aeroplanes. Two years before this syllabus came out, the Hadow Committee, this time concerned with the work of the primary school, had made its celebrated plea for education in terms of "activity and experience". Here was the earliest response.

Pressures of all kinds in the 1930s combined to strengthen the recreative element in physical education. While girls at Bedford and the other colleges were still constructing tables in the Ling tradition, the nation's womanhood was swept off its feet by "Keep Fit" and the Women's League of Health and Beauty. "Though 'Keep Fit' work is not educational gymnastics, it is based on the principles of the Swedish system," said the Board of Education in 1937.[84] The Swedish gymnasts did not think so. "It would be sad if the science of movement were to be entirely lost in the art of 'Keeping Fit' ", wrote one contributor to the *Journal* in 1938. She conceded that few would now want to teach "$\frac{1}{2}$ str. $\frac{1}{2}$ wg. $\frac{1}{2}$ kn. st., T backw. flex", as in Baron Nils Posse's "discarded textbook". But, "if the need for this exactitude is no longer felt, what is to take its place?"[85] The same thing troubled Dr Anna Broman, Madame Österberg's niece. "This 'Keep-Fit' movement may have very far-reaching results . . . We must, indeed, we shall be forced, to make it sound."

> It is you gymnasts, you educationally-trained gymnasts, who can save this reckless and uneducated enthusiasm for something real, something genuine, something fine. If you desert your own training . . . to run with the pack, you will be no better than the pack.[86]

One cannot help feeling that "the pack", in her eyes, meant girls who went "slobbering along the road with young men", for she regards "Keep Fit" and the like as playing for "sex appeal, for beauty or slimness". And the antidote? "I have been forced back more and more to the older, accurate, anatomical outlook on exercises."

There was no going back, however. The "Keep Fit" movement was simply one aspect, if the most publicised, of what now amounted to a national crusade to promote recreation for everybody. Its moving spirit, Phyllis Colson, was in fact an Old Student of Bedford College, and it was her brainchild, the Central Council of Recreative Physical Training which, as its royal president said later, "transformed the concept of recreation in Britain".[87] Whether or not moved by a desire to "make it sound", Miss Stansfeld, now aged seventy-six, joined Phyllis Colson and the Mayor of Bedford at a public meeting in 1936 to launch "Keep Fit" classes in the town. The somewhat disquieting example of Germany, where 4000 Olympic athletes had recently taken a training oath "whereby they pledged themselves to renounce all worldly pleasures" for the sake of the Fatherland, was present in some minds. But Miss Stansfeld, who was greeted with loud applause, addressed herself solely to the need to improve physique in Britain; starting, in Bedford, with "Keep Fit" classes for women and girls "from fifteen to ninety years of age (laughter)".[88] Bedford staff offered to help with the classes. In fact, the students in Lansdowne Road had already had a taste of "Keep Fit" in their course, while from 1934 "recreational gymnastics" appears as a subject distinct from gymnastics in the holiday courses run for Old Students.

Despite the anxieties of Dr Broman it was not "Keep Fit" which undermined Ling but the remarkable developments in dance that were being pioneered by Rudolf Laban. Dance destroyed Ling in the 1950s.

6
Change of Direction

I don't really think that Dance goes very well with Physical
Education. Dance is an exploration into human experience.
Veronica Sherborne, 1980[1]

Neither do men put new wine into old bottles.
Matthew ix.17

Those who finished their training at Bedford just after the end of the
Second World War see themselves, looking back, as latter-day pro-
ducts of a long-running assembly line which was just about to be
completely re-jigged. "The type of lesson we'd been taught to teach
was out-of-date suddenly."[2] In retrospect, the suddenness may be
exaggerated, but it is the case that the late forties and early fifties saw
the effective abandonment of Ling. The well-tried ways were discredited. Children were no longer to form in line or perform in
unison. Gymnastic tables, crammed into half a century of notebooks
from Molly Evans on, became redundant, and "In A Huge Bonnet
She Ate Little Jam Rolls" was left to the junk room of memory.

What this generation of gymnasts encountered was the displacement of Ling by Laban, a blurring of the line between gymnastics and
dance. In one sense, it was a rapid process; in another, it reflected
developments going back over fifty years. One could even say the
writing was already on the wall when the first students came to
Lansdowne Road, for the Edwardian heyday of Ling also saw the
rising star of Isadora Duncan.

Reconstructing the dances of antiquity from figures on Greek
vases, this amazing woman led a crusade to liberate movement from
the formalities of classical ballet. She had the courage, Laban wrote
later, "to demonstrate successfully that there exists in the flow of
man's movement some ordering principle which cannot be explained
in the usual rationalistic manner."[3] The first reaction of Bedford
students exposed to Greek dance in 1914 was rather more naive: they
were astonished to find that they were expected to perform barefoot.[4]
Two years later, when Freda Colwill became the first resident specialist in dancing, emancipation went one stage further. After a

struggle, she persuaded Miss Stansfeld to allow the dancers more suitable attire than their heavy serge gymnastic tunics. "Might we have crêpe de Chine, do you think?"[5]

Greek tunics and bare legs were obvious signs of freedom. The dances themselves were rather formal, exemplifying set positions. What was new, though, was the dancer's freedom to create her own sequences and development. In this respect, the Revived Greek Dance offered a different experience of movement from anything that had been available before. At this time, folk dancing and national dancing reigned supreme in the colleges.[6] When Bedford students, in the First World War, danced reels to entertain the Gordon Highlanders, this was in the mainstream of what they were taught, and would go on to teach in schools. In addition, they learnt modern ballroom dancing. "Every Friday night we got into our glad rags and put on kid gloves and went into the gymnasium."[7] There they were ceremoniously instructed by "an old-fashioned dancing master". But the foxtrots and quicksteps that he taught them, like the Scotch reels, were all "step" dances. What Isadora Duncan had pioneered was a *lyrical* form of dance expression. Her dances expressed "the life of her 'soul' ".[8] It cannot be supposed that Miss Stansfeld would have welcomed too much expression of a student's soul. "We are not theatricals", she told Miss Colwill, resisting a plea that national dances should be performed in national costume. And she was known to get "really upset" if girls went into a "soppy trance" when dancing.[9] Luckily, perhaps, Greek dance in the twenties owed more to Ruby Ginner than to Isadora Duncan. Soppiness would clearly have been incompatible with its Pyrrhic and Athletic forms. Even the Lyrical and the Bacchic offered little scope for unrestrained self-expression, since the object was to portray emotion as it seemed to have been portrayed by the Greeks. Ginner identified eight fundamental lines and thirteen fundamental angles of the arms. Thus, in joy, "the lines must be made lightly and gaily, the hands pointing outwards or the palms slightly turned up", while, in sorrow, "the hands will . . . turn downwards as a rule". Spiritual ecstasy required that "the hands . . . turn upwards, the eyes be raised".[10] Greek dancing was staple in colleges and girls' schools in the period between the wars. Bedford, however, from the early thirties, turned towards a more adventurous development.

93

Central European Dance

There is really no saying why this should have been so, why Freda Colwill in 1930 should have been summoned into the drawing-room to hear Miss Stansfeld lay before her a proposal, not for further attendance at the Ginner summer school in Stratford-on-Avon, but for a year's secondment to Vienna to learn the new Central European Dance. Miss Stansfeld was now seventy, had never been a dancer and had always mistrusted theatricality. She might so easily have shared the view of modern dance as "intrinsically self-concious" held by a former student of her own, Marion Squire, then Principal of Anstey.[11] Remarkably, she did not. On the contrary, Freda Colwill was sent to Vienna, to Gerti Bodenwieser, a pupil of Laban. And a year or two later, when she married, her successor, Joan Goodrich, was sent to Dresden, to his still more celebrated pupil, Mary Wigman. The result was, that long before 1938, when Laban himself took refuge in England, to be hailed as a guru up and down the land, modern dance was pioneered at Bedford College.

Since before the first War a modern dance movement had grown up in Europe, as in America, and Laban was its acknowledged leader. Born in Bratislava in 1879, his personal life, at least into the thirties, was no less exotic than Isadora Duncan's. His experiments in dance seem to have started early in the century when he lived for a time as a member of an art colony by Lake Maggiore and organised creative dance festivals which involved the local people. In 1916 he went to Zurich, started a eurhythmic ballet school, and apparently became involved with dubious quasi-masonic activities, many debts and many women. He was in the thick of Dadaism, which centred on Zurich; his school was a resort for all the dissidents of the arts; and in this fervid, surrealist atmosphere Laban developed the remarkable ideas which were to transform dance in Europe and eventually to be transplanted to the austerity of wartime England. As a recent study puts it:

> Movement choirs, notation, choreology . . . teaching styles, and ideas concerning space patterns and harmonies all had their genesis during this period.[12]

In the 1920s he returned to Germany and had soon established dance schools everywhere – Munich, Nuremberg, Stuttgart, Hamburg, Wurzberg, Essen – as many, his colleague Lisa Ullmann said later, as there were *Boots* on English street corners.[13] His reputation crossed the Channel. An article describing the dance form he created appears in 1924 in the *Journal of School Hygiene and Physical Education*:

> It has been called "positive" or "absolute" dance because it dispenses with any kind of external aid, seeking neither to be pantomime nor illustration of an idea or an event, but an independent art, possessing its own laws, which cannot be given in so many words, any more than the "absolute" music of an orchestra or . . . instrument can be given.[14]

Laban found the words, but many years later. At this time publication of his famous analysis of the laws of movement lay decades ahead, and his influence was largely spread by his pupils, especially through the work of Mary Wigman, whose Dresden school had already become the focal point of modern dance. As another writer in the *Journal* noted, she was hailed as the successor to Isadora Duncan, though her work was very different, reflecting, as it did, the aftermath of a European war. "Mary Wigman is the product of a country that has suffered desperately; of an age grim and changing, bewildered by new formulas and unsolved problems."[15]

By the time Joan Goodrich came to Dresden the unsolved problems had taken a new turn. It was 1933. The Weimar era, so favourable to artistic experiment, had ended, and the migration of dance had begun. Kurt Jooss, formerly a pupil of Laban, had fled from Germany with his company in the aftermath of the sensation created by his production of *The Green Table*, the ballet which displayed a new Art of Movement based on Laban's revolutionary theories, and, even more boldly, took for its theme the atrocity of militarism. Lisa Ullmann, already known as a leading exponent of Laban-movement, left Essen for England in 1934. Laban hung on. In 1933 he was still directing ballet at the Berlin State Opera, while Wigman had not yet been forced by the Nazis to close the Dresden school to which Joan Goodrich made her pilgrimage.

Before she set out, as she remembers, "I'd already decided that this was *my thing*."[16] The decision stemmed from her attendance at an international summer school to which Miss Stansfeld sent her when she accepted the college post. There she experienced Central European Dance, taught by Leslie Burrowes, herself just returned from studying under Wigman in Dresden, and was converted instantly. "The very first lesson I had, I felt different. I really knew that this was what I wanted." In Dresden, then, she "found" herself, training her body ("your body is your *instrument*", Wigman said) in the idiom of expressive movement. So much, indeed, did it prove to be "her thing" that they tried to persuade her to become a performer, but she came back, and went to Bedford, and introduced the new kind of dance.

Miss Stansfeld backed her, only insisting, "I'm afraid you must do *some* Greek and national, because that's what the headmistresses want."[17] The local physical training organisers were prudently invited to see a performance, "and they got hooked!" While as for the students, everyone capable of loving dance loved it, "even the big lumpy ones", in one recollection.[18] Some of them undoubtedly would disagree. There were some students, lumpy or not, who felt self-conscious with modern dance, as there were certainly others who found their own commitment to dance through Joan Goodrich.

> I loved the dance we had at college and that tipped me further into the world of dance.[19]

> I went into the first lesson, and I thought – well, we were all shivering and thinking, "Dance – what are we going to do? Never done any." And really rather dreading it . . . And she was just magic . . . I came out on air.[20]

"She was just magic, a magical dancer, the most magical teacher who ever taught me, to see her dance was just a joy!"[21] But they were not only captured by the dancer. A quality of the new form of dance was that it opened doors to creativity. They began to invent their own dances, to compose what came to be called dance-drama.

> We had made up dances before, but in the sense of putting together techniques and steps which we had learnt . . . Whereas here we began to make up our own movements. And this was very exciting.[22]

In these early days they were offered no theory. Weight, Space, Time and Flow had yet to be engraved upon their hearts.

> I loved it. I don't think I understood where it was getting to . . . I went out to teach it because I'd had the enjoyment.[23]

This was the response of a gifted student who later succeeded Joan Goodrich at the college. Indeed, Elizabeth Swallow's career demonstrates well how the influence of Laban filtered down to the level of English schoolgirls, before most people had heard of him. The line descends through Wigman in Dresden, Goodrich at Bedford, to the midland grammar school where Miss Swallow took her first post in 1939. Here, the folk memory of the early war years embraces not only air raid drill and evacuees, but "modern dance", an experience re-called as impinging on everyone, for movement was not seen, either by Laban or by his followers, as simply for those who moved rather well, in the conventional "lyrical" sense. "It is not artistic perfection or the creation and performance of sensational dances which is aimed at, but the beneficial effect of the creative activity of dancing upon the personality of the pupil," wrote Laban.[24] This view of every human being as a dancer was to establish immediate rapport with the child-centred educational ideals of post-war England. But in 1939 *Modern Educational Dance* had not been written and teachers such as Eliza-beth Swallow were very largely working on their own, building on their own experience of the new dance, with its inherent respect for personality.

> It doesn't matter what size you are, or who you are, you begin to control yourself and you express something . . . with what the Lord's given you . . . If he's given you a fat body then you express it with a fat body; if he's given you intelligence, then you express it not so much in movement but in intelligent movement.[25]

You express it also, she might have said, in working with others. For though Laban abandoned the "movement choirs" which he had pioneered in the twenties, group work remained a significant aspect of the development of modern dance, and one closely linked with its ideology of personal and social awareness.[26] This was one of the new experiences of the schoolgirls taught by Miss Swallow. Not only did they do their own choreography but the ballets they performed in those wartime summers, beside the grassed-over air raid shelters, were very largely the result of group interaction and improvisation.

When Laban came to England, then, in 1938, it was to find a bridgehead established. Jooss and Lisa Ullmann were based on Dartington. Leslie Burrowes had opened a Dance Centre in London, and Bedford students trained by Joan Goodrich were taking modern dance into schools. In 1938 Diana Jordan, a former Bedford student, published the first book on movement education to appear in England.[27] As a recent study points out, however, the fact that Laban himself at this stage turned from dance as a performing art to dance in education was largely fortuitous, and not unconnected with his need to earn money.[28] The turning point seems to have been 1941 when the Ling Association ran a special conference to explore the educational potential of dance. Joan Goodrich, acknowledged as "having done a great deal to establish Modern Dance in its educational aspect," gave the introductory lecture, and members were addressed, not only by leading exponents of the genre, but also by representatives of those on whom its future in the schools must depend: an H.M.I., a Physical Training Organiser. Laban himself was the star of the conference, which ended by concluding that "Modern Dance was a type of movement satisfying to mind, soul and body" and by resolving to approach the Board of Education for assistance in developing the work in schools.[29]

From this point the new kind of dance took off. It seemed to supply what had long been wanting: a means to develop with older pupils the movement training given at the primary stage through the freer *Syllabus* of 1933. At first, the modern dance holiday courses, run by Joan Goodrich, Diana Jordan and Lisa Ullmann, were the only means of training for teachers in Laban's principles of movement; but in 1945 Miss Ullmann opened the Art of Movement Studio in Manchester, which became a centre for Laban's research as well as offering courses in what was now called "Modern Educational Dance". In 1947, at the invitation of the Ministry of Education, a one-year course for teachers was started. Laban's book *Modern Educational Dance* appeared in 1948.

It says something for his extraordinary range that *The Times* obituarist, ten years later, managed to fill a good half column without even mentioning his work in education.[30] He is described as the inspiration "of the style of dancing which has . . . been called the free, natural or Central European style", and as the inventor of "Labanotation", "the most widely-used of all the notations that have attempted to set down in score the steps . . . of the choreographer". Of his work in England, the writer comments on his analysis of movement in industry and on the application of his skills to parachute-jumping in the R.A.F. The extent of his influence on education was the subject of a tribute a few days later.

Laban was an original thinker whose research is inadequately understood through his writings alone . . . but it is perpetuated in

the varied activities of thousands of former students. He offered
. . . not a system (excepting the notation) but a means of approach
to many contemporary problems, based on unprecedentedly
thorough research into the elements of human movement.[31]

Considering its status as holy writ, *Modern Educational Dance* is a
short book; a featherweight beside such a solid tome as Posse's *Special
Kinesiology*, and a featherweight, too, in the eyes of Laban's most
hostile critic in the 1960s, for its "undefined . . . ambiguous teaching
terminology".[32] However that may be, in the decade that elapsed
before his death in 1958, demand from the teaching world ensured
that it ran to five reprints. Intended as a guide for those who were
applying the new dance forms in school, it outlines basic movement
themes and the rudiments of a free dance technique, as well as
Laban's concept of the sphere of movement, which was fundamental
to his analysis. It also explores the value, in teaching, of movement
observation, an aspect very close to the concept of movement as
bound up with personality, which is the book's underlying theme. Far
from simply serving a functional role, movement, says Laban, is "an
independent power creating states of mind frequently stronger than
man's will".[33] With conviction drawn from his researches in industry,
he stresses the impact of movement on the mind. Modern dance
training, he says, must be based on knowledge of "the stimulating
power which movement exerts on the activities of the mind". And the
great need for this arises because in modern times the rich movement-
life of the pre-industrial epoch has been lost. The industrial worker
may be tied without respite to the performance of some simple movement sequence, and this, to Laban, is disastrous; not as it would have
been disastrous to Ling, or to Archibald Maclaren in his Oxford
Gymnasium – as tending to physiological imbalance – but as tending
to unhappiness and mental stress.

We know today that modern working habits frequently create
detrimental states of mind from which our whole civilisation is
bound to suffer if no compensation can be found.[34]

In seeing dance as a source of compensation, a means of re-discovering
that "body awareness" of which industrial man has been robbed,
Laban was at one with the Greek dance school. "The natural physical
rhythms of mankind are being slowly crushed out of existence," Ruby
Ginner had written years before, "the labourer no longer knows the

joy of the strong sweeping rhythms of his own body."[35] Her answer was deliberate relaxation, and acquaintance with the "unhurried dignity of the ancient ways of movement". Laban went much further. For him, the key to the "rich movement-life" so essential to happiness lay in the mastery, not of dance steps, but of the elements which he discerned as common to all forms of human movement, and classified in terms of *effort* and *shape*. His analysis, described in *Effort*, which he wrote with F.C. Lawrence in 1947, is linked to his study of industrial movement, and in this field he was not alone. But no one else came to it from his background and perhaps for that reason no one else had his insight into the double purpose of movement as both functional and expressive. *Modern Educational Dance* followed *Effort*, proposing themes which would introduce children to the factors of movement (Weight, Space, Time and Flow), to the basic "efforts" and the numberless "moods" produced by combining different elements. From this book the dancer emerges mixing movement with the subtlety and eye of a painter mixing colour.

Probably fewer were converted by the book than by contact with Laban and his disciples. This could be traumatic. Veronica Sherborne, who later made her own distinguished career in the field of movement for the handicapped, recalls the three days spent by Laban and Lisa Ullmann in the college in 1941.

> I felt that a kind of curtain had been pulled back, opening up my eyes so that I could suddenly see something I was looking for – which was Movement which had both physical and mental significance. Those three days probably changed my life.[36]

An Old Order

Changes in the life of the college were, of course, enforced at this time by the war; but they were not profound. While Chelsea students were moved out to Wales, and Dartford played hockey on the sands at Newquay, Bedford was not evacuated. Trenches were dug in the college gardens, a five-inch line was painted round the baths, students slept on mattresses in ground floor corridors, did fire-watching and land work, swotted in their eiderdowns, and, as the highlight of their Sunday tea-parties, produced a concoction of reconstituted egg. There was some relaxation in matters of dress. Students were no longer obliged to go hatted out to the games field or to the schools;

they played lacrosse now in ankle socks. But there was little change in
attitudes and discipline. The burden of work remained almost over-
whelming, the standards virtually unattainable, sarcasm frequent and
praise uncommon. The formal "crit. class" was discontinued but
tutors' critique of teaching practice seems to have been dreaded as
much as ever. A reference to "the nightmare of being critted" incon-
gruously follows one recollection of "teaching children to fall flat on
their faces on hearing machine guns".[37]

The manners and customs that cling like barnacles to the physical
presence of established places were not seriously disturbed at
Bedford. Dartford College could hardly have transplanted to the
shores of Newquay its time-honoured rule that only students in their
final year should use the covered way to the gymnasium.[38] But in
Lansdowne Road tradition still proclaimed: "No first year student
must EVER walk on the 'thirty-seven' side of the wall dividing
'thirty-seven' and 'thirty-five'."[39] Indeed, in one sense, wartime
conditions only served to reinforce the qualities in which this community already excelled – industry, self-control, dedication – and to
point up the "tremendous unity" of a place staffed by its own
alumnae.[40] As to the other side of the coin, "They were a fairly
narrow-minded lot," writes one, recalling the regimentation, "the
training to fit you into *their* concept of what a p.e. teacher *must* be."[41]
Another looks back on her training in the forties as "a stunting,
paralytic three years, during which one was used as a tool to achieve an
end-product".[42] But time brings reversals. In retrospect, the impreg-
nable fortress is seen to have been almost on the point of crumbling.
"They were part of an old order which was about to change after the
war. We were . . . beginning to be part of the new."[43]

Did Miss Stansfeld herself feel "part of an old order"? She was
eighty-five in 1945 when the war ended and she retired, the last
survivor by many years of those who had launched the specialist
colleges of women's physical education. At Dartford, Anstey,
Chelsea, Dunfermline and Liverpool, Principals had come and gone.
Sir George Newman, whose early support sustained the movement,
had died in the thirties. She had outlived her generation. On the other
hand, she had by no means outlived her capacity to respond to change.
"I am greatly interested in what you call 'Creative Gymnastics' ", she
wrote at eighty-nine to a young colleague then working in the States.[44]
While she remained in charge of the college she ran the show, no
question of that. "She is so positive," explains the steward in the

opening scene of *Saint Joan*, and that is also how Miss Stansfeld managed. "When she was firm she wasn't objectionable but she did things in a way quite her own, and neither students nor staff could resist it."[45] Nonetheless, the war years tired and depressed her. In 1944 she could not bring herself to organise the usual Old Students' Holiday Week, for, as she explained, it would have seemed out of place "in a tragic world oppressed by every form of cruelty. Thousands of people . . . have been torn from their homes and are only existing in the utmost misery. I could not have enjoyed it at all, and I can only hope you will forgive me."[46] It was some years later, though, before her firm hand, tending ever upwards in the manner alleged to betoken optimism and ambition, could be perceived to be tending down.

Just as Madame Österberg's college had been unsettled many years before, when her dominating influence was withdrawn, so Bedford entered a difficult phase in 1945 on Miss Stansfeld's retirement. Her successor was Cicely Read, who had been one of her early students and a college tutor since 1918. She was fifty-four. There is no means of knowing how long she felt she had been waiting in the wings but some at least suggest that "her time came too late". It certainly did come fifteen years later than if Miss Stansfeld had retired at seventy. But would "Birdie" Read, "a very thin, brittle woman, very able, very short-tempered, and an extremely good teacher of gymnastics",[47] have responded differently then?

"She was a highly tense, uptight woman."[48] Memories of her younger days confirm the impression of a clever, shy person, not incapable of warmth, but already deteriorating under stress. She would over-react to almost any situation. "I think you're a *silly little girl* and you'll regret this!" she railed at a student proposing to leave and take up training in physiotherapy.[49] She would fly off the handle in front of a class; lose control. She developed a twitch. And it crosses every mind that she must have been ill – for how long, no one is able to conjecture – but there is the fact that she died of a heart attack three years after taking on the Principalship.

In retrospect, it seems improbable that an effective successor to Miss Stansfeld could have been found from among her staff. They were, in a sense, collectively disqualified by years in that praetorian guard which, consciously or not, had served the function of deflecting odium from the leader. (Many, for instance, are recalled as sarcastic; one or two, hated; but Miss Stansfeld, never). They were also all very powerful characters kept in line by their special relationship, individually, with herself. Miss Read had not only to contend with all this but with the fact that Miss Stansfeld still existed. If her well-known figure could no longer be glimpsed in the drawing-room window as students changed classes, retirement had not taken her far from college. She remained the principal shareholder in Bedford Physical Training College Ltd, and chaired its meetings. She corresponded, naturally, with many Old Students, and came to college for Old Students' Day, when, it seems, she could behave rather badly. "She was very naughty; at the Demonstrations, she would talk to her neighbour about the Dance."[50]

Speaking of Miss Read's death in 1949, the eighty-nine year old mother-of-them-all praised "almost above everything" her absolute loyalty, "whatever her private opinions might be".[51] Absolute loyalty takes its toll, and at Bedford College, Cicely Read, who "for thirty years and a term . . . devoted herself with single-mindedness to the promotion of all its interests",[52] paid with her twitch, her terrible temper, and at last, perhaps, with her life.

She seems to have made few changes in the college. A lecturer appointed in 1947 found it then very much as it had been when she finished training fifteen years earlier. After some time teaching at Dartford, in Newquay, "To come back *here* was claustrophobic!"[53] "Bedford was a place where time had stood still," according to another who arrived the same year.[54] As for the students, girls who came to Bedford straight from the A.T.S. and other women's services "were amazed at the restrictions under which we lived . . . I remember our senior student, then aged about twenty-two, going in great trepidation to Miss Read to ask if we might all have the evening out 'just until 10.00 p.m.' to celebrate Princess Elizabeth's wedding."[55] Staff still poked around student rooms and complained about dirty hair brushes. Miss Read herself made the terrible discovery of a girl so heedless of college standards that she had actually gone back to bed on one bitter cold Sunday morning. Another, of left-wing views, was sent for, and told to desist from her "beastly red flag-wagging".[56] It was not easy, as one lecturer recalls, to be loyal to Miss Read and yet fair to the students.[57]

But it was not easy, Miss Read thought, probably, to keep your thumb in the hole in the dyke. She had some awareness of the need for change without the resilience to carry it through. One of her first moves, when appointed, had been to initiate a student council, affiliated to the N.U.S.; but when it met (with herself as president) and presented a list of items for discussion, she accepted only the most trivial.[58] A few months later, the students tried again, asking for one free evening a week (when they could hold meetings or wash their hair), for the freedom to go into hotels without their parents' written permission, for third year students to have the privilege of signing "away" for week-end leave, and for others to have two week-end passes a term. All these requests were disallowed.[59] Miss Read stood firm against encroachments on discipline.

On the other hand, the struggle for autonomy was now emerging as a many-headed hydra. Students not only asked for free time but for freedom to wear track suits and freedom to decide whether to subscribe to Dr Barnardo's. The teaching methods of younger staff reflected the trend towards freer education. Some of those described as being "less intrusive" in personal matters were the ones now venturing to introduce "almost dancing sequences" into their gymnastics. "Miss Read frowned on this."[60] In earlier days she had herself spoken up for change in gymnastics. Then, it seems, she held advanced ideas, and in one view at least, was only inhibited from experimenting with freer movement "because she had to have that sort of standard" – meaning, the perfectionist standard of Ling and of Miss Stansfeld.[61] On this reading, her "absolute loyalty" had a great deal to answer for. Change came too late for her, in the forties. By then, whatever she might once have been, she was "too rigidly a gymnast",[62] telling students they had "no sense of line"[63] at the very moment when, in every classroom, in every subject, lines were disappearing. It was just about this time that another gymnast, Ruth Morison, at the college in Liverpool, marched into her Principal's office and said, "I can't go on teaching 'Arms Bend' any longer!"[64] And modern educational gymnastics began.

At Bedford, the conflict between old and new appeared in a growing lack of sympathy between the older and younger staff. Elizabeth Swallow, in 1944, had been summoned back from her midland grammar school to replace Joan Goodrich, the "magical" teacher who had introduced her to modern dance. She and two others in their early twenties were Miss Stansfeld's last appointments, and they joined a staff which, even discounting the octogenarians, Miss Stansfeld and Miss Roberts (about to retire), was still well-weighted by those over forty. In the few years since she, as a student, had run about at the behest of Miss Read and others who were now her colleagues, Elizabeth Swallow had added experience to her own natural gifts as a teacher and her very forceful commitment to dance. More or less intuitively, it seems – certainly, without any grounding at this stage in the principles of child-centred education, she was in process of finding her own ways of "working from the child". She had her own ways, too, of dealing with students, and to the old guard they seemed excessively free and easy. Miss Read, as Principal, felt bound to rebuke her for calling students by their Christian names.[65] A kindred spirit, Veronica Sherborne, the first of the staff to have trained with Laban at the Art of Movement Studio, arrived in 1947. She too chafed against the formality, and against being treated by older colleagues more or less as if she were a student still.[66] But the real problem arose over dance; or rather, dance was the mirror reflecting a significant generation gap.

When Ruth Morison had protested that she could not teach "Arms Bend" any longer, she meant that movement was indivisible; that you could not follow Laban's principles for dance, helping every child to discover and develop her own movement potentiality, and then rap out commands in gymnastics. This was the kind of thinking that preceded the infiltration of gymnastics by dance. At Bedford, in the late 1940s, that infiltration had already begun. The gymnastics taken by the younger gymnasts were already "tinged with dance". At the same time, as one student reflects, the attention paid to her own bow legs in 1949 implied an assumption, even then, that she would be "standing in front of a class at attention for at least some part of the lesson".[67] Miss Read would certainly have assumed it. She took the students in their final year. Was she, as she appeared to eyes focussed on the merits of modern dance, now afraid for the future of gymnastics? Did she see her subject being swallowed up? If so, time has shown her fears were justified. Like those who fought the first extension of the franchise, she dreaded what actually came to pass. Unlike them, she had already made concessions. The formal account of the Demonstration presented by her students in 1948 before the Old Students shows her explaining "that all the different gymnastic movements had been learnt individually and freely, and that they had been practised in a common rhythm only for the purpose of demonstration". However, "for its climax the table reverted to completely orthodox vaults", and "equal with this climax, if not surpassing it . . . was the figure marching". The writer adds, "Miss Read's ability to create these movement mathematics and give them life is, in its perfection, almost unique."[68] The account continues with some description of *dances* presented at the Demonstration, ending with a sequence called "The Cycle of Life", "which seemed an attempt to portray the abstract. It had for sub-titles 'The Beginning', 'Childhood', 'Youth', 'Workers', 'Parenthood', 'Old Age', 'Death' and 'The Cycle of Life Continues'. Many past students liked these dances exceedingly but there were many who did not."

Behind the scenes, as the dances were prepared, there had at length been a confrontation.[69] "You can't do Old Age!" Miss Read had commanded, "Not with Miss Stansfeld sitting there!" Elizabeth Swallow had insisted that they should. For her it was a question of artistic integrity, and of her integrity as a teacher. The dance was not meant to be personal comment; it was the students' work and what they wanted. "You can cut that bit out!" She said, they could not. Nor, as the Principal suggested, could they recite a poem instead. The students backed her. To Cicely Read, it may have seemed that she egged them on. Either way, the students were present in both minds, and for both, the dispute related not only to freedom of expression in dance but also to freedom in the relationships of staff and students at the college. In the event, the dance was performed and, as reported, though many liked it, "there were many who did not". One of the audience, then in her thirties, recalls that it showed old age as "horribly frail", and that the eighty-eight year old Miss Stansfeld turned to her neighbour and said, "That's us!"[70]

A few months after this Demonstration Elizabeth Swallow left the college for the Art of Movement Studio in Manchester. Miss Read died early the following year.[71] Miss Stansfeld, practically eighty-nine, responded to this crisis by packing her bag and returning to No. 37. "Within a few hours . . . (she) was on her way to Bedford, and when the staff saw her walk up the path they felt again the sense of security and strength that she had ever given."[72] It is still remembered, the matriarch returning. "She came back to comfort us."[73] That was true, but there were other things. What was going to happen, now, to the college? The running of it rested with the two Vice-Principals; but the succession?

For the last time Miss Stansfeld deployed her lifelong strategy: ask an Old Student. The one she picked on, Phyllis Spafford, had been asked before; but that was forty years back, when the young Miss Spafford, having just left Bedford, declined an invitation to return, on the staff. Miss Spafford now was on the point of retirement from the

Secretaryship of the Ling Association; she again declined, resisting the idea that nobody else would fit the bill.

"Ask a lady doctor!"

"Find me one, then!"[74]

And at length Miss Spafford, in signal demonstration of that sense of service which marked them all, had agreed to come for two years.

Miss Stansfeld died towards the end of that period, in June 1951; her death, it was noted, breaking "the last direct link in the chain with the early work in this country of Madame Österberg".[75] The following autumn, a new Principal took up appointment and Bedford, like the other specialist colleges, headed for the problems of the post-war world.

7
Almost a Revolution

The colleges must not be isolated from the main training service;
they must be part of it.
McNair Report, 1944

The last ten years has seen something almost in the nature of a
revolution in these colleges.
Ruth Foster, H.M.I., 1960[1]

Possibly the post-war world began for the p.e. specialists in 1940
when they were told by a junior minister that they should look outside
their own little patch and contribute more to the life of the nation. He
even had the bad taste, as their guest, to joke about the name of their
professional body. What did "Ling Association" convey? "It might as
well be the Bell Heather Association; no one would be any the wiser."[2]

Two years later the colleges gave evidence before the McNair
Committee concerned with the supply, recruitment and training of
teachers. This they did with considerable pride in the female tradition
which they represented. Admitting the drawbacks of the isolation of
the specialist colleges from general teacher training, regretting the
expense of the course (unsubsidised)[3] and the limitation of students'
prospects as teachers on the non-graduate scale, they nonetheless
argued that advance in p.e. was "owing largely to the pioneer private
effort of the Founders of the Women's Physical Education Colleges".[4]
The striking improvement over twenty years in the health, bearing
and physique of girls could be traced to the influence of these colleges,
which had "grown up from individual enterprise, the result of the
conviction of certain women of outstanding personality that there was
a need for teachers with this training and outlook".[5] For men, there
was nothing comparable in England. They drew attention to the
research and development promoted by the colleges over the years, to
their international contacts and pursuit of new methods. If it was true
that they had once been places where students were instructed dog-
matically, that had changed long since. Nowadays, their whole
conception of training was in harmony with the view of education as
designed to promote the child's all-round development (a view the

Committee itself had stressed in its preliminary notes to witnesses).

A main concern of the McNair Committee was the huge problem of teacher supply certain to arise in the post-war world when "secondary education for all", already in prospect, should become a reality. Uppermost with the colleges, however, was a reluctance to increase supply by what they saw as a lowering of standards. Their thinking was conditioned more by their experience of specialised training and small institutions than by perceptions of the post-war scene. Indeed, their own memorandum concluded, "It may seem that much has been said of the past and very little of the future."[6]

That they had a future they did not doubt. "To College and its future!" was the principal toast, ten years later, in 1953, at the Dinner organised by Bedford Old Students to mark the college's half century.[7] Linked to this toast was "the memory of Miss Stansfeld". On such an occasion, understandably, the future had only a walk-on part; and even that was a projection of the past. One speaker urged, "we must keep the Olympic flame, which Miss Stansfeld lit for us, burning brightly." Another, forty years from her student days, confessed that "scarcely a day goes by without a problem arising which I instinctively solve by saying, "What would Miss Stansfeld have done?"

What indeed! Some that evening certainly thought that "Stan" would never have allowed the college to be "taken over". In 1952 it had passed to the control of Bedfordshire local Education Authority, after negotiations conducted by the new Principal, Miss Alexander, who now replied to the toast of "The College". Her speech, too, paid homage to the past but not exactly to that intimate past evoked for instance, by the speaker who exclaimed "We are all generations of one large family!" It was not Eileen Alexander's family. To the disquiet of some of those present, her appointment, two years back, had broken the chain of old *alumnae* who until then had staffed the college. Miss Alexander was Dartford-trained. Her speech alone, then, of the five that night, contained no anecdote, no Sunday bun-fights or shooting downstairs on a black tin tray or dancing reels with the Highland regiment. After judicious tribute to the past she turned, in broad terms, to the future, which was where her commitment lay.

She was then just over forty. The Old Students' president, Marion Squire, Principal of Anstey, who proposed the toast of "Bedford Physical Training College", alluded to her as "capable, courageous . . . someone who will adjust the balance of the pendulum to the requirements of the present day". Adjustment should be gradual, however. "We have come gradually a long way," Miss Squire said, "*Gradually* is the emphasis that should mark any real stable progress." Did it, perhaps, occur to her to wonder whether they still had time to be gradual? Marion Squire was a traditionalist and one devoted to the memory of Miss Stansfeld. To the new Principal things looked different.[8] Early on, she had come up against the fact that change could be abrupt, for the unfaltering stability of life as it was lived under "Stan" had not been paralleled at Dartford in her day. When she went there as a student in 1929, the pioneer college had been in upheaval, the Principal and others about to resign. After training, and a few years spent in a girls' boarding school and a grammar school, she had sought involvement in what was then the major area of change in education: the drive to follow up the Hadow Reports.

The vast majority of children, at this time, got all their teaching in the elementary schools. The move to introduce them to secondary schooling, following Hadow, took various forms, among them the setting up of senior schools with the kind of equipment and facilities appropriate to secondary education. "They were starting to build gymnasia" Eileen Alexander recalls, "but there was nobody to teach gymnastics, nobody qualified to use the apparatus." The Board of Education tackled this problem by laying on big summer school courses for elementary teachers who were anxious to supplement the limited experience of their general training. She went along to them, although such courses were not intended for specialists. "I wanted to find out how it was being done, how these senior school teachers were being trained." She also wanted to move abreast of developments in primary education, where the Hadow leaven was already at work through the new *Syllabus* of 1933. In student days she had done her stint of teaching in elementary school playgrounds but even then felt how little was offered, "a watering down of the secondary idea rather than a building up from underneath". Building up, "working from the child" was the breakthrough; and this new world was being made accessible earlier, in fact, to the elementary teacher than to the specialist elite. She sought it, therefore, where it could be found: in Scarborough summer schools; in evening classes organised for elementary teachers. "I was allowed in as a privilege." And she found it marvellous, an eye-opener. "I suddenly realised what tremendous scope there was and how I could use my limited material in an infinite variety of ways." The upshot of all this was that, at twenty-six, she was appointed to Homerton Training College to pioneer the special gymnastics course laid on there for elementary teachers as part of the official campaign to "level up".

There was certainly room for such levelling. Over the many years which had passed since Madame Österberg tackled the Board Schools and then abandoned them to form an elite, physical training for elementary children had subsisted on crumbs from the rich man's table. And still did. Whatever Hadow had planned, the thirties saw only limited progress in closing the gap between the Two Nations. From playgrounds to playing fields was one problem; another was the different quality of teaching. Indeed, one task of the elite all along (as training college lecturers, inspectors and organisers) had been to translate the ideal, as they knew it, into something practicable for the less privileged: rounders in the playground, rather than lacrosse; gymnastics done without fixed apparatus. The courses now laid on at Homerton and elsewhere, so far as they went, were a departure from this, aimed at those points where the gap was closing and schools had been reorganised. Many who attended were already teaching in senior schools, such as the Chesterton Girls' School in Cambridge, recently-built, with gymnasium and playing field. The time was to come when a much more thorough-going closing of the gap would be attempted; but, by then, it would not be a question of spreading the ideal so much as of changing it, and, in the process, of changing Bedford and the sisterhood of specialist colleges. That was in the future. In the 1930s, the senior school teachers who came to Homerton were very talented and very keen and Eileen Alexander's association with them was "one of the most thrilling parts" of her career.

The war cut it short. She spent several years running physical training in the A.T.S., then, after a spell as Vice-Principal of Homerton, became an Inspector in 1946. The Ministry of Education then was astir with the implications of the Butler Act. Out in the field, the senior schools were now called secondary modern schools, but that did not immediately provide gymnasia. She became familiar again with gross disparities: the well-found high school alongside others, of supposedly equal status, where forms had to be carried downstairs into the yard when a class took physical education. It was a time, however, for travelling hopefully. The considerable problems were problems of growth, and new approaches did not wait for new buildings. Like the other p.e. inspectors, she was identified with the re-thinking of physical education for primary children which was one of the fruits of these years. *Moving and Growing* and *Planning the Programme* were published in the early 1950s to replace the *Syllabus of Physical Training* issued by the Board in 1933. In contrast to that, they are child-centred, starting from a carefully-established base of natural development. Where the old text opens with more about Plato than about infancy, *Moving and Growing* starts by exploring the movement experience of the very young. While the old *Syllabus* had been the first to build upon the natural instinct of play, it had also been governed by the idea of posture. The new programme moved outward from the child: partly on lines of skill and adventure – climbing, balancing, overcoming obstacles – and partly towards expressive movement. Laban was not actually mentioned, but his work, as we know, had the Ministry's blessing, and his influence is perceptible. We read that the pursuit of skill alone is not enough, that movement must also be seen as an art and that this implies an attitude towards it

> quite different from our approach to swimming or gymnastics . . . because we shall be concerned not with movement as a means of performing some feat, but with its expressive quality . . .[9]

Through dance, which was not utilitarian, children could explore the qualities of movement. "It seems important that we should help children to enjoy as rich an experience in movement as we do in language."[10]

In different ways, then, the world from which Eileen Alexander came to Bedford in 1951 was a world of change but not, in essence, of that *gradual* change advocated by the Old Students' president in her speech at the Jubilee Dinner.

Nothing Must Ever Change Here

Arguably, Miss Stansfeld's death intensified the natural conservatism of the Old Students, and especially of that inner circle which was closest to the college. By now the Old Students' Association had over 1300 members and its impressive territorial map seemed to show that Bedford had carved up England.[11] A *mental* map would have shown, on the perimeter, the multitide of those for whom "College" existed as a kind of Mecca in the mind; closer in, those active participants in Old Students' Days and Holiday Weeks who sought professional and personal renewal from regular visits to Lansdowne Road; closer still, officials of the Old Student body, and those Old Students who staffed the college. Of these last groups, which overlapped, it could well be said, as at the Jubilee Dinner, "I do not know where the college ceases and the Old Students begin."[12] With some, a very evident sense of trusteeship expressed itself in pats-on-the-back for the current occupant of "thirty-seven" ("Miss Alexander has been wise enough to retain the intrinsic essence of the past while adjusting . . . to the needs of the present and future.")[13] Others were more forthright. Miss Squire for instance, did not hesitate to tell the new Principal, "Nothing must ever change here!"[14]

This advice came straight from that last ditch where Marion Squire was now entrenched, carrying on a battle, as Principal of Anstey, to keep her own college independent. The fact is that by now the sixty-year monopoly of the private colleges had been broken.[15] In 1947 two of the earliest had passed to the control of local authorities (Chelsea College came under Eastbourne and the Liverpool College under Lancashire). Bedford, when Miss Alexander was appointed, was on the brink of a similar change. The problem was money. For all their high standing, the colleges were wholly dependent on fees; their somewhat imposing Grade A world, in all its confidence, came down to that; and fees became a problem after the war.

The change of fortunes can easily be traced in the minutes of Miss Stansfeld's company, the Bedford Physical Training College Ltd. After its inception in 1930 the company had jogged along for twenty years, paying its six per cent dividend on preference and five per cent on ordinary shares. The pattern hardly changed, except in wartime, when the shareholders (all of them staff) voted loyally to waive their dividends for 1939 and 1940. After this, things went on as before, with careful management and narrow margins. But in 1950 the strain begins to show. That year they faced big items of expenditure, including the prospect of salary increases resulting from revision of the lecturers' scale. Fees were raised; an overdraft applied for; a loan accepted from Helen McMinn, the college secretary, and it was now acknowledged that local authority grants were "very vital" in relation to student intake.[16] The majority of students still paid their own fees but the number of county scholarship holders had built up since the 1930s. There was nothing mandatory about this, however. As always, grants depended on the goodwill of individual L.E.A.s; and now, with the Chelsea and Liverpool colleges, and even "Madame's college" at Dartford coming into the public sector,[17] why should authorities pay private fees?

In this context, the directors of the company (senior staff) looked at the future of Bedford. For the first six months of 1951, though with much scrutiny of balance sheets, debate on fee increases and economy, they decided to go on as before; and that, despite the published decision of the West Riding Education Authority (which in 1949 had opened its own women's p.e. college, Lady Mabel) to make no more grants at independent colleges.[18] The attitude of other education authorities had yet to be clarified. But that last hope, if it existed, was dispelled in June, at a meeting attended by Eileen Alexander.[19] Intake for the coming year was satisfactory but entrance applications for 1952 were down to only half of what might have been expected; and for good reason. Four authorities had now refused to make grants at Bedford, while it seemed that many were prepared to consider assisting students at independent colleges only if there were no places available at those maintained by L.E.A.s. For herself, Miss Alexander needed no convincing that the day of the private college had passed, and a majority shared this view. It was resolved to make approaches to Bedfordshire Local Education Authority.

Minuted among these anxious discussions about the future of Miss Stansfeld's college was news of her death, and of a last request: she had left a letter in which she asked that they allow the daughter of a former student to train free of charge, "should she decide to adopt Physical Education as a career". The directors took time from their consideration of falling rolls and rising expenses to agree that "every effort would be made" to carry out Miss Stansfeld's wish.[20] How soon, though, the wishes of the dead are outmoded! The arrangements they were then on the point of making would mean free tuition at Bedford College, and maintenance paid by the local authority, according to parental means.

The Authority took over on 1 August 1952 and Bedford Physical Training College Ltd went into voluntary liquidation. Miss Alexander's careful explanation to the Old Students of the need for the transfer was reassuring and left them, they said, with "a feeling of confidence for the future".[21] They were in any case much preoccupied with plans to celebrate the college's half century, and by the time all that had died down, work had begun on a superb new gymnasium, with sprung floor (heated from underneath), changing rooms, showers, and spectators' gallery. There was also improvement of

existing buildings, re-wiring, decoration, extra bathrooms. It would
have been hard to quarrel with all that. The conquerors, too, were
reassuring. At least one alderman went on record in praise of a college
with "not only a national but an international reputation".[22] It seemed
to be an honour to take it over. The new gymnasium was formally
opened in 1956 by Sir Frederick Mander, chairman of the Bedfordshire County Council. "Some people," he said, "had felt that the
College would lose its freedom, but this was not so."[23] If it was so, it
was hardly perceptible. Certainly, there was no conflict of aims. The
college's freedom, in practical terms, meant freedom for the Principal
to carry things forward within the context of a notable tradition, and
Bedfordshire was proud to endorse that tradition. The college's high
quality training should go on, but with more investment, better
facilities. To this end, the County was ready to buy adjoining houses
as they came on the market, and Miss Stansfeld's empire enlarged its
frontiers posthumously, with the ratepayers' backing. If freedom was
eroded in these early days, it was on the margin: in the kitchen, for
instance. To a college still rather small and domestic, substantial
bulk-buying was an innovation. Where contingencies had once been
met by the housekeeper, Miss Perkin, who would "just run down the
road", now huge vans drove up to the college. There were other,
related aspects. For as long as anyone could remember, the college
had bought its sports equipment from Hague's, in the High Street.

> Then, when we were taken over, we were suddenly told that we
> couldn't get any more from Mr Hague, but a Luton firm . . . we
> had to get everything from them, and it was very poor quality . . . I
> felt very guilty . . . because we didn't do anything to thank them for
> their service over the years and . . . they took a tremendous amount
> of trouble.[24]

It is a far cry from groceries and cricket bats to the life-and-death
questions of student supply which have come to dominate the college
world; nonetheless, the one relates to the other, in that, for those
within a public system, supplies of all kinds may be switched off and
on.

Bedford, and the other specialist colleges, came to this experience
late in the day. They were soon faced with its implications. Education
in the fifties and sixties was dominated by what, at times, seemed to be
a limitless demand for teachers. Even before the war had ended,
teachers were being pursued as urgently as if they had been miners or

munition workers. "The nation," wrote the McNair Committee, in 1944, "has woken up to the deficiencies of its public educational system." In terms, this meant that it was more than time to raise the school leaving age to fifteen, one advance which had been on the agenda almost continuously since the twenties, and was included in the Butler Act. The government's Emergency Training Scheme was launched in 1944. The leaving age went up three years later, but long before that it had become apparent that emergency measures were not enough; that the Act's requirements could not possibly be met, in the context of a rising birth rate, without expanding the teacher training system on a scale never dreamt of before. The post-war "bulge", and the raising of the leaving age, increased from five to seven million the number of children in grant-aided schools between 1946 and the early sixties;[25] by which time, the problem was compounded by extension of the period of teacher training. The introduction of a three-year course had been regarded, since the days of McNair, as fundamental to any attempt to raise the quality and status of teaching; but the change when it was made, in 1960, meant a loss that year of 10,000 teachers, and at a time when, once again, the birth rate was up beyond expectations.[26] The Advisory Council on teacher training worked through nightmares of arithmetic. In the end, acting on its recommendations, the government agreed to authorise no fewer than 24,000 additional places, a number equivalent to doubling the capacity of the general training colleges.[27]

For physical educationists, the crisis was linked to changes in the secondary schools. Here it was not only a question of numbers, as the post-war babies advanced in years, but of general reorganisation introduced by the Butler Act. Every child of secondary school age now attended a secondary school, and all these schools required the specialist provision which had once been a grammar school prerogative. The question was whether the biggest expansion in physical education since the days of Madame Österberg could, or should, be led by the specialist colleges. Years before, when the war had yet to end and the Act had yet to reach the statute book, they had assured the McNair Committee that it was undesirable for any college to exceed 150 students, a natural attitude at a time when most training colleges had less than 200 and some did not even reach the hundred mark. However, as the Committee had noted, the annual output of the specialist colleges was only about 210, which was not enough to meet current demand. Since then current demand had exploded. The colleges were now within the public sector, but still with an elite, rather inward-looking image. Should this be the image of growth in the sixties? The view of the National Advisory Council, was that these colleges should go on providing specialist training "of a high order"; but, they added, "It is widely accepted . . . that there is advantage for some specialists in living with and working alongside students who will teach other subjects."[28] The Council concluded, as McNair had done, that the p.e. specialists were isolated, and reviewed ways in which it might be appropriate to combine general and specialist training, "whether by developing specialist 'streams' in general colleges, or by introducing general training alongside the courses . . . in specialist colleges".[29] The Ministry decided to plump for the former. Three quarters of the extra places needed would be supplied by p.e. "wings" attached to selected general colleges, since, they felt, "there could be no certainty that large scale expansion of specialist courses would attract . . . enough . . . suitable candidates".[30] Naturally, a different view was taken by Bedford, Dartford and the rest. Eileen Alexander had already raised the question of Bedford's doubling in size to accommodate "semi-specialist" students of the kind whom it was proposed to train in the "wings".[31] The Ministry, however, saw Bedford at this stage in terms of "a small increase" in numbers, outside the great expansion crusade.[32] In February, 1959, Miss Alexander joined a deputation of college Principals and representatives of the Head Mistresses' Association which went to the Ministry to voice disquiet at the shortage of women p.e. teachers and at the government's handling of the problem. Crumbs from the official board that day seem to have amounted to little more than further promises of "minimal" expenditure. Subsequently, though, she managed to impress on the Bedfordshire Local Education Authority the possibility of enlarging the college to take 240 students.[33] The Ministry eventually approved this plan, and Bedford was excepted from the general rule of limited growth for such institutions.[34]

"One of our favourite national habits seems to be the setting up of anomalies", commented one critic at about this time, pointing out that yet another strand had now been added to the complex pattern of provision across general and specialist colleges.[35] The new "wing" courses had been introduced to produce specialists. "*Despite this, however*, it has been decided that the full three-year specialisation for women shall be retained."[36] That it could have been otherwise, may, perhaps have crossed some minds. Chronologically, 1960 was almost mid-way between the private era and that dread future when the Secretary of State closed five colleges a day before breakfast. From the psychological standpoint, however, it was much closer to the private days, when the worst fears of Bedford and the others did not include the fear of being shut down. Not that they could have feared this now. Nonetheless, there were anxious overtones to Miss Elaine Buxton's Question in the House in May 1959. The "wings", she said, were welcome, "but not as a replacement of the specialist colleges".[37]

In the event, as pressure to expand was piled on and piled on during the sixties, most of these colleges grew at a rate which stretched them almost to breaking point. "This year sees the beginning of big changes for the College," wrote Miss Alexander in 1960.[38] The Ministry had settled now to raise the intake from fifty to eighty; work had begun on "an extensive building programme": two new gymnasia, an indoor pool, a library, laboratories, lecture rooms. Two years on, and the new gymnasia ("Stansfeld" and "Read") were now complete, and the pool in use. But all around were buildings being ripped out and others constructed; old rooms were chopped about for central heating; there was even some chopping of term and vacation time to allow maximum scope to the contractor. Two years more, and the "extensive pro-gramme" had run its course, but another was planned. The target of 240 students overall had become a target of 360. "We shall be dis-turbed by . . . the builder's hammer for some years to come," wrote Miss Alexander. By this time, the main sources of pressure were the goverment's plan to raise the school leaving age to sixteen in 1970, and the huge expansion of teacher training envisaged in the Robbins Report. "More students, and yet more students, is the perpetual cry," she recorded. That was in 1965. In five years the college had doubled its numbers, while the annual intake over that period had shot up from fifty to a hundred and twenty. "Even this is not enough and the Government have asked colleges to find ways of increasing the annual intake by twenty per cent, by more intensive use of existing accom-modation. By what means . . . this further increase in numbers will be achieved I do not yet know." Was bulk-buying to apply to admis-sions? "It is one thing to talk of increasing the number of students accepted each year to 140, though quite another to find as many candidates of the right calibre." In 1966 she told the Old Students, "we are . . . defending ourselves against threats of a four-term year and other radical schemes of reorganisation which would endanger the quality of the training". Bedford, however, though grossly overcrowded, was not among the many colleges which had to make "box and cox" arrangements. Building went on. By 1968 a new dance studio had been completed and plans were in hand for more tutorial rooms, lecture rooms, common rooms, a craft room, and extension of the students' Union. The previous year the Secretary of State had set a new target for the early seventies: 111,000 teacher training places outside the universities – the Robbins figure.[39] By 1969 it was realised, however, that this number would be more than supplied by the expansion already authorised; the time had come, therefore, for "consolidation of the rapid growth of the past decade".[40]

It is almost like the end of a war. No one can work through the Ministry's reports without feeling hassled by the pressure of the sixties. As for Bedford, it is a relief, as the dust settles, to turn from site plans and furniture schedules to a tranquil scene: a small procession making its way across the gardens behind the houses along the north side of Lansdowne Road. The acquisition of adjoining property had at length gained the college clear access from "thirty-seven" right to the end, and it was the pleasure of Miss Alexander and some of the staff and student body to mark the achievement one summer's evening by a ceremonial stroll after dinner.[41] They had been spared the ten-storey hostels planned for some places. Indeed, their architect had won distinction from the Civic Trust for the care with which he fitted "these modest and charming buildings" unobtrusively into the neighbourhood.[42] It was nonetheless a transformation. The small procession walked in a world from which small colleges had disappeared.

The College Course

Remodelling of the courses was the main evidence of change on the inside. Miss Alexander had aimed from the start to open up the curriculum at Bedford by developing the study of education (in which the college lagged behind others), and of liberal subjects likely to enhance the students' understanding of their specialist work as well as to promote their personal development. Appointments in education, art and music had thus been made as a matter of priority well before expansion got under way; a nucleus of tutors outside p.e. was incorporated into the staff, and the students' work was diversified. It is clear that there had always been those who chafed against the narrowness of the training, and especially at the lack of aesthetic outlets: students who loved Yeats, who played the violin, who tried to get a dramatic club going. With the introduction now of special courses in English, drama, music and art, the forming of an orchestra and choir, and strong recruitment and ambitious work of music and dramatic societies, came a renaissance. The contrast with the past appeared not only in bricks and mortar, or even numbers, but in opportunity. The expansion of the college and increase in staff, wrote Miss Alexander in 1965, had led to important changes in training. Students who wished, could now prepare to teach English, or science, or art, or music in addition to physical education. They also had a host of practical options, including badminton, judo, squash, sailing, canoeing and subaqua.

It will be remembered that the college day, in the Stansfeld era, was filled to bursting, and that the more limited programme of that period occupied students all the hours there were. It is obvious, then, that pottery and poetry could not have come in unless other things went out.

"Something had to give."[43] What gave, in the end, was the last feature of the Ling tradition: the medical and remedial work. "What has happened to the training in School Remedials that used to be included in the syllabus in all recognised P.E. Colleges?" asked "Gymnast of the Old School" in *The Leaflet*.[44] Working in the general hospital of a town "in which there is also a women's p.e. college", she was astonished to be sent schoolchildren for flat foot exercises, and even to be told, "Please teach this student of the p.e. college some neck exercises for her stiff neck." "Gymnast of the Old School" was indeed witnessing what amounted to the end of an era. In Victorian England, remedial work had been the forerunner of Ling's teaching before his educational gymnastics took hold. It had formed an important element of Madame Österberg's venture in Hampstead, the means whereby Miss Anstey gained her own start, and the first enterprise of Margaret Stansfeld. The money she put up to buy No. 37 must have come partly from patients' fees. Her first contribution, in 1901, to Ling literature was an article on flat foot,[45] and Ling conferences over the years heard her speak on remedial matters. An important aspect of the work of the gym mistress from the days of Miss Buss to the 1950s had been to organise her own school clinic. Apart from all that, remedial gymnastics underpinned the powerful *therapeutic* ideology of Ling's system, which formed a main plank of the female tradition with which we are concerned. One manifestation of this interdependence was the very marked obsession with posture which dominated the twenties and thirties. Even as late as 1957 advertisements for "The Posture Recorder" were still appearing in *The Leaflet*.[46] But "when a school uses the 'Posture Recorder', what happens to children shown by this appliance to have a poor posture?" asked "Gymnast of the Old School". A major factor behind the phasing out of remedial work in the p.e. colleges was, of course, the elaboration of training and techniques in physiotherapy. Bedford students were no longer entered for the C.S.M.M.G. after 1946, and first years might rejoice that they were no longer summoned to act as "bodies" on cold plinths before breakfast. However, for members of the college staff who had been committed to remedial work, the change was no occasion for rejoicing. "We used to have a very flourishing clinic", was a statement of fact, but also an epitaph from one who felt College had changed too much. "*It* had changed, *I* hadn't."[47]

This, undoubtedly, was also the reaction of some Old Students, especially in the first years of the new Principal. Very great care was taken always to temper the wind to the Old Students, and to avoid disturbing the *manes* known to reside in Lansdowne Road. Allowing for the blandness of formal reports, the accounts of Old Students' Days for these twenty years indicate very considerable success. Those who admired the "speaking likeness" of Miss Stansfeld's portrait in 1952 and clustered in the garden the following year round the Jubilee cake "in College colours", were soon taken up with the new gymnasium, "which must be seen to be fully appreciated", and with the new dining hall where "we could see what an advantage it is for the whole of College to feed in one group". "The pace at which College is expanding is remarkable" was a fit opening for the 1960s. "College has grown . . . physically . . . mentally . . . and socially", "the newer additions . . . now seem like old friends". "How surprising," (at the end of the decade) "that so much has been built along these 'backs' where . . . we used to sleep out on our camp beds!" The sixties, indeed, had been a big box of goodies, with every year offering some new delight: pottery, painting, fabric printing, mini-skirted third years, judo, trampolining, college films and college music, including an extraordinary piece by Stockhausen. As to change and development in courses, "we could only feel a glow of pride that our old college was progressive in its thinking". At the Diamond Jubilee in 1963 this feeling was summed up by Phyllis Colson, one of the most distinguished Old Students: "How delighted Miss Stansfeld would have been to see College so spry, so full of growth, so modern, so independent – no slavish follower of someone else's pattern."[48]

The last phrase is interesting. Miss Colson herself was certainly no slavish follower. As orginator of the highly successful Central Council for Physical Recreation, she, like Madame Österberg, had marked a need and set herself to meet it, selling her idea to people who had never dreamt of it before.[49] But it was some years since any of the colleges had enjoyed that sort of independence. Since the 1950s they had all been bound, not slavishly, perhaps, but to a marked extent, to follow "someone else's pattern"; a pattern determined both by public funding and by forms of academic control. As to funds, their blooding in the public service had come with the Ministry's decision to invest in "wing" courses at general colleges, and then with the switch to high-pressure expansion. As to academic control, each of them, on being taken over by a local education authority, had become a consti-tuent member of an Area Training Organisation. The network of A.T.O's across the country was one outcome of McNair proposals which aimed to create a coherent training service out of a medley of separate colleges through regional grouping. From 1952, then, Bedford College had been a constituent of the Cambridge A.T.O.; and Bedford students prepared for the Certificate of the Cambridge Institute of Education. What difference did that make? In terms of content, we have seen that the new course ranged more widely than that for the London University Diploma in Theory and Practice of Physical Education, which it replaced. Behind this, though, was the fact that p.e. students were now following a course which had to be approved by the Cambridge Institute as part of a package for a whole group of colleges (of which Bedford was the only one to specialise in p.e.).[50] Theoretically, then, what went on at Bedford had ceased to be simply a matter for the specialists.

The implications of this become clearer if we move forward to the 1960s when Bedford, like other teacher training colleges, was con-cerned with the problem of the B.Ed. degree. The ideal of a graduate teaching profession had been endorsed by the Robbins Committee; it was up to the colleges, however, to get their submissions approved by universities. As one writer in *The Leaflet* forecast, "The universities will be in control and . . . [can] dictate terms . . . it may even be that some universities will reject the idea of a B.Ed. degree or perhaps regard individual subjects as unsuitable for degree study." Physical education was certainly one for which there would be no automatic acceptance, "indeed, it is likely to be severely questioned". "Will universities find acceptable a subject tagged as 'technical'?" he asked.[51] Bedford's experience with Cambridge University bore out some of these prognostications. In the first place, the Council of the Senate rejected the idea of an external B.Ed. (such as could have been taken at the colleges which belonged to the Cambridge Institute). Two years later, in 1968, a proposal for an *internal* B.Ed. went through.[52] The question then was whether physical education would be acceptable as a component. There was need, Miss Alexander told the Old Students, "for patient yet tenacious negotiation". "Somehow," as she put it, "a way must be found . . . so that Bedford students can graduate."[53] There was a world of meaning in "somehow". If Bedford students had been excluded it would undoubtedly have damaged the college; yet there was a limit to what could be done when all the trump cards were with the University. Miss Alexander toiled behind the scenes as Miss Davies had done a century before, in her struggle to get girls into the Cambridge Locals. It was a matter, now, as then, of convincing those who could convince others; a long job, and uncertain to the end. At length she was able to tell the Old Students that "the Council of the Senate have accepted the Physical Education Syllabus, and an Internal Honours Degree combining Education and Physical Education will be available to our students in Cambridge from 1971. I am sure," she added, "you will all appreciate the sense of relief with which this news was received."[54] But could Stan's Old Students really appreciate that the continued prosperity of "College" depended, these days, very much less on solidarity in Lansdowne Road than upon the verdict of an outside body? Stan had never sat in "fear and anxiety" through a meeting of the Council of the Cambridge Senate, "wondering what might happen".[55] Things had turned out well, but whatever the merits of the situation, it could scarcely be called independence.

The fellowship of Bedford

The organisational and administrative changes which, as we have seen, destroyed the autonomy of Bedford College from the 1950s, were, of course, reflections of change in society. To what extend did these social pressures modify not only courses and buildings but attitudes in Lansdowne Road? Here was a community which had been created in pursuance of an ideal. Authority and discipline were its cornerstones; loyalty and service were the ruling values which for half a century had knit together what was once described as "the fellowship of Bedford".[56] How did all this survive the broadening of recruitment, trebling of numbers, expansion of staff and individualism of the 1960s?

"Absolute loyalty", it will be remembered, had been singled out in the tribute to Miss Read. The "unswerving loyalty" and "selfless service" of others who had worked long years for the college were also saluted in these later days.[57] But the staff as a community had greatly changed. When Miss Alexander came in 1951 it was still small enough to be claustrophobic. By her retirement in 1971 it had increased four times in size and was very different in composition.[58] In 1952 she had made the first appointment of a male lecturer and of specialists from outside the field of physical education. When she left, a third of the lecturers were men, half taught subjects other than p.e., and only a sixth had been trained at Bedford. Another highly significant factor was that many now lived out of college. Convinced that residence in a college was "too confining", one earlier tutor, Doris Wilkie, had ventured to live out, braving the displeasure which met such a course in 1932.[59] For a generation no one followed suit. "College was one's life."[60] How demanding a life appears in the minutes of the Students' Council where we glimpse these single, professional women, not on the field or in the gymnasium so much as in their domestic role: waiting to lock up as the students come in. Later, when students were allowed more freedom, it was hard to break the habit of years. "I never liked to go to bed until my house were in."[61] In the late sixties, on a Saturday night, this could mean sitting up till 1.00 a.m.

The number of staff who lived outside college rose with the appointment of men and married women, and the *absolute* loyalty of earlier years could not eventually survive such appointments. But the concept died hard. Even in the sixties, thirty years after Doris Wilkie had faced Miss Stansfeld with her bungalow at Bromham, single women had to brace themselves to announce that they meant to live outside Bedford, as if such a move were slightly disloyal; despite the fact that, as in other colleges, an organised rota of "duty weeks" brought residential duties to non-resident staff. In Lansdowne Road this meant, among other things, stoking boilers and locking up houses late on Saturday and Sunday nights, as well as hanging on to see students in. It is said the married men jibbed at this. "The married men" jibbed at a number of things which unmarried women had long accepted, such as staff meetings held in the evenings and a five and a half day teaching week. By and by these things disappeared.[62]

But if loyalty had ceased to be indivisible, and private life, in a sense, had been invented, this did not mean any sudden turn-round in the concept of authority at Bedford. Authority, of course, in the later sixties, was coming under scrutiny at different levels, and not only in relation to the young. The Weaver Report on college government, published in 1966, had a lot to say about the relationship between college principals and their staff. "The principal should be, and should be seen to be, the acknowledged leader of the college community."[63] Miss Alexander was certainly that. However, the Report attached great importance to staff participation in college government and especially to the role of the academic board as a means to open up decision making. In practice, the existence of an academic board did not guarantee that any college would at once abandon "a chain of command in which impulses move only downwards",[64] and the impression is that staff at Bedford did not get very far along the Weaver road.

As for students, as one tutor puts it, "We still kept a very tight hold."[65] This very tight hold can be glimpsed for a decade through the minutes of the Students' Council before it was reorganised in 1962. With the Principal, as president, in attendance, and terms of reference which focussed attention largely on the quality of hockey socks, it cannot be claimed that the Students' Council approximated to a Marxist cell. Nonetheless, it was the scene, now and then, of confrontations between students and staff; and all the signs are that from such encounters, discipline emerged with barely a scratch. Despite growing numbers, areas of conflict were still such as would arise in a family: meals, clothes, and the time to come in.

Meals were a varied source of challenge. Could lunch be at one o'clock instead of ten past? Could "following" operate only at dinner? Could Sunday breakfast be optional? The students brought out practical arguments.[66] The staff responded on lines which suggest the very considerable importance attached to eating rituals in a structured society.[67] As for clothes, one question was tidiness ("because in our profession it is essential that we set an example") and another was propriety. In the 1950s the track suit gave rise to much the same problems as had been associated with the gym tunic at the turn of the century. Track suits came to Bedford in 1952 but they were only to be worn on the field. When student representatives proposed that they

be worn in the town, en route for hockey matches and athletics, Miss
Alexander reminded them:

> that we must safeguard against criticism from outside, and
> although we think of track suits as suitable clothing, many of the
> people living in Bedford do not. The wearing of track suits through
> the town would also lead to people going into shops with their track
> suits on, which would obviously not be desirable, and the excuse
> would be, "Oh well, I was on my way to the athletics track".[68]

Mutatis mutandis, this was the argument applied to the earliest young
ladies at Girton; and it would be hard to find a plainer instance of
"double conformity" a century later, than the case of the Bedford
student "not allowed to wear trousers when going to the town, yet
expected to cycle carrying a javelin".[69]

The Council's most persistent grievance, however, related to the
time of coming in on Sundays, a matter which different student
representatives pressed unavailingly over the years. The argument on
each occasion was a variant of that which took place in 1955 when it
was proposed that the time for coming in should be 11.00 p.m. on
Sundays, as on weekdays, instead of nine-thirty.

> In reply to this, Miss Alexander spoke of the need to maintain a
> high standard of academic and practical work . . . she considered
> that for the sake of the students' health the earlier night on a Sunday
> evening was essential . . . Although it was pointed out that students
> did not necessarily go to bed any earlier because they were in their
> houses by 9.30 p.m., the staff considered that they should have the
> chance to do so and should therefore keep Sunday as an early night
> in preparation for the week's work ahead.[70]

The minutes go on: "The year representatives still felt very strongly
about the proposal, but Miss Alexander did not consider that it was
possible for reasons of work and health." A "lengthy discussion"
three years later brought no change, "because the staff expected that if
half an hour extra was allowed it would not be very long before
students would want another half hour".[71] Three years after that the
students were still battling, pointing out that the extra half hour could
mean an extra four hours at home, in the case of a student living in
Bristol. The Principal remained unmoved.

Miss Alexander said that fares were very costly for such a long journey and only because grants given now are good ones are students able to travel in this way. She said that from the point of view of both our health and our work we should have one early night each week.[72]

Apart from the concern with health and stamina natural in a p.e. college, the very strong sense of responsibility for student welfare which pervades these minutes would probably be evident in the records of most women's training colleges at this time. College authorities, before 1969, stood *in loco parentis*, and said so. Rules about late leave, signing in, and male visitors were the general response to the hostel warden's habitual nightmare: the physical vulnerability of women. While Bedford, in the fifties, allowed male visitors in student rooms at week-ends only, and only up to 7.00 p.m.,[73] some training colleges were even stricter: Whitelands, Stockwell and Fishponds, for instance, admitted men only to public rooms, and in at least one (Roman Catholic) college, the public room in question had walls of glass. Only a fraction of college rules were concerned with safety, however. As the minutes of the Students' Council and memories of "petty restrictions" indicate, most reflected a concept of authority which had changed little over the years. Great efforts were being made in this period to liberalise the Bedford course. "We are trying to tell the students less," wrote the Principal in 1955, "to encourage them . . . to find out for themselves . . . think for themselves . . . rely less on being told."[74] But little seems to have been done in the fifties to apply this policy in social terms, unless we are to count the decision that college clocks should no longer be kept fast, to ensure that students were not late for their classes.[75]

To change the old training college style of authority called for something more than the changing of clocks. In the 1960s the Student Union, affiliated to the N.U.S., took the place of the Students' Council, but it was still "overlooked" by the Principal and served mainly as a forum for discussion. Not surprisingly, as time went on, the pressure mounted for greater freedom.[76] The Weaver Committee had recommended that "within reasonable bounds set up by the principal", students should have "freedom of association and expression and substantial responsibility for the democratic conduct and management of their own affairs and funds".[77] By the late sixties the gap at Bedford between what the Principal and students thought "reasonable" was becoming increasingly wide; even if, as one tutor recalls, "the national surge to stand on one's rights rather than on one's responsibilities had not [yet] attained complete dominance".[78] This very word "responsibilities" brings us back again to the ethos of Bedford and the sisterhood of specialist colleges. The universities had never dwelt largely on ideals of "responsibility" and "service"; the general colleges had their roots in the Victorian elementary school where the teacher was a kind of servant and responsibility lay with her betters; but in the Österberg-Stansfeld tradition, that female tradition with its curious blend of therapeutic, upper-crust and feminine values, the ideal of service to the community had always been prominent; and it was this, as well as authority, which seemed to be threatened by student power. "In these days of 'student power'," wrote Miss Alexander in 1970, praising the response of students as blood donors, "it is encouraging to see so many exercising their freedom in so positive a manner and with concern for those less fortunate than themselves."[79]

Among the blood donors were undoubtedly some who felt the Principal had not come to terms with the implications for college life of the law which had brought the age of majority down to eighteen the previous year, and some, too, who were already eager to "throw off the shackles of the Union Constitution."[80] But things had not stood still. If Bedford seemed remote from the larger dramas of the student revolution, there had nonetheless been significant changes, especially in the breaking down of the local isolation of Lansdowne Road. This had begun in 1963 when the college ran a sustained campaign to raise funds for "Freedom from Hunger", out of which developed what came to be Rag Week, in which other colleges were asked to join. The people of Bedford, once preserved from the sight of girls in track suits, were, by 1970 at least, confronted with them in bikinis, and the students' own view of that particular Rag gives a new slant to the concept of service.

> We would like to say thank you to the people of Bedford who did encourage and support us. To those others [less enthusiastic] we would say, "try to see us in a different light. We caused chaos, continually asked people for money, held up traffic with our parade, but we did collect £1000 for people less fortunate than ourselves. Surely you can suffer this inconvenience?"[81]

The opening up of contacts with other institutions including colleges for men,[82] the enterprise, democracy and freedom of the Rag, probably did as much to foster" 'the new image of Bedford students' in which we believe so earnestly"[83] as was achieved when they came, at length, to "throw off the shackles of the Union Constitution".

This last was not done in Miss Alexander's day. "I am a despot," she once told a colleague, adding, "benevolent, I hope." There was a Stan-like frankness about this which Stan, who was a realist, would have approved. She would also have been bound to approve the skill, even in somebody trained at Dartford, which had brought her college through the eye of the hurricane, though whether the tremendous pressures for change from 1960 could have been imagined by someone born in 1860 is another matter. As if her own reign of twenty years were part of a story for serialisation, Eileen Alexander's retirement coincided with the cessation of major building ("the unity of the campus is complete"),[84] and with the award of the Cambridge B.Ed. degree to the first batch of Bedford students. This, perhaps, gave her most satisfaction. "A damned nice thing," as Wellington put it, "the closest-run thing you ever saw in your life . . . I don't think it would have done if I had not been there."

8

Questions of Identity

First, what is our true identity? We must solve the disturbing problem of our academic illegitimacy.
A.W. Sedgwick, "Physical Education in the University", 1963[1]

Sooner or later the colleges will lose this special identity.
H.D. Fairclough, "Physical Education and the Robbins Report", 1965[2]

The need to establish the credentials of physical education as an academic study appropriate to a B.Ed. degree arose at a time when there was more internal dispute and uncertainty as to its nature than at any point since it came on the map. Beside the schism of the post-war years, pre-war friction about rhythm in gymnastics and whether one should introduce recreative movements between the formal groups laid down by Ling, seems superficial. In earlier days still, the force of conviction had carried the Swedish gymnasts to victory over the exponents of military drill, under one banner. It would not have served now. Indeed, two banners had had to be devised in the struggle for the London University B.Ed., to accommodate the different views of men and women.[3]

Men, in this narrative, were last caught sight of as the drill sergeants abhorred by Madame Österberg and as a few early converts to Ling.[4] From the start of the century until the Second War they encroached very little on the women's sphere of influence, partly because they had limited success in promoting gymnastics in secondary schools. Commander Grenfell, who had been so impressed by the work of Madame Österberg's students that he himself went for training in Stockholm and introduced Swedish gymnastics in the Navy, subsequently also taught them at Eton. But they had scarcely taken hold there when Grenfell moved on in 1909 to become Inspector of Physical Training in the medical department of the Board of Education, recently established under George Newman. As we know, the official support of Newman and his colleagues for the Swedish system was critical to its early success. But the Inspectorate, over the years, concerned itself mainly with the elementary schools; and whatever plaudits for the Swedish system appeared in the annual pronouncements of the

Board, most boys' grammar schools continued to mould themselves in the pattern of the public schools, where it would certainly have taken more than Grenfell's Etonian excursion to shake the overweening dominance of games. Grenfell had been succeeded at Eton by Reginald Roper and Commander Coote, both of whom had trained in Sweden, and who later introduced Swedish gymnastics at Bedales and Harrow respectively.[5] However, it was only at Bedales, where Roper went on teaching till 1923, that the experiment really "took". His influence was also apparent in the thirties in the innovatory physical education developed at Mill Hill and Queen Elizabeth's, Barnet,[6] but the mass of boys' schools was unaffected, and no specialist training developed for schoolmasters comparable with what was available to women.

In the reconstruction era after the First War the Board of Education tried to tackle this problem. It was admitted that "prospects and status have not been sufficiently good hitherto to attract many men of good education to take up physical training as a profession".[7] But with the prospect of openings for them in the new Day Continuation Schools and the growing need for county organisers, the Board launched a training course for men at Sheffield. It survived only till 1923, hit, like the Day Continuation Schools themselves, by the economies of the recession.[8] So, once again, there was no physical training course available in England for men teachers (apart from the element included in the curricula of general colleges); and nothing further was done to supply it till 1930, when the Carnegie Trust, persuaded that lack of specialist courses "militated against the full development of this essential branch of a boy's training", decided to fund a new college at Leeds.[9] It is worth noting that Carnegie College was deliberately launched in a different pattern from that of the specialist women's colleges. It was not desirable, said the Board, "that the subject should be in the hands of those whose qualification is limited to physical training".[10] Carnegie, therefore, (and later, Loughborough, where a similar course was started) offered a one-year training to men who were already qualified teachers. Men were thus trained, from the early thirties, in the less rarefied and specialised style later approved by the McNair Committee, and, later still, embodied in the "wing" colleges. The male tradition, slight as it was, stemmed from that opening-out of education which was observable before the war but came to fruition after 1945, while the deep roots of the women's colleges reached to a Victorian subsoil of privilege. The sense of Two Nations lingered with them. "I have been told," said one writer to *The Leaflet*, "of the principal of one of our three-year colleges who considers it a 'waste of training' if her students go to teach in secondary modern schools." Admittedly, there could be problems. While such schools might be well-equipped, "there is the task of building up a tradition for the subject, as well as coming to terms with the different abilities, attitudes and environmental conditions of the pupils".[11] Some found this experience traumatic.[12] Certainly, the women's colleges, post-war, went on sending most of their students to the grammar schools and independent schools; and Bedford (despite the fact that Miss Alexander had come with experience of the wider scene) seems to have been no different from the rest. The development, from the 1960s of comprehensive schooling, (which was often mixed), further eroded their historical base.

He/She

If women's physical education had a different starting point from men's, it was also travelling in a different direction. Gymnastics, it was said now, meant different things in England "according to . . . the sex of the individual".[13] Briefly, by the fifties, Laban's influence had "overridden the boundaries of dance" and permeated physical education, a development unwelcome to many men.

In retrospect it seems hardly surprising that the concept of "movement" should have transformed gymnastics, and that, as the new approach filtered down, an ever-growing number of gymnasts should decide that they "could not go on teaching 'Arms Bend' any longer."[14] Here was a change far more profound than Björkstén's development of rhythm in the thirties. In some respects it was identifiably part of the current revolution in teaching. "We no longer think merely of giving instruction . . . but we set out to provide the environment . . . and give the stimulus which will help the individual to grow and develop naturally."[15] That explanation, by a gymnast, could just as well have come at that time from a history or mathematics teacher, who would also have felt at home with the view that "we accept and welcome . . . individual differences, recognising in them a vast field of potential ability of every kind".[16] To move away from directed work and learning based on imitation, to teach the children rather than the subject, had become a broadly accepted goal; but could the history or mathematics teacher draw on such a radical ideology as the concept of movement developed by Laban? "This work of Mr Laban may well prove to be even more important than that of Ling", wrote one who had trained in the old system.[17] The new gymnastics aimed overall to develop children's "body awareness" through experience of the movement factors of Time, Weight, Space and Flow. The teacher would choose a movement theme. "She may set them the task of finding different ways of curling and stretching, or of moving high and low, or straight and twisted, or near themselves and far from themselves".[18] They would find that a movement could be done in different ways, "quickly, slowly, strongly, lightly, directly, or flexibly". As for apparatus, "instead of teaching specific skills invented by Ling" the teacher would set problems "capable of many different solutions" and the children would solve them in their own way.

The new gymnastics was not so much a product, as a by-product of Laban analysis. The Art of Movement Studio which Lisa Ullmann started in Manchester was set up for dance. The word "gymnastics" was rarely heard there and it was Ruth Morison of I.M. Marsh College who transferred what she had learnt at the Studio to gymnastic teaching in the 1940s. Other colleges followed suit. Bedford, which had pioneered modern dance, was slower to cast out formal gymnastics. A new young lecturer, Margaret Rosewarne, who joined the college in 1950, found it still largely Swedish-based. But a year or two later Miss Alexander sent her to the Art of Movement Studio and she returned to teach "movement education". In 1952 we come across movement in the Old Students' holiday course under the somewhat tentative heading, "Freedom within a limited framework". They were given guidance on planning the lesson ("The most important factor . . . is the Theme"), and found themselves discussing such questions as "whether quality or shape of movement" was the more important, and "whether gymnastics is not becoming more and more like modern dance".[19] It was certainly becoming less and less like the figure marching which Miss Read had presented at her last Demonstration in 1948. The display in 1957, for instance, took for its focus, "shape and pattern". "Long, spread, rounded and screwed shapes were used by students on the floor and on apparatus . . . Later the students worked in pairs . . . pushing and pulling against each other, showing symmetry and asymmetry."[20] A film which was to have wide circulation, *The Development of Movement Themes in the Gymnasium*, was made by the college two years later.

That movement acquired a capital "M", and a new terminology (Movement Training, Movement Education, the Art of Movement) is proof of an advance which had strong official backing. The Ministry's support for the Art of Movement Studio from its early days can be linked with the appointment as staff inspector for physical education of Ruth Foster, who promoted Movement as Newman had promoted the Swedish system. An endless stream of teachers went to the Studio. "Just how much ministerial pressure really exists I found . . . impossible to estimate," wrote an older gymnast in 1954, returning to England after many years abroad.[21] She thought some teachers, trained in the old style, were afraid of being thought old fashioned by their H.M.I. and took vacation courses because they felt "promotion and future success depend on their mastery of the Art of Movement as interpreted by Laban." Some tried to adopt "what they think are new methods without properly understanding or believing in them". (It was precisely to such teachers, "who are puzzled by present day trends", that Ruth Morison addressed her essay *Educational Gymnastics* in 1956.)

If there was some confusion among teachers this was partly a reflection of the fact that the new approach could not, of its nature, provide the rock-like certainties of Ling. Indeed, as the pages of *The Leaflet* show, its boundaries remained a subject for debate: "Are movement training and gymnastics synonymous?"; "The Movement Approach: a need for clarification"; "Dance and Gymnastics: the Border Line". Always supposing that a border line existed. Those who were most committed to Movement did not recognise any such division. Gymnastic teaching, as Ruth Foster saw it, was like mastering the fundamentals of a language "which could be used pertinently and flexibly for all purposes".[22] Such large, all-purpose claims for Movement did not appeal to those who were not devotees of Laban; that is, to the majority of men. Here is the origin of that split which has been one of the most striking phenomena of recent educational history. Divisions in a discipline are common enough, but they are not usually aligned with sex. "I find it difficult to conceive of men's/women's geography, mathematics etc.," says one writer.[23] In fact, historically, there is no other subject where the split could have happened as it did in physical education. In this field, where women were leaders, the war brought not only a change of direction but a chance for the men to get out from under.

Very few men had been involved with Laban's entry into education. Whether his talents would have found that outlet if circumstances had not brought him to England into the little coterie of women who were *teaching* dance, no one can tell; but it was certainly they who set the ball rolling in the early forties.[24] At that time, many of the men were away, entirely cut off from such developments and subjected to the very different experience of combat and commando training. When the war ended, "Physical education broke out of the gymnasium and the playing fields and spread to the mountains and rivers" in activities which capitalised on an element of danger.[25] While within the gymnasium men became interested in pressing, to new levels and with new techniques, the *physiological* approach to gymnastics. *The Leaflet* reflects this approach in the fifties under such headings as "Training for Strength", "The place of strength and stamina in physical education", "Tests and measurements and the physical educationist". The Triple Thrust Dynamometer appears (measuring "chest thrust, chest pull and grip"), while Leeds University pioneered the development of circuit training, a method employed by the American Army to maintain fitness during the war.[26] This, and other techniques for exploiting the principle of "overload" in physical exercise, achieved immense popularity with men.

The influence of Leeds is highly significant. In the middle fifties the University, in conjunction with Carnegie College, launched, for men, a diploma course in physical education which gave the *entree* to post-graduate studies and all that that could mean in terms of careers. Carnegie claimed proudly in 1955 that

> Much, perhaps most, of the pioneering work in Physical Education in University departments which has developed during the war and during the present decade has been in the hands of Carnegie students.[27]

It is true that women played very little part in developing p.e. at university level, either at Leeds, Manchester, or Birmingham (where from 1946 the subject could be taken as an element in a first degree). At Leeds, women students were not admitted to the diploma course till 1966, after the appointment of a Bedford-trained lecturer, Irene Glaister. Considering the way that things moved later, their lack of involvement at academic levels was probably crucial to the influence of women, as was also, probably, their relative indifference to "scientific measurement" in physical education. In the 1970s, as we shall see, everything hung on academic viability, and, in the struggle to establish that, *measurability* was very persuasive. Eventually, it could be said, the force of their reaction against the physiological tradition of gymnastics tended to isolate women.

Men were inclined to explain the whole thing in terms of the personal influence of Laban. The tremendous appeal of the Art of Movement became associated, in their eyes, with a mystic cult of female groupies. "You never hear of Laban working with a *man*," according to one man.[28] Another draws attention to the disproportionate amount of space in the *Laban Art of Movement Guild Magazine* taken up with anecdotes about the Master.[29] The women, says a man who went to the Studio (for there were men there, especially later on, when Movement began to seem a good career prospect), were largely uncritical of what was taught, interpreting any kind of challenging remark as a form of attack on Laban.[30] By contrast, who would not turn with relief to the Triple Thrust Dynamometer?

Laban's personal charm is undisputed, but there are other things to consider, relevant to the female tradition. It was argued earlier that the therapeutic aspect of Ling's work appealed strongly to women; also that the ethos of gymnastic teaching was very much bound up with ideals of service which had strong affinities with "womanliness". Comparable ideals were writ large in Movement, which from the first claimed social ends. Writing of the founding of the Art of Movement Studio by Lisa Ullmann, Laban spoke of her "unerring humanitarian drive". Movement, he said, "can and should be used as a positive force in our civilisation. We can, and do, understand others through their movements; we can, and do, contact and help others through movement."[31] What this meant in practice, appears in different ways. Group work was very important, for instance. "Group dancing," wrote Sylvia Bodmer, an early exponent of Laban's work, "aims at letting the dancers experience through the combining power of movement a real feeling of co-operation and unity."[32] Group dance was valuable psychologically, in the experience of one (male) student who did not otherwise rate dance very high. "It brought us as a group very close together . . . at a time when morale was very low."[33] "There is a crying need . . . for people to co-operate, to work with . . . respect for each other's qualities," wrote one Movement lecturer;[34] and certainly respect was fundamental to the concept of Movement. Respect, arising from the recognition of the different movement qualities of different individuals, inspired its marked uncompetitiveness. Whereas, it was said, the old gymnastics left many children with a sense of failure, in Movement "no one need feel inferior", a claim which took on additional meaning when movement training was applied to the handicapped. "Movement," wrote Veronica Sherborne, whose early contact with Laban at Bedford ultimately led to distinction in this field, "can help the mentally handicapped child . . . to be involved in himself, to experience himself." Such children often lacked a sense of "I".[35]

The "bulging biceps" and "movement maniacs" caricature of the fifties, then, reflects significantly different attitudes from men and women towards competition. There was also the feeling with many men that Movement undermined the purpose of gymnastics: the acquisition of strength and skills. "This teaching approach," wrote A.D. Munrow, head of the Physical Education Department at Birmingham University, "appears to involve an abandonment of the specifically physical and physiological aims of gymnastics."[36] Was it claimed, he asked, that Basic Movement was "a fundamental approach to all forms of skill?" He noted that vaulting had almost disappeared. As for "the general gymnastic qualities of mobility, strength and endurance", was it felt that these could be disregarded?[37]

The women, at many a holiday conference, had argued round the question of skills. With movement training, "the specific techniques of any major skill" could be easily learnt, according to one group in 1952. "The body twist in lacrosse, leaping in netball, the gliding in breast stroke" could all be translated into Laban's factors of Weight, Space and Time.[38] At some of the colleges (though not at Bedford) games were certainly coached in this way.[39] The pith of Munrow's question, however, was whether generalised movement training was as good a preparation for specific skills as the old-fashioned way of simply practising them. How else, he asked, could one experience such things as "the really shattering degree of tension evoked during impact . . . at take-off in a long jump?"[40] He was doubtful, too, about the problem-solving method taken to extremes, as was at least one student who came to Bedford in the early fifties when, it seems, "You were given a rope and told to be strong and get to the top of it." ("Luckily, I had been at Cheltenham, where they were still telling you how you climbed a rope.")[41]

Munrow's challenge was taken up by Marjorie Randall, a college lecturer and Bedford Old Student, in 1961 with her book *Basic Movement*. Her first reaction had been to acknowledge a lack of athleticism in movement training,[42] but she argued now that while the gym lesson was no longer designed "purely to meet the ends of strength and suppleness", these ends would, in fact, be met incidentally. "I believe that girls taught by modern methods become far more mobile than their less fortunate contemporaries."[43] "Children work so much harder at movements of their own choice, in their own time . . . that their powers of endurance are greater than of yore."[44] As for skill, she did not claim that movement training led automatically to skill in tennis; but the girl who had acquired "body awareness" (which she equated with Munrow's quality, "personal skill") should have an advantage. If games were taught only through skill drills, anyway, the result was often the ironing-out of talent. "Rather let these skills be superimposed upon a high level of personal skill or body awareness acquired through the elastic and imaginative training obtained from Basic Movement."[45]

The debate was inconclusive. A form of Movement/Anti-Movement sex war went on right through the 1960s and had still enough steam at the end of the decade to inspire two satirical pieces in *The Leaflet*. "Sacred Cows" (which was written by a woman) pinpointed the follies of the Movement lobby:

> The first sacred cow . . . is the one which maintains stoutly that a basic vocabulary is used in the universal language of all movement and it is only through doing either modern educational gymnastics or modern educational dance that this fundamental material can be learned. Therefore, to follow either of these pursuits should make a human body more able to move in water, shoot arrows or row a boat.[46]

This triggered off a sequel, "Sacred Bull", from a man who loathed the shibboleths of male gym teachers:

> Thou shalt never refer to "Movement". Rather shoudst thou speak of P.T. and remember – "The Skills" *are* the opposite of "Movement". Also remember to guffaw loudly when thou hearest the term "The Art and Science of Movement".[47]

He may have been over-sanguine in hoping that the sacred animals might graze together and their offspring inherit "the best of both strains", but the 1970s brought them closer. Munrow, in his later writing, for instance, was readier to acknowledge the merits of Movement;[48] while movement teaching, even before Olympic gymnastics brought new emphasis on skills, showed a tendency to become more structured. By the late seventies it was rather old-fashioned to make a fetish of problem-solving. "Find how many ways you can get over this mat" – the kind of thing Bedford students called "ed. grov.", or educational grovelling – found favour now mainly with the old style lecturer. By now, also, it is hard to imagine that many teachers went in for the soul-searching which one Bedford-trained expert, in 1970, seemed to think should follow every movement class:

> Did John/Jane fulfil the movement task on the floor? What was his/her answer to the problem? Has he/she learnt to control his/her body weight coming down to the floor? Where and how did he/she work during the climax of the lesson on apparatus?[49]

Even at the time this sort of thing had proved too much for less earnest women.

> There is surely cause for concern when an apparently serious article, without a shred of redeeming humour, asks us soberly to consider possible answers to a question such as: "Where does the right hand go while John/Jane is in the air?"

If there was to be self-interrogation, then, said this writer,

> let all teachers, male and female, of physical education/movement/ art or science of movement, attempt an honest answer to: "Could/ might some/all children/colleagues think/imagine I/we am/are out of my/our tiny Chinese mind(s)?"[50]

Another correspondent on the subject entreated, "Let us, please, in the women's P.E. world, come down to earth from those Labanistic clouds!"

The Three-Legged Race

Coming down to earth, it is widely known, has, in a different sense, been the experience of everyone connected with teacher training from about 1971. True, in a massive reduction of the colleges, few have plummeted like grouse at a shoot. Rather, their descent has been prolonged and uncertain, sometimes more like the movement of a kite, which, when almost grazing the ground, may lift off on a sudden upstream and soar again, or eventually tumble. It is too soon to write the history of what has been called the "end of an era",[51] for the business of remodelling, (or, some would say, dismantling) the teacher training sector is still going on. We are anyway only concerned with one aspect; the effect of such changes on the female tradition.

"I suppose," Miss Alexander had told the Old Students in August 1971, "it would be true to say that during this last year, everyone concerned with the training of teachers has been living under the shadow of the James Committee." So began her last "Principal's Letter". Her successor as Principal, Mrs Bowen-West, picked up the reference in the opening paragraphs of her first letter, the following year. They were now "in the stark light" of the James Report, "but the shadows are still about us". What were these shadows, an outsider might ask, following so soon on prodigious expansion and the much-coveted B.Ed. degree? Neither, in fact, had done much to resolve the basic problems of teacher training, nor to improve its public image. Despite the impact of McNair and Robbins, the colleges were still very far from being integrated into the field of higher education. Critics said the quality of training was poor, the new B.Ed. degrees ill-thought-out; and that while the colleges churned out teachers, standards in the schools were actually slipping. The James Committee, then, was given a wide brief to look at the future of teacher training and it came up with a set of proposals which would have amounted to complete re-structuring. In particular, it recommended a break with the ʈraditional "concurrent" course, in which the student's personal education was combined with learning to teach. James proposed that the teaching commitment (and professional training) be deferred to the end of a two-year course of higher education which potential teachers would share with aspirants to other professions, as they did at university. The implications of all this were enormous, and for none more than the specialist colleges. In the whole galaxy of teacher training they, it might be said, had most to lose by such a transformation, for they throve on commitment. Enlarged in size, diversified in range, twenty years removed from the death of Stan, Bedford, like the others, remained a place where learning and training lay very much alongside, and where demands were made from the start on students as prospective teachers. The new Principal, Pat Bowen-West, had asked herself when she took on the job whether the specialist college had a future. Government committees from the days of McNair had posed the same question. Was this the answer?

It was, perhaps, with the government's White Paper, published in the wake of the James Report, that awareness slowly dawned that there *were* no answers; that they were moving into an era when answers either could not be given or were given in a kind of New-speak. Thus, the government's White Paper was entitled, "Education: A Framework for Expansion", yet it was actually a framework for contraction, so far as the colleges were concerned. Questions of concurrent or consecutive training were overshadowed as it came home to them that it was intended to merge teacher training in the public sector of higher education, not only as a means of opening it out, but of adding to the general pool places no longer required for teachers. This would be achieved in various ways. It was thought some colleges might join with polytechnics or with colleges of further education; others might combine among themselves to form large, diversified institutions. "Some must face the possibility that . . . they will have to be converted to new purposes; some may need to close."[52] Or, as Bedford's new Principal put it in her letter to the Old Students, "what has been described as 'the gravy boat' of the 1960s . . . is fast becoming a retrenchment."[53]

Behind retrenchment were the awkward facts of a falling birth rate and growing recession. The famous Circular 7/73, whereby the Department of Education called on local education authorities to submit plans to reorganise the colleges, estimated that by 1981 something like 65,000 places would suffice for initial teacher training (there were 114,000). That projection, by the end of the seventies, had been cut to 35,000, but it seemed extraordinary enough at the time. The "Drift through Chaos" following this Circular has been vividly described elsewhere.[54] Colleges large enough to diversify (which meant 1000–2000 students), made a bid for the glittering prizes and saw themselves as polytechnics of the arts. Others, small or badly located, were consumed with apprehension. "In some quarters, lecturers, who only two years ago were on the crest of the expansion wave, now faced cut-backs and were frantically trying to design new courses to stay in business." Survival kits were made and re-made. "Whole new schemes for courses had to be scrapped . . . because College A would not now merge with College B but with Polytechnic X."[55] One way or another, they shot the rapids, and when the craft could be seen for the spray, some had disappeared and some were lashed together to form all manner of curious vessels. Bedfordshire produced one of the rarest: a clumsy three-decker, made by combining the p.e. college in Lansdowne Road with Bedford's general training college and its college of further education.

"This College," Mrs Bowen-West had written to the County in

1974, "would be very reluctant to lose its separate identity."[56] Its separate identity was lost, officially, in 1976 when the three-fold College of Higher Education came into existence. Around this time, the separate identities of the whole sisterhood of specialist colleges disappeared. The smallest of them, Anstey, was taken into Birmingham Polytechnic; Dartford merged with Thames Polytechnic, Chelsea with Brighton Polytechnic, I.M. Marsh with Liverpool Polytechnic. The one free-standing survivor was Nonington, founded only in 1938; but it survived without initial teacher training.

The Bedford merger had been the outcome of three years' hard negotiation, both between the County and the colleges and between the County and the central Department. While the haggling was still going on, the Department cut its estimate of places needed, and in Bedfordshire, as elsewhere, the argument grew bitter as people struggled over a smaller slice of cake.[57] The Chief Education Officer pressed for more places, urging the Department to take into account the fact that one of the Bedford colleges chanced to be a specialist institution. "It follows that, in a sense, the accident which brought Margaret Stansfeld, the founder of the College, to Bedford is now being allowed to work to the Authority's disadvantage."[58] This piece of casuistry failed, however, to achieve an increase in the County's share, now reduced to 600 places or little more than half the capacity of the p.e. and the general college combined.[59] It had been obvious from the start that neither was large enough to stand on its own. Further, the Department pressed the view that a new, combined institution, which would not be restricted to the liberal arts but took in also the vocational element of further education, would be likelier to survive. So it came about. Stan's old college, still based on 37 Lansdowne Road, was joined with the training college at Polhill, (which, despite its thirteen-storey tower block, was, in origin, the Froebel College, founded in 1882) and Mander College of Further Education, formerly the Bedford technical college, which had been established in 1919. This third runner in the three-legged race, with 8000 students, part-time and full-time, was a giant beside its partners, and the three moved forward with the awkward gait which might be expected of such a combination.

That this race was a race for survival had been made plain by Mrs Bowen-West to the Old Students long before the merger. When it came to giving them unpalatable facts, she had the advantage over Miss Alexander of being one of them, trained at Bedford; indeed, a member of the last generation which could claim to have been admitted by Stan. Times had changed, though. "Our aspirations, our interests and our strengths must . . . be linked," she said, "to those of our neighbours," adding that decisions about the future "ultimately . . . will be out of our hands".[60] By now about forty per cent of Old Students had never known the college as a private institution. It was perhaps the other sixty per cent that the new Principal had in mind when she looked back to 1952 and the takeover by the Local Authority. That had been a wise move at the time, "for it assured survival".[61] Now, twenty years later, it was again a question of survival.

Temperamentally, and from her own experience, Pat Bowen-West was a notable survivor. She had done what was comparatively rare in the fifties: combined a career with marriage and motherhood. She had been widowed young, with young children. Professionally, she had worked her way in the conventional p.e. field: a grammar school; a post as county organiser; later on, physical education lecturer in three different colleges of education. She had spent a year at the Art of Movement Studio and another at the London Institute, taking a diploma in philosophy of education. She came to Bedford straight from the rival – or, one might say, alternative – world of a "wing" college. In that environment (the sixties' contribution to broadening the narrowness of specialist training), it was not unnatural to speculate sometimes on whether a college like Bedford had a future. By the time she was established in Lansdowne Road, the question had become, whether any of them had.

The cuts following Circular 7/73 proved, in fact, to be only a beginning. As the birth rate still declined and the recession deepened, the Department in London cut and cut again its estimate of pupils for the coming years, and of the number of teachers needed. In the first round, thirteen institutions had been told to "discontinue initial training"; another twenty-three were marked out in the second, some of them reprieved later on. No grand total can be said to exist, for the process continues, but by 1981 out of 152 colleges of education at the start, it seems that only twenty-eight remained free-standing and twenty-five had closed. The rest had merged with other institutions, (a few with universities, most with polytechnics, with each other and with colleges of further education). Some of these refugees from the storm have found the refuge itself precarious. Anstey (merged with Birmingham Polytechnic) will effectively expire in 1984 when the last intake of p.e. students has worked through the course. Very much the same thing has happened to Dartford: and 1985, the centenary year of the college Madame Österberg founded, will mark the cessation there of teacher training.

As for Bedford, in its new existence, change has been of a very different order from any resulting from that earlier survival bid which brought it into the public sector. In order to be viable, the new institution had to have a structure designed to minimise the separatist tendencies of its three elements. The college Principals were thus transmuted into Deputy Directors under a chief who was appointed from outside. The academic work was reorganised in Schools, based on the site which seemed most appropriate; (students and staff work on all three).[62] The constitution of the Academic Board had to be devised to reflect the interests of the different Schools and the wide-ranging work of the college. Its twenty sub-committees are only a part of the bureaucracy called into existence. Administration centres on Mander. On paper, "Bedford" has disappeared.

In practice, of course, the erosion of identity is a very much slower process. There are certain factors which tend to retain it, as a clay soil tends to hold water, though it all drains away in the end. One of these factors at Bedford is the site. Attention has already been drawn to the fact that, alone among the sisterhood of colleges, Bedford never left the place where it was born. It was not evacuated during the War, and, partly owing to the pressure of Old Students, did not move out when it had to expand, in the 1960s. It is possible, then, for a student today, who has never heard of Stan, to feel the same inhibition about coming through the front door of "thirty-seven" as was ingrained in Stanny's Stues. "I defy the rules, but you do have guilt," says one, while another adds, "I heard the other day that it's all right if you're not in a track suit."[63] The p.e. work is still based at Lansdowne, in the School of Human Movement Studies, and for students who live there it is easy still to see it as a college from which they go forth to certain lectures on other sites. Many still come, as they did before, because a teacher, relative or friend has been there. They have heard about "Bedford" in advance and when they get there they hear more about it from their college "mother", an older student to whom the newcomer is assigned. Those who were mothered by the last generation to know the old college have only just left. The context of this mothering is residence at Lansdowne. In the early days after the merger all the p.e. students lived there and the atmosphere was very little changed. "I knew everyone," one of them remembers, "can't say I know half the college now."[64] She means, apparently, p.e. students, some of whom now live on the Polhill site, in the former college of education. "They pop in to college." (She adds, in parenthesis, "What I call college, which is Lansdowne.") In the early days, she recalls, it was as much as anyone could do to go from Lansdowne to Polhill for lectures, let alone live there. "You didn't go to Polhill. You tried to miss your lectures at Polhill." Because of the distance? "Because they lived on the reputation of the p.e. college." The word "reputation" has a pre-war ring, evoking years in which Bedford and Dartford were "the Oxford and Cambridge of physical training." The feeling against Polhill subsided, it seems, as students who knew about the old days left. Though p.e. students still wear the sweatshirt of the College of Physical Education, "Give it another couple of years and you probably won't notice the difference." Some of her fellow students insist that there *is* a difference, apart from the feeling. The p.e. student and the type who goes in for primary school teaching are entirely different.

Whatever the difference, it is very slight beside the difference which divides them both from the further education students at Mander. There is probably no way in which several thousand sixteen-to-eighteen year-olds, (apprentice hairdressers, engineers, builders, typists and the rest), mostly part-time and living at home, can make common cause with a few hundred others, resident, adult, working for degrees. The Students' Union building was erected at Mander. But they are too *young*, say the Lansdowne students, they don't know how to use it; they don't understand about student politics and student government. And on top of that, we're given our degrees alongside people getting "O" level certificates. The blend of further and higher education also poses problems for the staff. At the teaching level it has brought new work; to some it has even brought new insights, for the resources of Lansdowne Road, especially in drama, music and art, have been opened up more to local people through this link with the much less privileged world of further education.[65] At the level of policy-making, however, the gulf between "further" and "higher" remains. Competition for scarce resources tends to express itself on these lines in the debates of the Academic Board, the constitution of which was designed to reflect the balance of the institution. That balance, naturally, tilts towards Mander, where five of the nine schools are located, and Human Movement people do not find it easy to justify a Dance degree to engineers. The Articles of Government may refer sometimes to "the teaching staff as a whole", but no whole exists, and old loyalties hang on.

They are, however, an ambivalent shadow of *loyalty* as it was once experienced. That monolithic quality of earlier days was shattered by Circular 7/73, and at some point in the ensuing struggle had to retreat from the old idea of "College" sufficiently to take in the new one, if only for the reason that hanging together was preferable to hanging separately. Where loyalty had been a prime virtue in staff, it fell to the Principal, in the old days, to embody that which called forth loyalty: high ideals. We read of Stan that "nothing second-rate would do";[66] of Miss Squire's "unswerving adherence to the highest standards";[67] of Miss Drummond ("The Drum") of Dunfermline as "one who responded with all her strength to the call of duty".[68] These Old Roman Virtues are not discredited; but they are no help in the present situation. By 1971 when the college's last Principal, Pat Bowen-West, took up her appointment, resilience and a talent for responding to change were among the most valuable qualities which any Principal could embody. At Bedford they were first called into play by the changing relationship of staff and students. It was then that pressure to "throw off the shackles" of the old Students' Union came to a head and a new, autonomous Union was created. This and other things – from a student bar to student Governors – were not introduced without the exercise of some of the skills now required of the former Principal as Deputy Director responsible for Lansdowne in all the hazards of the three-legged race. The only role she has which remains unchanged is as president of the Old Students' body, now, in a sense, the main repository of the old identity of "College".

When the Old Students come every year, as they still do, in numbers, to Lansdowne Road, they are certainly not coming to the Lansdowne "site" of the Bedford College of Higher Education. They take the place over. They bring "College" with them. It will be some time before all that feeling, all that *loyalty* runs into the sand. Meanwhile, their badge has the old initials "B.P.T.C.", which do not even reflect the changed nomenclature of thirty years back. That, perhaps, is neither here nor there; for insofar as a female tradition resided in the physical actuality of a group of specialist colleges, it was destroyed in the 1970s.

Men Again

That tradition, though, as we have seen, was also very much a matter of influence. From the 1880s to the 1950s, what was understood by physical education had been substantially defined by women. Women account for six out of nine in *Nine Pioneers in Physical Education*, the booklet produced to mark the sixty-fifth year of the Physical Education [Ling] Association. But by 1964, when this booklet came out, the shift away from women had already begun. In 1960, only one of four speakers on physical education at the British Association conference was a woman. The specialist colleges did not contribute, but the university departments of p.e. were much in evidence. If this seems to reflect the changing power base, so do the topics. Miss Foster spoke on Movement; Mr Munrow, on the application of mechanics to physical skills, and Dr Floyd on patterns of muscle activity. The Director of the Department of Physical Education at Manchester University, in his introduction, explained that the intellectual level of men in p.e. had changed since the days when boys were taught by ex-Army instructors. For girls, he acknowledged, it had been different, adding rather oddly "and we should have been unwise to leave a woman out of our list of contributors to this symposium".[69] There were other developments, only just perceptible in 1964, which reinforced the shift away from women. One was the challenge to the specialist hegemony from the "wing" colleges (women's and men's); another, the erosion of the female base through the steady loss of grammar schools and girls' schools. A third, less obvious but no less significant, was the considerable and mounting pressure to academicise physical education. In that respect, the heat is still on.

It had first been turned on in the 1960s with the movement for the B.Ed. degree. The dream of a graduate teaching profession began at last to approach reality when it was endorsed in the Robbins Report, but this, as we saw from Bedford's experience, did not automatically open the door either to acceptance of the B.Ed. degree by particular universities, or to the admission of physical education as a potential degree component. Clearly, though, there was little future for any subject that was left outside, and there was fierce determination to get in. Physical educationists bent their minds to the problem of "degree worthiness", and, if the literature is anything to go by, none more eagerly than the men. Indeed, in the view of one Bedford lecturer, they were ready to pre-empt the field. The B.Ed. Study Group set up in the sixties by the Physical Education Association consisted, as Margaret Rosewarne-Jenkins pointed out, of five men and only one woman. It had no member to represent the numerous women p.e.

lecturers and both the professional associations were represented by male delegates. "It appears," she wrote in *The Leaflet*, "that our men colleagues were invited to assume almost entire responsibility for this planning."[70] The answer came that it was surely irrelevant whether the constituent associations were represented by men or women. "Universities in their courses of study do not differentiate between men and women."[71] She pointed out, however, that in physical education the divergence of view between the sexes was so great that it had actually been acknowledged in the Study Group's terms of reference. "How can even the most fair-minded of men . . . be expected to make proposals completely relevant to the work in women's P.E.?"[72] Whether others felt this, the existence of the split was seen as an obstacle to "degree worthiness". Some of those responsible for B.Ed. syllabuses tried to paper over it; others worked round it. "Physical Education," wrote one male lecturer, "has suffered overlong from the dichotomy that the two-sex approach perpetuates."[73] He advised combining the men's and women's colleges, to give them balance, "and add status to our subject". By this time (1965) academic status had emerged as the goal.

"Has Physical Education an academic future?" "What is the intellectual content of Physical Education?" When such questions were asked in the early sixties the answers were were not very reassuring, for the subject appeared to be something of a ragbag. The problem was defined by one writer who admitted

> It is difficult to think of any example in Physical Education of ideas which are ours alone . . . Our subject is at present a vast and loosely-integrated body of diverse material, too general, too superficial, and too dependent on allied fields to satisfy the ideals of university study.

Before convincing others, they must convince themselves "that our subject needs to be academic".

> First, what is our true identity? We must solve the disturbing problem of our academic illegitimacy, and show that there is in Physical Education some area of knowledge which is not already adequately studied by allied disciplines.[74]

From the mêlée of ensuing debate emerged some thoughts on lines of advance. What they needed most, wrote Gordon Curl, was an adequate definition of working concepts in which our knowledge of Physical Education can be handled. Too long we have relied on common sense and intuition, but now that we aspire to the status of science, our pre-scientific rule of thumb methods must give way to the exact and precise formulation of new and more negotiable concepts . . .

If "physical education" was part of "education", then it had techniques, theories and values. Of these, *values* were the most important.

Our techniques and theories are becoming more reliable, but what is the use of knowing the right way to our destination if we have no means of knowing whether the destination itself is the right one? Such a study of *values* in Physical Education comes within that discipline known as the Philosophy of Physical Education.[75]

That philosophy, riding high in the education world of the 1960s, should have been called in aid is not surprising. It is for philosophy to sort out meaning, and there was certainly a crisis of meaning, an identity crisis, in physical education, exposed to some extent at college level by the drive for the B.Ed. degree, but also extending to teachers in the schools. A handbook to encourage teachers to form their own philosophy of physical education and clear their own minds on why they taught the subject, enjoyed considerable success at this time.[76] More sophisticated, if less supportive, were the deliberations of those who teased out the "concept" of physical education to the point where it seemed very doubtful whether it was *education* at all.[77] Did its activities amount to more than "skills with limited cognitive content"? Were not its aims very largely instrumental? Was it not, despite the high-flown language, possibly really physical *training*? A study group set up to debate the "concept" was criticised for begging such vital questions. "To assume that 'physical education' is an area of educational activity is an assumption of immense proportions," declared one writer in 1970, "it is no longer any use saying that we all know this is true." What he wanted were "trained philosophers" to sort out "the vast array of terms, words, ideas etc. which are supposed to tell us what we mean by the theory and practice of 'physical education'."[78]

When "trained philosophers" got their teeth into the vast array of terms and words they had no difficulty in pointing out that these were reflections of muddled thinking. What did a well-known exponent of dance mean, for instance, by attributing to it "a special integrating role" as an art form? What was meant by saying that "Physical" Education should be described as "Movement" Education since the teacher dealt with children "who think, feel and do"? "We need to ask what is presupposed in talk about 'the integration of doing, thinking and feeling'. What is the conceptual relationship between thought and action, between thinking and feeling, between intending and doing, and between reason and emotion?"[79] The way to clarify the "concept", it seemed, was to focus on questions of meaning. But not everybody felt equal to it. There was "general reluctance" at one conference "to discuss, in depth, issues and ideas that required a philosophical analysis rather than . . . a practical interpretation".[80] Some felt that "philosophical ideas were of no great value to the majority".[81] Others, though, deplored such an attitude as likely to invite scorn from other educationists and to ensure that physical education remained "at the bottom of the educational hierarchy".[82] Could it not be, asked A.D. Munrow, "that other people in education evaluate our subject by what we say about it?"[83] While another lecturer "wholeheartedly" agreed that "the status of our subject is related to our ability to discuss it with philosophical and sociological foundation".[84]

In the decade which has followed since the early seventies there has been no lack of philosophical discussion. Conference papers, doctoral theses, books and articles abound. Reputations have certainly been made – it may even be that Chairs have been won through assiduous philosophical digging in this hitherto neglected spot. Like a nation that is on the move, a rising discipline seeks new outlets, and the ascendancy established by Professor R.S. Peters and Professor Paul Hirst for philosophy of education in the 1960s naturally built up a kind of colonising pressure. Physical education, obsessed with the need to justify itself in academic terms, was certainly ripe for colonisation.

That most of the colonists have been men is not sufficiently explained by the fact that more men than women are "trained philosophers". It is just those areas of physical education in which women predominate – Movement and Dance – that have proved most receptive to the insights of philosophy; but while women form the mainstay in the conference halls, they are substantially addressed by men. Can the philosophical advance be explained, partly at least, on a different level? Men, say some of those women who look back to the world that was ruled by the specialist colleges, started to push very hard for careers. Certainly, the B.Ed. opened the door of graduate status to the physical educationist; and after that came post-graduate status: the M.Phils and M.A.s and Ph.D.s that the men went after particularly. "In a competitive Phys. Ed. world, you're looking at your future," one man comments, thinking of his time at the Art of Movement Studio in the early sixties, well before the days when the philosophy bandwagon started rolling. At that time, the bandwagon was Movement and Laban, and it brought some men to the Art of Movement Studio who were not very interested in either. However, "it was suddenly an incoming thing and it was needed in the colleges and they were wanting to get men doing it. The promotion aspect was very very good. I think [men] were getting . . . lecturing jobs through Movement".[85] Later, perhaps, through Philosophy of Movement?

However that might be, the colonisation of p.e. by other subjects through the B.Ed. degree led, some felt, to college courses becoming excessively theoretical and to a widening of the gap between "college theory and school reality". By now the "specialist" course contained "Sociology and P.E., Psychology and P.E., Philosophy and P.E., Bio-mechanical analysis of P.E., Art of movement and P.E., Statistical evaluation of P.E., and, the cynic might add, the 'practice' of P.E."[86] *The Leaflet*, as early as 1967, had been criticised for giving too much space to mediocre essays in p.e. philosophy and not enough to practical hints for teachers.[87] "Skewing the proper shape of the subject" to meet the requirements of a B.Ed. syllabus was deplored by Munrow in the early seventies.[88] However, at about the time he was deploring it, a shrewd outsider's advice to those who were concerned with physical education in the post-James era was that they should find

> some intellectual leverage, as opposed to physical and technical clout, not to intellectualise their subject but to identify its nature and justify its contribution in terms which their colleagues and the students in higher education will be able to understand and accept . . .[89]

The line between "finding some intellectual leverage" and "intellectualising their subject" was a fine one, especially at a time when, as the writer allowed, "Hopefully, we are poised on the threshold of an era of mass higher education."

As we know, they were also poised on the threshold of an era of mass economy; and once survival came to be seen in terms of the capacity to offer courses likely to prove attractive to students who did not necessarily wish to teach, the pressure to intellectualise was immense. What else produced those degree submissions, each as big as a telephone directory, which from the middle 1970s landed on the doorstep of the C.N.A.A.? The Council for National Academic Awards had been set up in 1964 to validate non-university degrees. Ten years later it was inundated with proposals from colleges of education: first, for approval of their own "B.Eds."; then, for validation of B.A. degrees. By now, validation of a B.A. degree was what an Equity card is to an actor: a licence to enter the open market, without which he is likely to starve. Indeed, the resemblance is closer still, for, to get his card, the actor must have acted, though he cannot easily act without one; and the college, to get its degree approved, must show that it can teach at university level (outside the limits of teacher training), which is hard to show without the licence to try.

"Bedford" did not clear this hurdle till 1980, when, with much trouble, it gained approval for a B.A. Honours (Sports Studies) degree. "These non-teaching degrees are vital in attracting students to fill the gap left by the cut in the teacher training numbers",[90] Mrs Bowen-West had told the Old Students. Two years later she was able to inform them of the "long-awaited and important breakthrough".[91] Historically, though, it is less the breakthrough than the struggle itself that is interesting, for even on the time scale of the C.N.A.A., a four-year struggle counts as a long one and indicates a notable clash of view.

At one level, Bedford's problems were no different from anyone else's: they had to put across to empanelled experts the concept and structure of their degree. However, the reason that they failed to do so lay, it seemed to them, in its innovatory nature. It was a new departure. Their proposal, as planned (and twice rejected) was not for Sports Studies but for Human Movement Studies, a very different thing. The degree they wanted would, in fact, have been the first of its kind, based on the study and *evaluation* of intentional human action. Scientific methods, as they pointed out, could explain but could not evaluate movement. For that, a much wider range of factors, including personality and motivation, intentions and context, had to be brought in. Their approach was linked with the work of the philosophers who had been preoccupied with movement and dance.[92]

The "experts" met this first-of-a-species with the fusillade of questions about focus, structure, and the relationship of this to that, customary to them, and shot it dead. Its sponsors felt the anguish of pioneers bested by the establishment. And something more. There is another light in which this business can be viewed: there are ways in which it seems to echo the He/She, Movement/Anti-Movement war. The "experts", certainly, were not all men, but men were most significant among them and it was the "men's view" that came over: the bio-mechanical approach to movement, the voice of exercise physiology, which seeks to *measure* rather than evaluate, and is linked, historically, with circuit training rather than with the insights of Laban. One memory of the struggle, from the losing side, is that it was "essentially a conflict between male and female concepts of the area of study". The human movement studies approach, in that view, *"might* have been acceptable had we not wished to make Sport (sacred to the male macho image) the first option [in the new degree]".[93] The records of the 1976 submission show that "it was not clear [to the C.N.A.A. panel] what was the relevance of human movement studies to a study of sport and recreation". It was still not clear to them four years later, by which time the college felt bound to settle for the compromise of a Sports Studies degree.

Things had been different in the 1930s when Stan's college first moved out into the world of external validation. That was for the London University Diploma and there was certainly no He/She element in the associated consultations. There were several men on the Advisory Committee which ran the Diploma but they were doctors, or others committed, as were the women, to the gospel of Swedish gymnastics. A most conspicuous group of members were the Principals of the specialist colleges; but that was in the heyday of the female tradition.

Conclusion

What place should the physical training colleges have in women's history? That they scarcely appear in conventional accounts of the fight for education is not strange, for they came into existence rather late in the day and, effectively, without confrontation. In 1870, when a sheep was let loose in the midst of a medical lecture in Edinburgh, and some years later, when a bloomered effigy riding a bicycle was hung up in Cambridge, this was an expression of the tension and resentment provoked by what has been well-described as the breaking down of symbolic boundaries.[1] The bloomered gymnast of the 1890s was, of course, the sister of the bloomered cyclist, and would have made just as good an effigy, but there were no young men to hang her up. To all intents and purposes she slipped in unnoticed, because she was not entering the world of men.

The fact that the pioneers of physical training staked their ground *outside* the male citadel, seems, then, to set them slightly apart from the feminist movement of their own day. Does it bring them closer to the movement of ours? Gaining access to men's education, that great Matterhorn of the Victorians, does not impress contemporary feminists, who see it as a "con" which serves patriarchal values and ask themselves whether it might not be better if women "left" the system and became outsiders.[2] But it goes without saying that "outside" in this sense does not mean what it would have meant to Madame Österberg. It is not Dartford, but Virginia Woolf's dream of a women's college rejecting male values that is evoked by the feminist model of "non-hierarchical and non-competitive" education which "seeks to change, rather than reproduce the present structure of society".[3] It would be hard to imagine a community less in tune with this than the p.e. college, which started out as a faithful reproduction of the structure of Victorian society (but that there was no masculine element), and exemplified the spirit of autocracy at least as long as anywhere in England. There were even features of this special world which increased the stature of the autocrat. The way in which the colleges were founded, for instance, each of them springing up round one person in furtherance of the gymnastic ideal, produced the most complete identification of that person with the ideal. Bedford students did not distinguish between loyalty to Stan and to the principles of Ling; one might add, "and to the principles of Life", for that is what some still remember: "Miss Stansfeld taught me a way of life."[4] This focussing on the one great figure was not, of course, peculiar to physical education. The charismatic Principal or Headmistress was well-known through the inter-war years and still around in the 1960s. But the single-minded thrust of the Swedish ideal, and the personal commitment of personal ownership (lasting, at Bedford, to the mid-twentieth century) gave a dimension to the central figure in the p.e. college which was unique. This sort of thing is not likely to appeal to feminists nourished in the present day by the vision and experience of sisterhood. Nonetheless, the successful formulation of physical education as a school subject, and the building of the institutional complex which sustained it, was a remarkable achievement, and one for which women were wholly responsible.

Just as the making of this female tradition does not fit neatly into women's history, so it might be said that the factors undermining it do not all relate specifically to women. In particular, the specialist colleges, like all others in the public sector, have been drastically pulled about in the cuts and crises of recent years, and the effects of that upheaval (tangible and otherwise) are bound to be far-reaching. This does not seem, though, sufficient in itself to account for the decline in women's influence. It does not necessarily follow, because the colleges have been merged, that women specialists should have lost the headstart which they once had in physical education. Yet this has happened. "There are very few women left in any posts of responsibility."[5] Men are in charge now of human movement studies at what remains of the specialist colleges of Anstey, Dartford, I.M. Marsh, Lady Mabel, and at many former "wings" (though not at Bedford). At the institutional level, the female tradition is clearly not immune to the tendency for women to lose power in education, a tendency observable across the board, from the Oxford college to the infants' school. In terms of the influence they exert, women are still important in dance, but degree work in dance is substantially located at the polytechnics, where it forms part of a broader programme in performing arts. It is in the area of dance and aesthetics that philosophy has made it main contribution, and almost all the philosophers are men.

Broadly, there seem to be two ways of approaching the complex decline of this female tradition. One (of which one gets a hint now and then from those trained in it), is that it reflects the strong career drive of the men, once started. In the old world of the specialist colleges, you didn't push yourself forward for a job.

> The women always worked on the grapevine. People used to ring up and say, Look, you ought to apply for that . . . you weren't supposed to, in some kind of a way, think yourself good enough to do it . . . you used to be invited to apply. There was a big grapevine . . . it was all part of the very close community of the p.e. world, which was female . . . All that broke down.[6]

It broke with the breaking down of separate spheres when men began to teach in colleges like Bedford, and schools went over to co-education. This breaking down of separate spheres is also central to the other approach, but here it looks less like men breaking *into*, than women (rather late in the day) coming *out of* their small stockade. They were obliged to come out, in effect, by the need for external validation. The specialist colleges, as we know, did not resemble Virginia Woolf's fancy, and sought endorsement from the world outside. In the thirties they gained it from London University very much on their own terms; indeed, it could be said that, to all intents and purposes, the period of self-validation extended until they came into the public sector. When that happened, when they became members of Area Training Organisations, when they had to sue for the B.Ed. degree, and later, when they had to get B.Ed. and B.A. proposals through the C.N.A.A., they entered a world which was full of other interests, and which was also full of men. Men had already gained a foothold, for instance, for physical education in the universities, where the women had done very little. Whichever approach seems the more convincing (and they are by no means mutually exclusive), the history of what has been called a female tradition raises pertinent questions for anyone concerned with the balance of influence between men and women in a mixed society.

Notes

Abbreviations

INT   Interview (former Bedford students are listed under their maiden names and the dates when they were at college are bracketted after the name.)

LR   Letter

QN   Questionnaire

RS   Reminiscence

Report   Report of Bedford Physical Training College Students' Association

PP.   Parliamentary Papers

B.P.T.C.   Bedford Physical Training College

J.P.E.   *Journal of Physical Education*

B.J.P.E.   *British Journal of Physical Education*

Introduction

[1] Eleanor Rathbone, "Changes in public life", in Ray Strachey ed., *Our Freedom and its results* (London, 1936), p. 57.

[2] Although women's colleges were established at both Oxford and Cambridge from the 1870s, women were not admitted to full membership of Oxford University until 1920 and of Cambridge University until 1947.

[3] Dale Spender, *Invisible Women* (London, 1982), p. 23.

[4] See esp. Sara Delamont, "The Contradictions in Ladies' Education", in Sara Delamont and Lorna Duffin eds., *The Nineteenth Century Woman* (London, 1978); Carol Dyhouse, *Girsl Growing Up In Late Victorian And Edwardian England* (London, 1981), esp. ch. 2.

[5] Dyhouse, op. cit., pp. 64, 65. See also Sheila Fletcher, *Feminists and Bureaucrats* (Cambridge, 1980), for an account of the efforts made by the Endowed Schools Commissioners to get women onto governing bodies. (The Endowed Schools Commissioners were, of course, men.)

[6] Spender, op. cit., p.127.

[7] Virginia Woolf, *Three Guineas* (London, 1943), pp.62–4. First pub. 1938.

[8] Peter McIntosh, *Physical Education in England since 1800* (London, 1968), which remains the best general account.

[9] Quoted in Colin Crunden, *A History of Anstey College of Physical Education* (Anstey College, 1974), p.44. My italics.

[10] A.D. Munrow, *Physical Education* (London, 1972), p.156. Munrow was Director of Physical Education at Birmingham University, the first in England to accept physical education as an element in a first degree.

[11] Jonathan May, *Madame Bergman-Österberg* (London, 1969), p. 81.
[12] Spender, op. cit., p.23.

1 *The Nineteenth Century*

[1] National Association for the Promotion of Social Science, *Transactions* (1869), p.361.
[2] Thomas Hughes, *Tom Brown's Schooldays* (London, 1981), p.271. First pub. 1856.
[3] Archibald Maclaren, *Physical Education* (Oxford, 1895), p. lxx.
[4] See, for instance, Patricia Branca, *Silent Sisterhood* (London, 1975), Sara Delamont and Lorna Duffin eds., *The Nineteenth Century Woman* (London, 1978), and Martha Vicinus ed., *Suffer and Be Still* (Bloomington, 1972).
[5] Frances Power Cobbe, *Life* (2 vols., London, 1894), vol.1, p.47.
[6] Ibid., p.65.
[7] Elizabeth Wordsworth, *Glimpses of the Past* (London, 1912), p.39.
[8] Quoted in Christabel Coleridge, *Charlotte Mary Yonge* (London, 1903), p.125.
[9] Herbert Spencer, *Education: Intellectual, Moral and Physical* (London, 1902), p.169. First pub. 1861.
[10] A photograph dating from the 1850s which shows the see-saw and a group of girls still exists in the archives of the school.
[11] PP. 1867–68, XXVIII.4., Schools Inquiry Commission, vol.5, Minutes of Evidence QQ 11,623–7.
[12] A.T. Schofield, "Notes of a lecture on 'The Physical Education of Girls' " 1889 (G.P.D.S.T. Archives) quoted in Pauline Bell, "A history of physical education in girls' public schools, 1870–1920," unpub. M.Ed. thesis (Manchester, 1978).
[13] Annie Ridley, *Frances Mary Buss* (1895), p.203. The gentle, rhythmic style that appealed to Miss Buss is evoked too, by the Victorian drill song:

Swinging, swinging, onward we go,
Rising, falling, gently and low,
Turning, bending, marching along,
Swinging, singing, sweetly our song.

Quoted in Celia Haddon, *Great Days and Jolly Days* (1977), p. 52.
[14] PP. 1867–68, XXVIII.8., Schools Inquiry Commission, vol.9, Mr J.G. Fitch's Report, p.299.
[15] Cobbe, op. cit., p.65.
[16] PP. 1867-68 XXVIII. 8., Schools Inquiry Commission, vol. 9, Mr J.G. Fitch's Report, p.299.
[17] Ibid., Mr J. Bryce's Report, p. 818.

18 PP. 1867–68 XXVIII.7., Schools Inquiry Commission, vol.8, Mr H.M. Bompas's Report, p.63.

19 PP. 1867–68, XXVIII.6., Schools Inquiry Commission, vol.7, Mr D.R. Fearon's Report, pp.390–1.

20 PP. 1867-68 XXVIII.8., Schools Inquiry Commission, vol.9, Mr J.G. Fitch's report, pp. 401–10.

21 *Special Reports on Educational Subjects* (1898), vol.2, p.155.

22 John Bailey ed., *The Diary of Lady Frederick Cavendish* (London, 1927), p.22. For a brief reference to the encouragment of women's cricket in the eighteenth century by the Duke of Dorset, see *Chambers' Encyclopedia*.

23 PP. 1867–68, XXVIII.4., Schools Inquiry Commission, vol.5, Minutes of Evidence, p.739.

24 Ibid., p.740.

25 For an account of the struggle to achieve this see Sheila Fletcher, *Feminists and Bureaucrats* (Cambridge, 1980).

26 Alice Zimmern, *The Renaissance of Girls' Education in England* (London, 1898).

27 National Association for the Promotion of Social Science, *Transactions* (1860), p.594.

28 Quoted in Peter C. McIntosh, *Physical Education in England since 1800* (London, 1952), p.98.

29 McIntosh, op. cit., pp. 102–3.

30 For Roth's campaign see McIntosh, op. cit., and Terrence J. Surridge, "Mathias Roth", *Physical Education Year Book* (1973-4), pp.10-12.

31 Abstract of a paper on School Hygiene and Scientific Physical Education, read at the Social Science Congress, Brighton, 12 Oct. 1875. And see *Transactions* of the Social Science Association (1875), pp.470–2.

32 London School Board minutes (1 Feb. 1871).

33 Minutes of a sub-committee (of School Management Committee of London School Board) appointed 27 Nov. 1878 to enquire into the necessity of having a more complete system of Physical Education for Girls (11 Dec. 1878).

34 London School Board Minutes (18 Dec. 1878).

35 Concordia Löfving, *On Physical Education and its place in a Rational System of Education* (London, 1882), p.62, quoted in Ida M. Webb, "Women's Physical Education in Great Britain 1800–1966', Unpub. M.Ed. thesis (Leicester, 1967), p.64, n.15.

36 *The Times* (14 July 1881), p.7.

37 Jonathan May, *Madame Bergman-Österberg* (London, 1969), p.15.

38 Madame Bergman-Österberg, Report to the School Management Committee of the London School Board, Jan. 1888 (C10 Dartford College Archives). She goes on to say that lawn tennis had been introduced at several schools in Hackney and Finsbury, and Fives at a school in Ratcliffe.

[39] A.D. Munrow, "Looking back and looking forward in Gymnastics", *Physical Education*, vol. 48, no.143 (Mar. 1956), p.18.

[40] Evidence to the Cross Commission, June 1887 (PP. 1887, XXX p.376, Q 52,177 and p.378, Q 52,219).

[41] Ibid., p.377, Q 52,180 (But, for a different view, see Mary Scharlieb and Alice Ravenhill, "Physical Training in Stockholm and Copenhagen", *Nineteenth Century* (Dec. 1906), p.989: "Without doubt, free standing movements alone are an insufficient form of physical training.").

[42] Ibid., p.376, Q 52,158.

[43] *The Times* (25 June 1883), p.8.

[44] *Daily News* (July 1884), quoted in May, op. cit., pp.22-3

[45] Webb op. cit., pp.72, 77–8, 79–80.

[46] "Interview with Madame Bergman-Österberg", *Woman's Herald* (20 June 1891). The writer implies that the "untrammelled" conditions described here related to Miss Bergman's six years with the School Board but has surely mis-read her interview notes.

[47] Cross Commission (PP. 1887, XXX, p.378, Q 52,205).

[48] Madame Bergman-Österberg, *The Training of Teachers in Methods of Physical Education*, undated (C 6/8 Dartford College Archives). For reference to the eugenics movement, see ch. 2.

[49] Madame Bergman–Österberg, "Physical Training as a Profession", paper to Women's Congress (3 July 1899), pp. vi–vii.

[50] Private papers of Mrs Adair Impey, quoted in Webb, op. cit., pp. 193–4.

[51] Österberg, *Professional Women on their Professions* (1891), quoted in May op. cit., p.34.

[52] "Interview with Madame Bergman-Österberg", *Woman's Herald* (20 June 1891).

2. *Too Good to Fail*

[1] For Cambridge attitudes see R. McWilliams-Tullberg, *Women at Cambridge* (London, 1975); for grammar school attitudes see Sheila Fletcher, *Feminists and Bureaucrats* (Cambridge, 1980).

[2] Arabella Kenealy, L.R.C.P., "Woman as an Athlete", *The Nineteenth Century*, XLV (April 1899), pp. 635–45.

[3] Herbert Spencer, *Education: Intellectual, Moral and Physical* (1861), p.179.

[4] Henry Maudsley, "Sex in Mind and in Education", *Fortnightly Review*, n.s. 15 (1874), pp.466–83.

[5] Withers Moore in *The Lancet*, 2 (1886), p.315. For an account of the medical opposition to women's higher education, see Joan Burstyn, *Victorian Education and the Ideal of Womanhood* (London, 1980), ch.5.

[6] Quoted in D.D. Molyneux, "Early Excursions by Birmingham Women into Games and Sports", *Physical Education*, vol. 51, no.153 (July 1959), pp.46–54.

[7] Quoted in Pauline Bell, "A History of physical education in girls' public schools 1870–1920", unpub. M.Ed. thesis (Manchester, 1978), p.160.

[8] Historians of Edwardian Britain have lately paid a good deal of attention to this area. For recent analysis of some of its complexities, see Charles Webster (ed.), *Biology, Medicine and Society 1840-1940* (Cambridge, 1981); for discussion of some implications for women, see Carol Dyhouse, "Social Darwinistic ideas and the Development of women's education in England, 1880–1920", *History of Education*, vol.5, no.1, (1976), pp. 41–58.

[9] Arabella Kenealy, "Woman as an Athlete: A Rejoinder", *The Nineteenth Century*, XLV (June 1899), pp.924–5.

[10] Mary Scharlieb, "Recreational Activities of Girls During Adolescence" (1911), quoted in Carol Dyhouse, *Girls Growing Up in Late Victorian and Edwardian England* (1981), p.130.

[11] Dr Jane Walker, speaking at a conference of the National Union of Women Workers, quoted in Paul Atkinson, "Fitness, Feminism and Schooling", in Delamont & Duffin eds., *The Nineteenth Century Woman*, p.127.

[12] Sara Burstall, quoted in Atkinson, loc. cit.

[13] Österberg, "Physical Training as a Profession", Women's International Congress (3 July 1899), p.iii.

[14] Ibid., p.v.

[15] Ibid., p.iv.

[16] Österberg, "Physical Education", 1905 (C6/5 Dartford Archives), p.7.

[17] Letter, 3 June 1965, from C. Macnee (Dartford 1909–11) to Jonathan May (C9/10 Dartford College Archives).

[18] Quoted in May, *Madame Bergman-Österberg*, p.52.

[19] Kenealy, "A Rejoinder", p.927.

[20] Österberg, "Physical Education", p.5.

[21] Österberg, "The Physical Education of Girls in England", c.1913 (C 6/6 Dartford College Archives), p.5.

[22] "Interview with Madame Bergman-Osterberg", *Woman's Herald* (20 June 1891).

[23] Jonathan May, *Madame Bergman-Österberg* (1969), pp. 121–2.

[24] *Ling Association Supplement* (Aug.–Sept. 1915), quoting *Journal of Education* (Sept. 1915).

[25] "Interview with Madame Bergman-Österbeg", *Woman's Herald* (20 June 1891).

[26] For details of the regime in Hampstead and at Dartford see Jonathan May, *Madame Bergman-Österberg* (1969).

[27] Quoted in May, op. cit., p. 76.

[28] Ibid., p. 94.

[29] Österberg, "Physical Training as a Profession", Women's International Congress (1899), p.v.

[30] Ibid.

[31] Österberg, "The Physical Education of Girls in England", p.5.

[32] Österberg, "Physical Education", p.3.

[33] Ibid.

[34] Molyneux, op. cit.

[35] Quoted in *Englishwomen's Review* (1887), p.429.

[36] Miss P. Lawrence, Headmistress of Roedean School, "Games and Athletics in Secondary Schools for Girls", *Special Reports on Educational Subjects*, vol. 2 (1898), p. 152.

[37] Jane Frances Dove, "Cultivation of the Body", in Dorothea Beale, Lucy Soulsby, Jane Frances Dove, *Work and Play in Girls' Schools* (London, 1898), pp. 400–1.

[38] Lawrence, op cit., p. 155.

[39] This kind of distinction between the two types of school is explored in J.S. Pederson, "The Reform of Women's Secondary and Higher Education in Nineteenth-Century England", unpub. Ph.D. thesis (Berkeley, California, 1974).

[40] Lawrence, op. cit., p. 150.

[41] Dove, op. cit., pp. 401–2.

[42] Lawrence, op. cit., p. 145. (St Leonard's had been carrying on the same crusade since its foundation in 1877).

[43] Both Miss Dove and Miss Lawrence regarded football as unsuitable for girls on account of its roughness but some girls of the period seem to have enjoyed it. The Girls' Public Day School Trust *Centenary Review* records that in 1884 there was a football club at the Brighton High School and that football was played in the early days at Nottingham High School. M.C. Bradbrook's *That Infidel Place* records that the earliest students at Girton tried to play football but Miss Davies forbade it. There is a reference to schoolgirl football in Angela Brazil's *The Fortunes of Philippa* (1906). In 1922, according to an *Evening Standard* report, the girls in Messrs Lyons' athletics club were "specially fond of football".

[44] Quoted in Pauline Bell, "A history of physical education in girls' public schools 1870–1920" unpub. M.Ed. thesis (Manchester, 1978), p.74.

[45] Quoted in Margaret Claydon, "How Strong the Girls Grow", unpub. M.Sc. thesis (London, 1982), p.63.

[46] F. Cecily Steadman, *In the days of Miss Beale* (London, 1931), pp.83–4.

[47] May, op. cit., p.74.

[48] I am obliged to Margaret Claydon for pointing out that at the North London Collegiate School, which did not take up the Swedish system, games were coached in the old "amateur" tradition until the 1920s.

[49] Österberg, "Physical Education", p.5.

[50] Österberg, "The Training of Teachers in Methods of Physical Education", p.3.

[51] Österberg, "The Physical Education of Girls in England", pp.6–7.

[52] Bell, op. cit., p.147.

[53] Österberg, "The Training of Teachers in Methods of Physical Education", p.5.

[54] For an account of the discussion between Lord Lyttelton, Chief Endowed Schools Commissioner, and Emily Davies on the merits of the Laws of Health for girls, see Sheila Fletcher, *Feminists and Bureaucrats* (Cambridge, 1980), p.109. For the Laws of Health syllabus adopted at the North London Collegiate School, see Claydon, op. cit., Appendix 3.

[55] Quoted in May, op. cit., p.75.

[56] For a list of appointments gained by Old Students by 1915 and a list of schools from which students were drawn in 1914 see May, op. cit., Appendixes III and IV.

[57] Letter from Grenfell to Österberg (26 Mar. 1905), quoted in May, op. cit., p.102.

[58] Letter from Badley to Österberg (24 Nov. 1907), quoted in May, op. cit., p.105.

[59] Mary Hankinson, "The Teaching of Gymnastics", in Edith J. Morley ed., *Women Workers in Seven Professions* (1913).

[60] The Interdepartmental Committee on Physical Deterioration reported in 1904.

[61] George Newman, *The Building of a Nation's Health* (London, 1939), p.267.

[62] For an account see P.C. McIntosh, *Physical Education in England since 1800* (London, 1952), pp.149–51.

[63] *Ling Association Supplement* (June 1905). It is not actually clear whether all these training colleges were for elementary teachers.

[64] *Journal of Scientific Physical Training*, vol.II no.2 (1910), p.2.

[65] A.P. Graves, "Physical Education in Primary Schools", *Contemporary Review* (June 1904).

[66] *Journal of Education* (Sept. 1915).

[67] For a very useful account of all the colleges see I.M. Webb, "Women's Physical Education in Great Britain 1800–1965", Unpub. M.Ed. thesis (Leicester, 1967).

[68] *Journal of Scientific Physical Training*, vol. VIII (1915–16), pp.14–17.

[69] May, op. cit., pp.77–8. Mrs Adair Impey, a former Dartford student active in the matter of the Ling Association, recalled that Madame Österberg had told her "she had never envisaged a professional association operating on democratic lines as a separate thing from her college". *The Leaflet* (May 1959), p.27.

[70] She wanted to transfer her college to the nation. This did not come about but Sir Gerge Newman, Chief Medical Officer to the Board of Education, and Dame Janet Campbell, a doctor in his department, took the initiative in forming a board of trustees to govern Dartford. This does not seem to have secured its stability. In the next ten years there were four different

Principals, three of whom were not trained gymnasts. Dartford had a bad patch in 1930 with great dissatisfaction among staff and students, but when Miss Greenall was appointed Principal things settled down, at least till the upheaval of evacuation in the Second World War.

3 Ling in the Ascendant

1 See John Stansfeld, *History of the Family of Stansfeld of Stansfeld in the parish of Halifax and its numerous branches* (1885). Reminiscences of Margaret Stansfeld, including a very brief account of her early life by her sister, Florence Stansfeld, were published by Bedford College after her death in 1951, in a booklet entitled *Margaret Stansfeld*. There is an article about her by Marion Squire in *Nine Pioneers in Physical Education* (published in 1964 to mark the sixty-fifth anniversary of the founding of the Ling Association). There are brief references to her in Jonathan May, *Madame Bergman-Österberg* (1969).

2 Österberg, "Physical Training as a Profession", Women's International Congress (3 July 1899), p.v.

3 INT 1980 Joan Goodrich (1922–5).

4 K.M. Westaway ed., *A History of Bedford High School* (Bedford, 1932), p.49.

5 C 15/3 Dartford College Archives.

6 Ibid.

7 Undated letter from Eva Evans (née Cook) pupil at Bedford High School in 1897.

8 Public Record Office Ed. 35/10. Report on Inspection of Bedford High School, 1906.

9 F. Cecily Steadman, *In the days of Miss Beale* (London, 1931), p.48. The reference is to Cheltenham in 1889. Miss Lawrence's account of games at Roedean in *Special Reports on Educational Subjects* (1898) also touches on the problem of athletic costume, as do the early records of the Ling Association. For a recent discussion of the influence of dress see Marie Pointon, "Factors influencing the participation of women and girls in physical education, physical recreation and sport in Great Britain during the period 1850–1920", *History of Education Bulletin*, 24 (Autumn 1979).

10 C15/3 Dartford College Archives.

11 LR 1973 Freda Young (1903–5).

12 LR1973 Ida Hadley (1903–5).

13 LR 1973 Freda Young (1903–5).

14 LR 1943 B.H. Haldane (1906–8).

15 Ibid.

16 LR 1943 D.P. Payne (1903–5).

17 Ibid.

¹⁸ LR 1973 Margaret Graham (1908–10).

¹⁹ Ibid.

²⁰ Ibid.

²¹ LR 1943 B.H. Haldane (1906–8).

²² Baron Nils Posse, *The Special Kinesiology of Educational Gymnastics* (Boston, 1903), p. vi.

²³ Ibid., p.v.

²⁴ Ibid., p.8.

²⁵ Ibid., p.10.

²⁶ Ibid., p.40.

²⁷ Ibid., p.378.

²⁸ LR 1973 Molly Evans (1904–6). Molly Evans' notebooks and textbooks are in Bedford College Archives.

²⁹ *In A Huge Bonnet She Ate Little Jam Rolls*: the initial letter of each word recalls a stage in the sequence. Thus:

*I*ntroduction:	a loosening up exercise, marching in lines or running in a circle.
*A*rm:	standing in lines, arms swinging sideways and upwards in an infinite variety.
*H*ead:	cross sitting, head turning etc.
*B*alance:	horizontal half standing i.e. on one leg, or walking on a bar.
*S*houlder:	handstands, working at the wall bars, arm flinging.
*A*bdominal:	lying, leg raising or big trunk movements.
*J*umps:	vaulting.
*R*espiration:	the final inspiration, often "heel lifting, breath in; heel sinking, breath out".

Some students recall a slightly different version: In A Huge Bonnet She Ate Large Messy Jam Rolls.

³⁰ For a discussion of the course in "Home Science and Economics" introduced by King's College for Women in 1908, see Carol Dyhouse, *Girls Growing up in Late Victorian and Edwardian England* (London, 1981), pp. 168–9.

³¹ See ch.5.

³² Volkhovsky, V., "The Swedish System – a defence", *Journal of Scientific Physical Training*, vol.2, no.2 (1910).

³³ *Journal of Scientific Physical Training* (Spring 1910), quoted in Sara Burstall and M.A. Douglas eds., *Public Schools for Girls* (1911), p.214.

³⁴ Quoted in Burstall and Douglas, loc. cit.

³⁵ Volkhovsky, op. cit.

³⁶ Quoted in Burstall and Douglas, loc. cit.

³⁷ Miss Pater (Bedford Modern School for Girls), quoted in Pauline Bell, "A history of physical education in girls' public schools 1870–1920", unpub.

M.Ed. thesis (Manchester, 1978), p.123.

[38] LR 1973 Phyllis Spafford (1908–10).

[39] Volkhovsky, op. cit.

[40] Posse, op. cit., pp.25ff.

[41] LR 1973 Ida Hadley (1903–5).

[42] LR *c*. 1943 D.P. Payne (1903–5).

[43] LR 1973 Phllis Spafford (1908–10).

[44] LR *c*. 1943 Freda Young (1903–5).

[45] LR 1973 Phyllis Spafford (1908–10).

[46] Mary Hankinson, "The Teaching of Gymnastics", in Edith J. Morley ed., *Women Workers in Seven Professions* (1913), gives about 44 hours in total for a typical week's work in the second-year course at "one of the colleges" (*excluding* private study and matches). The breakdown is: gymnastics (6 hours), remedial gymnastics (5), treating patients in clinic (5), anatomy (6), physiology (2), hygiene (2), vaulting (2) dancing (3½); games (2 hours, four afternoons per week); class singing (two ½ hour lessons plus ¼ hour daily practice); "and each student teaches in the elementary schools three half hours a week and also gets some practice in the high school".

[47] Mrs Adair Impey in *The Leaflet*, vol.60, no.4 (May 1959), p.27.

[48] *Ling Association Annual Report* (1902).

[49] The course was run at Bournemouth High School and did not survive the First World War.

[50] "At the turn of the century the Swedish system was conducted by word of command and no musical accompaniment was used. Exponents of the British system (an eclectic system) used music, particularly for floor exercises. During the twentieth century there have been phases when 'music' was an integral part of gymnastic lessons and times when it was 'frowned' upon and forbidden by the 'purists'. Currently (1975) music is an integral part of the Olympic Gymnastics and Jazz Gymnastics systems but not of Modern Educational Gymnastics." I.M. Webb, "The History of Chelsea College of Physical Education with special reference to curriculum development 1898–1973". Unpub. Ph.D. thesis (Leicester, 1977), p.124.

[51] I.M. Webb, "Women's Physical Education in Great Britain 1800–1965", (Unpub. M.Ed. thesis (Leicester, 1967), p.289.

[52] Peter C. McIntosh, *Physical Education in England since* 1800 (1968), p.150.

[53] *Ling Association Supplement* (April 1903).

[54] George Newman, *The Building of a Nation's Health* (1939), p.271.

[55] Quoted in Webb, op. cit., p.305.

[56] *Ling Association Annual Report* (1909). (Mrs Adair Impey opening discussion on "The Problems arising from the training of Elementary Teachers".)

[57] Quoted in Webb op. cit., p.299. It was also proposed that a uniform syllabus be supplied to each Centre and two extra-mural examiners be appointed.

[58] *Journal of Scientific Physical Training*, vol. III, no.8 (Spring 1911), p.43.

[59] LR 1943 K.H. Scott (1905–7). There are shades of the drill sergeant here!

[60] *Ling Association Supplement* (Feb. 1902).

[61] *Ling Association Annual Report* (1900).

[62] Journal of Scientific Physical Training, vol.I, no. 1 (Oct. 1908).

[63] Österberg, "The Training of Teachers in Methods of Physical Education", (C 6/8 Dartford College Archives, undated).

[64] INT 1980 Freda Colwill (1913–15).

[65] Phyllis Colson, "College Tradition" in Report of Old Students' Day, Diamond Jubilee 1963.

[66] Ibid.

[67] INT 1980 A. Carr (1918–1920).

4 Stanny's Stues

[1] *Nine Pioneers in Physical Education* (1964), pp.5–8.

[2] LR 1943 Freda Young 1903–5; LR 1943 Ida Hadley 1903–5.

[3] Quoted in M. Bradbrook, *That Infidel Place* (1969), p.31.

[4] LR 1943 Jeannie Webb 1903–5.

[5] Freda Young, "First Memorial Lecture" (10 March 1953), p.12.

[6] Ibid.

[7] LR *c*. 1943 D.P. Payne (1903–5). The reading aloud was discontinued as the college grew in size but the custom still remained of groups of students taking coffee with Miss Stansfeld after dinner.

[8] Payne, op. cit.

[9] The intake rose from thirteen in 1903 to over fifty in 1943, when the college had over 130 students. As for buildings, in addition to "thirty-seven", two more houses in Lansdowne Road had been acquired by the First World War. In 1914 a new gymnasium was built. By the Second World War there were a dozen houses, a new science laboratory and the Sydney Road playing fields. The course was extended from two to three years in 1919.

[10] *Jubilee Report*, p.15.

[11] Quoted in J.S. Pederson, "The Reform of Women's Secondary and Higher Education in 19th Century England: A Study in Elite Groups", unpub. Ph.D. thesis (University of California, Berkeley, 1974), pp.370–1. Miss Davies affirmed: "Our college is not a place for 'young girls', any more than the other colleges are for young boys. It is a place for young women."

[12] See *Introduction* n.9, for Anstey. "Stanny's Stues" was the nickname current with some of the boys at Bedford School.

[13] Pederson, op. cit., p.398.

[14] Carol Dyhouse, *Girls Growing Up in late Victorian and Edwardian England* (1981), p.72.

[15] A better-known Victorian case is that of the educational pioneer and

feminist Barbara Bodichon, who, by arrangement, lived apart from her French husband (domiciled in Algiers) for several months of the year, to the great scandal of some of her acquaintance. In his short biography of Madame Bergman Österberg, Jonathan May is at pains to point out that Dr Österberg warmly supported his wife's work, and was often to be seen at Dartford where "with flame-coloured beard, top hat, and morning coat" he cut a striking figure on the cycling track.

16 *Nine Pioneers in Physical Education* (1964), p.16.

17 Colin Crunden, *A History of Anstey College of Physical Education 1897— 1972* (1974), p.8.

18 INT 1980 Freda Colwill (1913–15). Madame Österberg is also described as having "no church or religious affiliations".

19 INT 1980 A. Carr (1918–21).

20 Pederson, op. cit., pp.406ff, singles out a group of "saintly" headmistresses as distinct from those who were more "civic-minded". Miss Anstey, among the heads of p.e. colleges, seems to have had strong religious motivation, largely coloured by theosophy.

21 LR 1979 Peggy Finn.

22 INT 1980 Joan Goodrich (1922–5).

23 INT 1980 Molly Tod (1923–6).

24 INT 1980 Freda Colwill (1913–15).

25 INT 1980 Elizabeth Swallow (1936–9).

26 INT 1980 Rena Stratford (1925–8).

27 INT 1980 Erica Bache (1943–6).

28 INT 1980 Mary Feaver (1930–3).

29 INT 1980 Jean Lindsay (1927–30).

30 INT 1980 Freda Colwill (1913–15).

31 Ibid.

32 INT 1977 Phyllis Spafford (1908–10).

33 INT 1980 Rhona Lewis (1932–5).

34 RS 1943 (1920–3 Set).

35 INT 1980 Rena Stratford (1925–8).

36 Ibid.

37 Ibid.

38 INT 1980 Joan Goodrich (1922–5).

39 Encouraged by example: "I shall never forget the revelation I had one day when I was alone and unseen in the Gym . . . and Miss Stansfeld came in from teaching in the High School looking so exhausted that I thought she would drop as she almost dragged herself up the length of the room. That day we had such a rousing and stimulating lesson that we all excelled ourselves . . . 'So –' I thought, 'that is how you treat fatigue when you are a gym mistress!' " J.H. Wicksteed (1905–7).

40 INT 1980 Joan Goodrich (1922–5).

"Junior leg" (so-called because it seemed to afflict beginners) is Osgood-Schlatter's disease. Pain and swelling is caused by stress on the insertion of the patella tendon into the tibial tuberosity.

41 Josephone Tey, *Miss Pym Disposes* (London, 1957), p.34. First published 1946.
42 INT 1980 Freda Colwill (1913–15).
43 LR 1976 Grace Phillips (1923–6).
44 Fees, as at Dartford, were on a par with those of women's colleges at Oxford and Cambridge, which ranged from £90 to £105 p.a. before the First World War. In 1913 the cost of training at a residential physical training college was given as about £100 p.a. (Mary Hankinson, "The Teaching of Gymnastics", in Edith Morley, *Women Workers in Seven Professions*). From Cash Book entries for Bedford in the 1930s, it looks as if the fees then were about £150 p.a.; but the entries vary so much for individuals that it is hard to be precise
45 RS Joan Gibson (1938–41).
46 INT 1980 Jean Lindsay (1927–30). Ida Webb found in a study of Chelsea College that over half her sample of former Chelsea students chose that college because school staff were trained there. See "The History of Chelsea College of Physical Education with special reference to curriculum development 1898–1973", unpub. Ph.D. thesis (Leicester, 1977), p.254.
47 INT 1980 Jean Lindsay (1927–30).
48 INT 1980 Irene Fardon (1940–3).
49 INT 1980 Pat Frith (1943–6).
50 INT 1980 Elizabeth Swallow (1936–9).
51 QN 1978 Nancy Lusty (1927–30).
52 INT 1980 Margery Richards (1938–41).
53 INT 1980 Freda Colwill (1913–15). She was speaking of lacrosse but the same might well have been said of hockey. The Old Students' *Report* to the present day has its regular entry for International Honours in these and other games.
54 Ida Webb's researches show that the same was true of many entrants to Chelsea at this time.
55 INT 1980 Molly Tod (1923–6).
56 INT 1980 Jean Lindsay (1927–30).
57 She goes on, "Movement is necessary for growth for girls as much as for boys and should be encouraged instead of repressed. Long walks in files are most injurious, as each child having to keep step with longer or shorter legs, a harmful strain on back and legs is produced and the back is allowed to fall into a curved position from fatigue, while free movements as in hockey, cricket etc., afford most healthful exercise."
58 The Rev. Bevis Thompson, reported in *Ling Association Supplement* (June 1909). My italics.

59 Quoted in May, *Madame Bergman-Österberg*, p.45.

60 Ibid., p.87. What outraged this young man was the wearing of a tunic on a *public* ground (the Dartford girl was playing in a county match). Early Bedford students wore gym tunics when playing on the private grounds at Girton and Newnham, but elsewhere played in regulation skirts, six or seven inches off the ground. See *Report* (1975), p.26.

61 Marion Squire, *Report* (1953), p.14.

62 This is self-evident in respect of the Diploma each college awarded. The Ling Association's Diploma, introduced in 1904, was awarded by the gymnasts' own professional body. The London University Diploma which succeeded it in 1931 was the product of an advisory committee on which the college Principals figured large (see ch.8). Not until the colleges were absorbed into Area Training Organisations in the 1950s (see ch.7) were their courses really subject to *external* validation.

63 Quoted in May, op. cit., p.60.

64 RS 1943 (1926–9 Set).

65 LR 1973 Molly Evans (1904–6).

66 INT 1980 Erica Bache (1943–6).

67 RS 1943 (1926–9 Set).

68 Bache, op. cit., In the Victorian family-type girls' school, control was often exercised on a highly personal basis. "I say that I don't love them, that is always enough," was one headmistress's technique in the 1860s (see Dyhouse, *Girls Growing Up in Late Victorian and Edwardian England*, p.47). The Bedford reproof was meant to gain effect from the fact that the tutor and the student's mother had been contemporaries at the college.

69 INT 1980 Rhona Lewis (1932–5).

70 INT 1980 Margery Richards (1928–31).

71 INT 1980 Mary Feaver (1930–3).

72 INT 1980 Joan Goodrich (1922–5).

73 INT 1980 Erica Bache (1943–6).

74 INT 1980 Holly Graham (1929–32).

75 RS 1943 (1938–41 Set).

76 The chaperone rules (which meant that a woman student could not go to tea in a man's room unless she took a friend with her) had been abolished a year or two before. There was signing-out procedure for the evenings and women had to be in by 11.00p.m. But there was none of the minute-by-minute supervision exercised at Bedford, Dartford and the rest. Student rooms were private, lectures not compulsory, and working habits a matter of choice.

77 *Journal of Scientific Physical Training*, vol. VIII (1915–16), p.14.

78 Games Club Minutes, 16 July 1946. There is an interesting contrast with the autonomous organisation of games by the girls at St Leonard's, School, St Andrews, in its early days. I am obliged to Jane Claydon for pointing out

that the p.e. staff room there is still called "the captains' room" and the games captains enter without knocking.

79 RS 1943 K. Anson (1937–40).

80 Barbara Stephen, *Emily Davies and Girton College* (1927), p.31. The following is typical of many similar comments from Bedford: "I find that the happiness and gaiety of that time are the memories that are still with me . . . We trained before the time of the magnificent new gymnasium . . . but we did not miss any of the joys, for we were a small community living in an atmosphere of good will and hard work." K.W. Scott 1905–7.

81 QN 1978 Eira Davies (1922–4).

82 RS 1944 Audrey Hobbs (1921–4).

83 "*The Bran Tub*", Senior Students' Entertainment (1929).

84 RS 1943 Sylvia Buzzard (1926–9).

85 QN 1978 Eira Davies (1922–4).

86 LR 1943 Freda Young (1903–5), describing Isabel Stevenson of the same Set.

87 RS 1943 (1938–41 Set).

88 *Report*, (1945), p.15.

89 Ibid., (1922–4), D.M. Wilkie "Holiday Week 1922".

90 LR 1973 Phyllis Spafford (1908–10).

91 Molly Petit and Ida Hadley of the first Set, were appointed in 1906.

92 INT 1980 I. Nowell Smith (Dartford 1928–31; Bedford Staff 1948–70).

93 This company provided yet another forum for the exercise of influence at Bedford by the same group of people wearing different hats. Miss Stansfeld, of course, was not only Principal, but also president of the Old Students' Association and governing director of the company. Ida Hadley and Molly Petit were not only tutors but treasurer and secretary of the Old Students' Association and directors of the company. Helen McMinn was secretary to the company and to the college, and assistant secretary to the Old Students' Association; and so on.

94 INT 1980 Holly Graham (1929–32).

95 Eileen Alexander (Principal of Bedford 1952–71) recalls that when she trained at Dartford (1929–32) "we used to regard the Bedford students with fear". Dartford didn't play Bedford then – "we would have been afraid of losing".

96 INT 1980 Freda Colwill (1913–15).

97 INT 1980 Mary Feaver (1930–3).

98 *Report* (1975). p.29.

99 For further reference to Miss Wilkie's living at Bromham, see ch.7.

100 *Ling Association Supplement* (April 1911).

101 The Gymnastic Teachers' Suffrage Society was launched by Mary Hankinson during the Ling Association's holiday course in January 1909, at a meeting critical of W.S.P.U. methods. Its activities are reported in the

Association's monthly supplements. I have been unable to trace any records.

[102] The play was written by Mary Hankinson. See *Nine Pioneers in Physical Education* (1964), p.20.

[103] INT 1980 Freda Colwill (1913–15).

[104] In the small world of the specialist colleges there were very few Principal-ships – and what else could be considered promotion? Some, like Joan Goodrich, the specialist in dance (1933–46), felt the need to get out into more mixed society. She joined the Inspectorate in 1946.

[105] INT 1980 Pat Frith (1943–6).

[106] Ibid.

[107] INT 1980 Jean Lindsay (1927–30).

[108] INT 1980 Betty Donaldson (1930–3).

[109] INT 1980 Elizabeth Swallow (1936–9).

[110] INT 1980 Mary Feaver (1930–3).

[111] INT 1980 Freda Colwill (1913–15).

[112] Miss Wordsworth, of Lady Margaret Hall. See Dyhouse, op. cit., p.73. The social prestige of marriage for women, much later on, is shown by the fact that at Anstey College in 1934, the only married woman on the staff went in to dinner ahead of the Principal! (Crunden, *History of Anstey College*, p.44). One cannot see that happening in Lansdowne Road; but then, Miss Squire of Anstey was much more conservative than Miss Stansfeld, whose student she had been.

[113] Some of her early students thought her very good looking and speculated on why she had not married. It was accepted that *fathers* were "taken" with her, and that a handsome father was an asset at the interview when applying for admission to the college. There are many stories of her tenderness and humour in regard to the First World War soldiers in Bedford. "One night, Stanny was coming up the road from '17' when one of the Scotsmen called out: 'Good night, dearie!' Immediately she retorted: 'You wouldn't say that if you saw me under the lamplight!' " *Report* (1975), p.30.

[114] Miss Stansfeld's services to her profession were acknowledged in 1939 by the award of the O.B.E. She was also the first Englishwoman to be presented with the Swedish *Grand-titre honorifique de la Fédération Inter-nationale de Gymnastique Ling*.

5 A Sacred Trust

[1] H. Crichton Miller, "The Emotional Development of Boys and Girls", *Journal of Scientific Physical Training*, XIII 1920–1), pp.49–51.

[2] The data that follows is based on information in the members' address lists in the reports of the Old Students' Association but may not be precisely

accurate; it is not always clear, for instance, whether a professional address relates to a school or to private practice.

[3] Phyllis Spafford was secretary of the Ling Association 1931–49. Phyllis Colson founded the C.C.R.P.T. in 1935 and was its secretary till 1963 (see n.87 below).

[4] Arabella Kenealy, *Feminism and Sex Extinction* (London, 1920), p.138.

[5] *The Lancet* (14 May 1921).

[6] Ibid. (21 May 1921).

[7] In 1890 a committee of academic women, with Mrs Henry Sidgwick as secretary, published *Health Statistics of Women Students of Cambridge and Oxford and their Sisters*.

[8] *The Lancet* (18 June 1921).

[9] Ibid. (29 Oct. 1921).

[10] *Journal of Scientific Physical Training*, vol. XIII (1920–1), p.59.

[11] Ibid., vol. XIV (1921–2), pp. 50–4.

[12] Loc. cit. Only sixty-three per cent of the gymnasts breast-fed for three months or more, as compared with seventy-five per cent Girton students and seventy-three per cent non-collegiates.

[13] In 1921, twenty-three per cent of the Bedford Old Students seem to have been married (the 1921 *Report* notes 71 married members in a total membership of 310). This compares with twenty-seven per cent gymnasts married in the Ling study. The study notes that the marriage rate is "still rising", and the Bedford *Report* for 1934 records thirty-five per cent Old Students married, regarding this percentage as "distinctly high". A breakdown of entries in the *Report* for 1980 shows fifty-seven per cent married.

[14] The birth announcements of Bedford Old Students for 1914–24 show 51 girls and 31 boys. This is a significant difference. (N.B. No *Report* for 1917 available) However, birth announcements in *Reports* 1914–80 show a slight surplus of males, as in the population generally.

[15] Angela Brazil, *The Nicest Girl in the School* (1910).

[16] LR 1981 Rhona Lewis (1932–5). It is interesting that Miss Stansfeld hardly appears in the photograph albums of the different Sets, and when she does, has always been "snapped" unawares.

[17] *The Times* (5 Jan. 1922), reporting discussion on "Schoolgirls and Games" at the conference of Educational Associations.

[18] Quoted in the *Daily Mail* (5 Jan. 1922).

[19] "It is hardly possible at present, to specify the usual age of retirement for gymnastic teachers, but when a woman becomes too old for regular school teaching she can organise, supervise and inspect, or continue to practise remedial work, which includes massage." Mary Hankinson, "The Teaching of Gymnastics", in Edith J. Morley ed., *Women Workers in Seven Professions* (1913).

[20] INT 1980 Barbara Fletcher (Bournemouth High School 1927–35).

[21] Ibid.

[22] Miss Moller, Principal of Lady Mabel College, reported in *The Leaflet*, vol. 54, no.1 (Jan.–Feb. 1953).

[23] LR 1981 Rhona Lewis (1932–5).

[24] INT 1981 Margaret Boyd (1932–5).

[25] Ibid.

[26] LR 1981 Holly Graham (1929–32).

[27] Ibid.

[28] Phyllis Colson, "College Tradition", in Report of Old Students' Day, Diamond Jubilee 1963.

[29] Holly Graham, op. cit.

[30] She is so described in Mary Price and Nonits Glenday, *Reluctant Revolutionaries* (1974), p.74. The point is taken up by Paul Atkinson, "Fitness, Feminism and Schooling", in Sara Delamont and Lorna Duffin eds., *The Nineteenth Century Woman* (1978).

[31] Principal of Gipsy Hill Training College, quoted in *Times Educational Supplement* (18 Oct. 1917), p.400. I am indebted to Alison Oram for drawing my attention to this.

[32] Phyllis Colson, "College Tradition", in Report of Old Students' Day, Diamond Jubilee 1963.

[33] Margaret Boyd, op. cit.

[34] INT 1980 Betty Donaldson (1930–3). The Old Students' *Report* for 1930–1 shows that roughly a tenth of those employed were teaching abroad, the largest single group in Africa.

[35] Holly Graham, op. cit.

[36] INT 1980 Eileen Alexander (Dartford-trained, Principal of Bedford 1952–71).

[37] Winifred Whiting, "Retrospect and a Point of View", *Physical Education* vol.48, no.144 (July 1956), pp.35–47.

[38] Quoted in *The Leaflet*, vol.63, no.7 (Aug.–Sept.1962). Mary Hankinson in *Women Workers in Seven Professions* (1913), gives £60–80 p.a. as the usual starting salary (resident) and £100–120 p.a. (non-resident).

[39] Clara Collet, *The Economic Position of Educated Working Women* (1890), gives £105–120 p.a. (non-resident) rising slowly to £140–150p.a. for the Cambridge women; for elementary teachers, see Asher Tropp, *The School Teachers* (1957), Appendix B.

[40] Collet, op. cit., pp.72-3.

[41] Ibid.

[42] *Journal of School Hygiene and Physical Education*, XV (1922–3), p.79.

[43] Mary Hankinson, op. cit. "The three Government inspectors start at £200 rising to £400 with first-class travelling expenses and the four women organisers employed by the London County Council Education Committee start at £175 rising . . . to £240 plus actual travelling expenses."

[44] *Journal of Scientific Physical Training*, vol. 1, no. 2 (Feb. 1909), p.28. Mary Hankinson, op. cit., draws attention to the fact that women have often to compete with men for the very few organisers' jobs "and even in cases where both men and women inspectors are employed . . . the men's salaries are considerably higher, despite the fact that most women give up professional work on marriage, either voluntarily or compulsorily, and have, therefore, a shorter time in which to recover the cost of their training, whereas if they do not marry, they have to make provision for old age and in many cases to contribute to the support of others besides themselves".

[45] *Ling Association Supplement* (April 1913).

[46] Ibid. (June 1913), p.29.

[47] Ibid.

[48] Österberg, "Physical Education", 1905, p.4 (C 6/5 Dartford College Archives).

[49] "Report of Annual Conference, July 1924", *The Leaflet* (Aug.–Sept. 1924).

[50] Minutes of Burnham Committee's Committee of Reference No.2 (Secondary and Technical Schools) 9 Oct. 1925. Public Record Office Ed. 108/24. For those trained gymnasts already in the schools the outlook was brighter since authorities had *power* to pay non-graduates on the graduate scale, and were asked to accept a lower standard than that laid down by the Burnham Committee when considering the claims of such teachers. They were also recommended to recognise as graduates teachers appointed before 1912 whose service had been meritorious. The Ling Association lost no time, naturally, in advising its members to press such claims. For a useful account of this tedious business see *Journal of Physical Education*, XLII (March 1950), pp.80–3.

[51] *The Leaflet* (Oct. 1930), pp. 67–9.

[52] Quoted in I.M. Webb, "Women's Physical Education in Great Britain 1800–1966", unpub. M.Ed. thesis (Leicester, 1967), pp. 332–3, n.86.

[53] Professor Winifred Cullis's report (Bedford College Archives) warmly approved the science teaching, declared the college "admirably organised" and the students provided with the opportunity to secure "a first-class all-round training".

[54] Memorandum, Bedford College Archive file labelled "Notes and Reports McNair Committee".

[55] LR 1981 Rhona Lewis (1932–5).

[56] LR 1981 Holly Graham (1929–32).

[57] "The hands and feet people" (domestic science and gym mistresses) were on the women's non-graduate scale. Over the period 1935–38, for teachers outside London this scale was £174–306 (annual increment £9). Women graduates got £216–384 (annual increment £12). Men's salaries at their maximum exceeded women's in the ratio 5:4. In 1931 *all* teachers suffered a ten per cent cut, which was restored in two stages, in 1934 and 1935.

[58] *Journal of School Hygiene and Physical Education*, XXII (1929–30), p.121.
[59] *The Leaflet*, (May 1927), prints this *cri-de-coeur* from a gym mistress:

> I read the Ling Leaflet and C.S.M.M.G.
> And my word, I pity the poor modern "she"!
> Why not put on trousers, and say you're a "he",
> And do half the work for much more L.S.D.!
> You're wanted to housekeep, and wanted to nurse,
> And wanted to manage accounts and the purse,
> A Protestant needed and not an R.C.!
> Give Gym and give Massage, and also R.E.,
> Teach swimming and dancing, and hygiene and "Guides",
> Subsidiary subjects and form work besides!
> And take supervision, and march the girls out,
> And play games and coach them – there won't be a doubt
> That none will reach sixty, nor yet forty-five,
> Without being, surely, more dead than alive!

[60] Phyllis Colson (1923–6); see n.28 above.
[61] INT 1981 Margaret Boyd (1932–5).
[62] LR 1981 Holly Graham (1929–32).
[63] LR 1981 Rhona Lewis (1932–5).
[64] Phyllis Colson, op. cit.
[65] *Journal of School Hygiene and Physical Education*, XV (1922–3), p.81.
[66] *The Leaflet* (Nov. 1931), p.92.
[67] INT 1980 Elizabeth Swallow (1936–9).
[68] Quoted by May Fountain, Principal of Chelsea College of Physical Education in foreword to first English edition of Elli Björkstén, *Principles of Gymnastics for Women and Girls: Part I* (1937).
[69] *Journal of Scientific Physical Training*, XIII (1920–1), p.27.
[70] *Report* (1920–1), p.10.
[71] *Journal of Scientific Physical Training*, XIII (1920–1), p.27.
[72] See ch.3.
[73] Elli Björkstén, *Principles of Gymnastics for Women and Girls: Part I* (1937), pp.15–16.
[74] *The Leaflet* (Aug.–Sept. 1924).
[75] *Journal of School Hygiene and Physical Education*, XVI (1923–4), p.67.
[76] Ibid., p.152.
[77] Ibid., p.69.
[78] *The Leaflet*, (Nov. 1927), p.70.
[79] *Journal of School Hygiene and Physical Education*, XXII (1929–30), p.46.
[80] *Journal of Physical Education*, XLII (Mar. 1950), p.87.
[81] *Journal of School Hygiene and Physical Education*, vol. XXII (1929–30), pp.113–121.

[82] Quoted in May, *Madame Bergman-Österberg*, p.53.

[83] See I.M. Webb, "Women's Physical Education in Great Britain 1800–1965", unpub. M.Ed. thesis (Leicester, 1967), p.355.

[84] Board of Education, *Recreation and Physical Fitness for Girls and Women* (1937), p.9.

[85] *Journal of Physical Education and School Hygiene*, XXX (1938), pp.41–2.

[86] Ibid., pp.99–105.

[87] Quoted from the Duke of Edinburgh's foreword to H. Justin Evans, *Service to Sport: The Story of the CCPR – 1935 to 1972* pub. by the Sports Council, 1974. See especially chs. 2,10,11 and 12 for an account of the work of Phyllis Colson (1904–1973). Having trained at Bedford (1923–6), and taught in girls' secondary schools until 1930, she worked as assistant to Phyllis Spafford, organising physical education for the National Council of Girls' Clubs. Struck by the recreational needs of young people at a time when the vast majority of children left school at fourteen, she hit on the idea of creating a body to co-ordinate the efforts of the many sports groups, youth organisations, educational authorities, industrial firms and individuals willing and able to provide facilities. The Central Council of Recreative Physical Training, which at once attracted interest and distinguished patronage, was the result, and Phyllis Colson was its general secretary till her retirement in 1963.

[88] *Bedfordshire Times and Independent* (10 July 1936).

6 Change of Direction

[1] INT 1980 Veronica Tyndale-Biscoe (1940–3).

[2] INT 1980 Erica Bache (1943–6).

[3] Rudolf Laban, *Modern Educational Dance* (London, 1948), p.6.

[4] *Report* (1975), p.27.

[5] INT 1980 Freda Colwill (1913–15).

[6] Though colleges had their own idiosyncrasies. See Colin Crunden, *A History of Anstey College* (1974), pp.19–20 for an account of Aesthetic Dancing there in the early twentieth century.

[7] Colwill, op. cit.

[8] Laban, op. cit., p.5.

[9] LR 1980 V. Hayman (1937–40).

[10] Ruby Ginner, *The Revived Greek Dance* (1933), p.145. An early Bedford student, Effie Williams, assisted Ginner in building her technique.

[11] I.M. Webb, "Women's Physical Education in Great Britain 1880–1965", unpub. M.Ed. thesis (Leicester, 1967), p.137.

[12] John Foster, *The Influences of Rudolf Laban* (1977), p.16.

[13] I am indebted for this recollection to Nan Hill.

[14] *Journal of School Hygiene and Physical Education*, vol. XVI (1924), p.139.

¹⁵ Ibid., vol. XXIV (1931–2), p.131.

¹⁶ INT 1980 Joan Goodrich (1922–5).

¹⁷ Ibid.

¹⁸ INT 1980 Elizabeth Swallow (1936–9).

¹⁹ INT 1980 Diana Gamble (1938–41).

²⁰ Swallow, op. cit.

²¹ Ibid.

²² Gamble, op. cit.

²³ Swallow, op. cit.

²⁴ Laban, *Modern Educational Dance*, p.11. The experience of pupils at Queen Elizabeth's Girls' Grammar School, Mansfield, is recalled by the present writer and others.

²⁵ Swallow, op. cit.

²⁶ See, for instance, Sylvia Bodmer, "Group Dancing", *Journal of Physical Education*, XXXV, no.106.

²⁷ *The Dance as Education* (1938). Diana Jordan does not acknowledge Laban's influence in this book but pays tribute to it in *Childhood and Movement* (1966).

²⁸ Foster, op. cit., p.31.

²⁹ *The Leaflet* (June 1941), pp.80–3.

³⁰ *The Times* (3 July 1958).

³¹ *The Times* (8 July 1958).

³² Gordon Curl, "A critical study of Rudolph von Laban's theory and practice of movement", unpub. M.Ed. thesis (Leicester, 1967), quoted in Foster, op. cit., p.126.

³³ Laban, *Modern Educational Dance*, p.6.

³⁴ Ibid., p.6.

³⁵ Ginner, op. cit., pp.18–19.

³⁶ INT 1980 Veronica Tyndale-Biscoe (1940–3), who came back on the Bedford Staff 1947–9, after training at the Art of Movement Studio, but eventually made her main career in the field of movement for mentally handicapped children. As Veronica Sherborne she has published, and made films, on this subject. She is at present Senior Lecturer in the School of Special Education at Bristol Polytechnic. See also n.1, above, and ch.8.

³⁷ Unsigned RS (1938–41).

³⁸ INT 1980 I. Nowell-Smith (Dartford Staff 1940–7, Bedford Staff 1948–70).

³⁹ LR Joan Gibson (1938–41).

⁴⁰ Ibid.

⁴¹ LR Betty Alliston (1943–6).

⁴² LR Joan Carrington (1943–6).

⁴³ Alliston, op. cit.,

⁴⁴ Letter from Stansfeld to Mary Feaver (3 Aug. 1949).

[45] INT 1980 Rena Stratford (1925–8).

[46] *Report* (1944), p.4.

[47] INT 1980 Pat Frith (1943–6).

[48] INT 1980 Jean Lindsay (1927–30).

[49] INT 1980 Marjorie Fletcher (1938–9).

[50] Nowell-Smith, op. cit.

[51] *Report* (1949), p.11.

[52] Ibid., p.5.

[53] INT 1980 Holly Graham (1929–32).

[54] Tyndale-Biscoe, op. cit.

[55] LR Joan Stevenson (1946–9).

[56] Ibid.

[57] Lindsay, op. cit.

[58] Student Council Minutes (14 Mar. 1946). She accepted proposals relating to the organisation of games and to the provision of college notepaper; she rejected proposals that Sunday breakfast should be voluntary and that third year students should be allowed to sign out for week-end leave.

[59] Student Council Minutes (28 Oct.1946).

[60] Stevenson, op. cit.

[61] INT 1980 Mary Feaver (1930–3).

[62] INT 1980 Elizabeth Swallow (1936–9).

[63] Stevenson, op. cit.

[64] Quoted in I.M. Webb, op. cit., p.374. Ruth Morison had attended Laban's classes in Manchester. Liverpool students under her direction first demonstrated modern educational gymnastics at the Ling Conference in 1947.

[65] INT 1980 Elizabeth Swallow (1936–9).

[66] Tyndale-Biscoe, op. cit.

[67] Stevenson, op. cit.

[68] *Report* (1948), pp.13–14.

[69] Swallow, op. cit.

[70] Nowell-Smith. op. cit.

[71] Miss Read's most distinguished professional achievement had been to devise and conduct the women's gymnastics' demonstration at the Festival of Youth in Wembley Stadium in 1937. 350 students from Anstey, Bedford, Chelsea and Dartford took part.

[72] Freda Young, "First Memorial Lecture" (10 March 1953).

[73] Graham, op. cit.

[74] INT 1977 Phyllis Spafford (1908–1910).

[75] "An appreciation of Miss Stansfeld by Miss Helen Drummond M.A., Principal of Dunfermline College of Physical Education", *Report* (1951).

7 *Almost a Revolution*

1 *The Leaflet*, vol.61, no.5 (June 1960), p.34.
2 Ibid., vol.39, no.5 (May 1940), reporting Kenneth Lindsay, Parliamentary Secretary to the Board of Education speaking on "The Service of Youth" at L.P.E.A. Easter holiday course.
3 McNair reckoned the fees (£150 p.a. at Chelsea and £165 p.a. at Dartford) were about £100 p.a. higher than those at the general training colleges.
4 "The Training of Teachers of Physical Education", submitted to the McNair Committee by the Association of Principals of Colleges of Physical Education, and circulated as Paper 22.
5 Ibid. (See also the paper in the Bedford College Archives headed "Notes of the Association of Principals etc.")
6 Ibid.
7 For the account which follows see Bedford Old Students' Association, *Jubilee Report* (1953), pp.12–19.
8 The account which follows is based on an interview with Eileen Alexander in 1980.
9 *Moving and Growing* (1952), p.60.
10 Ibid., p.61.
11 *Report* (1926–7), p.30.
12 *Jubilee Report*, (1953), p.16.
13 Phyllis Colson, Diamond Jubilee Address 1963, p.9.
14 INT 1980 Eileen Alexander.
15 The McNair Committee had recommended that the p.e. colleges should be grant-aided. Anstey stood out till 1955 and was the last to lose its independence; see also n.17 below.
16 B.P.T.C. Ltd., minutes (21 Mar., 29 May, 24 July and 2 Oct. 1950).
17 Dartford became a direct-grant college in 1951. It was taken over by the L.C.C. in 1961.
18 B.P.T.C. Ltd., minutes (6 Jan. 1951).
19 Ibid., (13 June 1951).
20 Ibid., (16 Oct. 1951).
21 *Report* (1952), p.12.
22 *The Leaflet* (Aug.–Sept. 1956), p.37.
23 Ibid.
24 INT 1980 I. Nowell-Smith (Staff 1949–70).
25 John Lawson and Harold Silver, *A Social History of Education in England* (1973), p.428. The figures are for England and Wales.
26 Ministry of Education, *Education in 1958*, p.78.
27 National Advisory Council on the Training and Supply of Teachers, *Report*, (1960), p.1.
28 Ibid., p.5.

[29] National Advisory Council, *Report* (1958), p.9.

[30] Ministry of Education, *Education on 1958*, p.81, *Education in 1959*, p.58. Out of an extra 675 places, 515 were to be supplied by p.e. "wings" attached to the following women's colleges: Avery Hill, Bishop Lonsdale, Bishop Otter, Coventry, Endsleigh, Barry, Neville's Cross, and St Mary's Cheltenham. A "wing" was also established at one specialist college, I.M. Marsh. Entry to the courses was to be thirty students annually. "Wings" were also established at various men's colleges.

[31] Eileen Alexander to L.E.A., 5 Nov. 1958. She had discussed this with Ruth Foster H.M.I. the previous October. (An arrangement of the kind she proposed was in fact accepted for I.M. Marsh.)

[32] Ministry to L.E.A., 12 Feb. 1959.

[33] Eileen Alexander to L.E.A., 13 Apr. 1959.

[34] See the account by Ruth Foster H.M.I., *The Leaflet*, vol. 61, no.5 (June 1960), p.34.

[35] *The Leaflet*, vol.61, no.6 (July 1960), p.39. Considering women alone, the choice would now be: p.e. as main subject at a general training college, with possibility of specialised one year supplementary course to follow; three-year course at specialist college; three-year "wing" course at general college, which would cover another teaching subject as well as p.e.

[36] Ibid., my italics.

[37] Hansard, *Parliamentary Debates*, vol.605, no.109, col.529–530 (7 May 1959).

[38] *Report* (1960), p.5. The details for subsequent years, which follow, come from accounts in the *Reports* for those years.

[39] Ministry of Education, *Education in 1967*, p.62.

[40] Ministry of Education, *Education in 1969*, p.61.

[41] INT 1980 Eileen Alexander.

[42] *Report* (1967), p.13.

[43] INT 1982 Margaret Hesketh (education lecturer, 1952–76).

[44] *The Leaflet*, vol.58, no.9 (Nov. 1957), p.61.

[45] *Ling Association Supplement* (April 1901). Her statement "Flat feet, again, are natural to some races i.e. Negroes and Jews" reads oddly today.

[46] The "Posture Recorder" had been invented by Reginald Roper.

[47] INT 1980 Molly Tod (1923–6), who taught remedials at Bedford from 1934. The clinic was phased out in 1964, and remedial teaching in 1967, the year Molly Tod retired.

[48] Phyllis Colson, Diamond Jubilee Address 1963, p.9.

[49] See ch.5, n.87, above.

[50] The general colleges were: Balls Park, Bedford (formerly Froebel), Hockerill, Homerton, Keswick Hall, Putteridgebury, Saffron Walden, St Osyth, and Wall Hall.

[51] *The Leaflet*, vol.66, no.2 (March 1965), p.14.

[52] The problem of satisfying the *residence* qualifications for an internal Cambridge degree was got round by allowing students who had completed the three-year Certificate course (to a high standard) in their own colleges, to spend the fourth year at Cambridge. They were given B.A. status, and took a B.Ed. course taught jointly by lecturers from the University and from their own colleges.

[53] *Report* (1968), p.8.

[54] *Report* (1969), p.10.

[55] LR 1982 Eileen Alexander, who feels that the case was not pre-judged against physical education at Cambridge as it was in some universities. Concern for the likely calibre of students was, she thinks, assuaged by the fact that Bedford students had for some years attended anatomy lectures at Cambridge. In 1972, two of the three "Firsts" in the Cambridge B.Ed. went to Bedford students.

[56] Miss Alexander used this phrase in her retirement speech, *Report* (1971), p.11.

[57] Tributes to Holly Graham (retired 1971) and Molly Tod (retired 1967).

[58] In 1951 there were ten full-time staff, apart from the Principal. In 1971, there were more than forty.

[59] *Report* (1963), p.29.

[60] INT 1980 I. Nowell-Smith (Bedford Staff 1949–70).

[61] INT 1980 Molly Tod (1923–6, Bedford Staff 1934–67).

[62] Saturday morning teaching was discontinued in 1966.

[63] Report of the Study Group on "The Government of Colleges of Education" (1966), p.130.

[64] Ibid., p.132.

[65] INT 1980 Holly Graham (1929–32, Staff 1947–71).

[66] The students argued that the extra ten minutes in the middle of the day could be spent more profitably *after* lunch; that the "following" system was breaking down; that it would be a treat to be able to "lie in" on the one day when it was possible to do so.

[67] The staff were prepared to try one o'clock lunch but warned that if "the dignity of the dining room" was disturbed by latecomers, the experiment would cease. "Following" at dinner only was accepted, but with the reminder that "it is important that the dining room should be a social place and that everyone should make an effort to make 'following' successful". The Principal was unwilling to consider voluntary attendance at Sunday breakfast.

[68] Student Council minutes (17 Nov. 1959).

[69] RS 1978 Beryl Dray (1960–3).

[70] Student Council Minutes (24 May 1955).

[71] Ibid., (5 Nov. 1958). In 1960, "the new M 1 bus", arriving from London at 9.44 p.m. provided a lever, but the staff responded that late leave called for

a special reason; "this did not include a few extra hours at home". Later that year a battery of reasons (times of church services and television plays, of transport from Oxford, Cambridge, London and the North) was advanced, but without success.

[72] Ibid., (24 Feb. 1961).
[73] Ibid., (29 Nov. 1951).
[74] *Report* (1955), p.12.
[75] Student Council Minutes (3 July 1956).
[76] The story is that, on one occasion, N.U.S. representatives, arriving at the college to seek strike support from Bedford students (who were then absent on teaching practice) were more or less seen off by the Principal.
[77] Report of the Study Group on "The Government of Colleges of Education" (1966), p.31.
[78] LR 1981 Margot Jefferis (English tutor 1964–8).
[79] *Report* (1970), p.10.
[80] Ibid., (1972), p.19.
[81] Ibid., (1970), p.25.
[82] Shuttleworth College of Agriculture and Silsoe College of Agricultural Engineering.
[83] *Report* (1971), p.24.
[84] Ibid., (1971), p.10.

8 *Questions of Identity*

[1] *Journal of Physical Education*, vol.55, no.104 (Mar. 1963), p.15.
[2] *The Leaflet*, vol. 66, no.2 (Mar. 1965), p.15.
[3] A.D. Munrow, *Physical Education* (1972), p.158. The London University B.Ed. had alternative syllabuses, A and B. Syllabus A, which was general in character, was chosen by most men and some women; syllabus B, which was dance-oriented, was chosen almost exclusively by women.
[4] See ch.2.
[5] See McIntosh, *Physical Education in England since 1800, passim*, for Grenfell, Roper and Coote. See *Nine Pioneers in Physical Education* (1964), for Grenfell and Roper. See chs. 3 and 5 for references to early, ephemeral efforts to provide specialist training for men.
[6] The work at Mill Hill and Queen Elizabeth's Barnet is described in appendixes to McIntosh, op. cit.
[7] Report of Chief Medical Officer, Board of Education (1918), p.164.
[8] The work of Henry Cole, who was responsible for the Sheffield course, is described in *Nine Pioneers in Physical Education*.
[9] *Journal of School Hygiene and Physical Education*, XXIV (1931–2), pp. 76–8.
[10] Report of Chief Medical Officer, Board of Education (1931), p.82.
[11] *The Leaflet*, vol.57, no.10 (Dec. 1956), p.60.

[12] Vivian Lewis (trained at Anstey 1938–41) recalls the shock of moving from independent schools to a "tough" secondary modern in the 1950s. "There was just no tradition; the hall was just used as a place where they had assembly and things like that; certainly not any gymnastics or dancing."

[13] Marjorie Randall, *Basic Movement* (1961), p.12.

[14] See ch.6.

[15] Ruth Morison, *Educational Gymnastics* (1956), p.3.

[16] Ibid., p.4.

[17] *Physical Education*, vol.48, no.144 (July 1956), p.39.

[18] Morison, op. cit., p.7.

[19] *Report* (1952), pp.12–15.

[20] *The Leaflet*, vol.58, no.7 (Aug.–Sept. 1957), p.48. (Account by Holly Graham.)

[21] Ibid., vol.55, no.6 (July 1954).

[22] Ibid., vol.57, no.1 (Jan.–Feb. 1956), pp.2–3.

[23] Ibid., vol.66, no.2 (Mar. 1965), p.15.

[24] See ch.6.

[25] R.S. Harper, Director, Department of Physical Education, Manchester University, reported in the *British Association for the Advancement of Science*, vol. XIV, no.64 (Mar. 1960), p.413.

[26] Circuit training was developed at Leeds by G.T. Adamson and R.E. Morgan and promoted in their book, *Circuit Training* (1957).

[27] *The Leaflet*, vol.56, no.7 (Aug.–Sept. 1955), p.7.

[28] INT 1982 Jake Downey.

[29] John Foster, *The Influences of Rudolph Laban* (1977), p.75.

[30] Downey, op. cit. David Best, *Philosophy and Human Movement* (1978), p.36, comments, "Talking to followers of Laban often reminds one of talking to doctrinaire Marxists, Freudians and extreme fundamentalist religious believers. It seems to be taken as axiomatic that the Great Man could say no wrong – any errors or self-contradictions are hastily attributed to his followers' faulty interpretations."

[31] Rudolf Laban, "The Work of the Art of Movement Studio", *J.P.E.*, XLVI, no.137, (Mar. 1954), pp.23–30.

[32] Sylvia Bodmer, "Group Dancing", *J.P.E.*, XXXV, no.106 (1943), p.135.

[33] "Student opinion on Modern Educational Dance", *The Leaflet*, vol.69, no.8 (1968), p.71.

[34] Hilary Corlett (ex-Bedford), in *B.J.P.E.*, vol.1, no.2 (Mar. 1970), p.37.

[35] *Studio 25* (1971), p.57. (Celebrating the twenty-fifth anniversary of the Art of Movement Studio.) And see ch.6, n.36 above.

[36] A.D. Munrow, "Looking Back and looking forward in Gymnastics", *J.P.E.* vol.48, no.143 (Mar. 1956), p.21.

[37] A.D. Munrow, *Pure and Applied Gymnastics* (1955), p.242.

[38] *The Leaflet*, vol.53, no.5 (June 1952), p.73.

[39] "Some colleges have gone further than others . . . and would show you how the elements of Time, Space, Weight and Flow, which you have already seen applied to gymnastics and dancing could be equally effectively used in teaching water skills, diving and lacrosse." C.M. Webster, "The Training of the Woman Teacher of Physical Education", *J.P.E.*, vol.50, no.151. (Nov.1958), p.86. Dartford was one such college.

[40] Munrow, *Pure and Applied Gymnastics*, p.195.

[41] INT 1982 Christine Heath (1951–4).

[42] Marjorie Randall, "The Movement Approach – A Need for clarification", *J.P.E.*, vol.48, no.1, (Mar. 1956), p.16.

[43] *Basic Movement* (1961), p.84.

[44] Ibid., p.85.

[45] Ibid., pp.76–7.

[46] J. Myrle James, "Sacred Cows", *The Leaflet*, vol.69, no.12 (Dec. 1968), pp.86–7.

[47] B. Fryer, "Sacred Bull", *The Leaflet*, vol.70, no.1 (Jan.–Feb. 1969), p.34.

[48] See A.D. Munrow, *Physical Education* (1972). For evidence of men's interest in the sixties, see, e.g. G.S. Aaron, "Gymnastics and/or Functional Movement for Boys", *Physical Education Year Book* (1963); Robert Harrold, "Dance and the Educational Pattern", *The Leaflet* (July 1964).

[49] Hilary Corlett, "Modern Educational Gymnastics Today" Part Two. *B.J.P.E.*, vol.1, no.3 (May 1970), p.63.

[50] J. Myrle James (author of "Sacred Cows"), *B.J.P.E.*, vol.2, no.1 (Jan. 1971), p.9.

[51] H.C. Dent, *The Training of Teachers in England and Wales* (1977), title of ch.24.

[52] *Education: A Framework for Expansion* (1972), p.44.

[53] *Report* (1972), p.10.

[54] See David Hencke, *Colleges in Crisis* (London, 1978).

[55] Hencke, op. cit., p.61.

[56] 24 Apr. 1974, to Chief Education Officer.

[57] Bedfordshire's problem was exacerbated by the fact that local government reorganisation had brought Luton into the county, with Putteridge Bury College of Education. In the end, after a north/south conflict, it was decided to locate the whole "ration" of teacher training places in the north (Bedford) and to close the teacher training college in the south (Putteridge Bury).

[58] Chief Education Officer to Department of Education and Science, 2 June 1975.

[59] In 1975 there were 450 places at Bedford College of Physical Education and 660 at Bedford College of Education.

[60] *Report* (1973), p.9.

[61] *Report* (1974), p.13.

[62] The Mander site has the Schools of Engineering, Building, Business Studies, Science and Maths, Social Service Studies. The Polhill site has the Schools of Education and Humanities. The Lansdowne site has the School of Art, Drama, Music, and the School of Human Movement Studies.

[63] INT 1982 current students (Sarah Braithwaite, Jenny Furlong, Jane High, Janet Schofield), and Marion Wall (administrative secretary, Students' Union).

[64] Ibid.

[65] INT 1982 Sylvia Worthington (Head of School of Art, Music and Drama 1976–1980).

[66] *Report* (1951), p.5.

[67] *The Leaflet*, vol. 56, no.1 (Jan.–Feb. 1955), p.3.

[68] Ibid., vol.69, no.1 (Jan.–Feb. 1968), p.3.

[69] *British Association for the Advancement of Science*, vol. XIV, no.64, (Mar. 1960), p.412.

[70] *The Leaflet*, vol.66, no.9 (Nov. 1965).

[71] Ibid., vol.66, no.10 (Dec. 1965),

[72] Ibid., vol. 67, no. 1 (Jan.–Feb. 1966).

[73] Hubert D. Fairclough, lecturer in Physical Education, University of Exeter, "Physical Education and the Robbins Report", *The Leaflet*, vol.66, no.2 (Mar. 1965), p.15.

[74] A.W. Sedgwick "Physical Education in the University", *J.P.E.*, vol.55, no.104 (Mar. 1963), pp.13–15.

[75] *The Leaflet*, vol.66, no.1(Jan.-Feb. 1965), p.5

[76] M.G. Mason and A.G.L. Ventre, *Elements of Physical Education: Philosophical Aspects* (1965).

[77] See, for instance, R. Carlisle, "The Concept of Physical Education" and Mollie Adams, "The Concept of Physical Education II", in *Proceedings of the Annual Conference of the Philosophy of Education Society of Great Britain*, (Jan. 1969).

[78] B.W. Jelfs, "Thinking about the Meaning of Physical Education", *B.J.P.E.*, vol.1, no.6 (Nov. 1970).

[79] Peter Renshaw, "Physical Education, the Need for Philosophical Clarification", *Education for Teaching* (Spring 1972).

[80] B.W. Jelfs, quoted in Renshaw, op. cit.

[81] Margaret Talbot, "Letters to the Editor", *B.J.P.E.*, vol.2, no.6 (Nov. 1971).

[82] Ibid.

[83] Quoted in Renshaw, op. cit.

[84] Talbot, op. cit.

[85] INT 1982 Jake Downey.

[86] *B.J.P.E.*, vol.3, no.3 (May 1972), p.37.

[87] *The Leaflet*, vol.68, no.5 (June 1967), p.36.

88 A.D. Munrow, *Physical Education* (1972), p.205. He cited such statements as "only through notation can movement be made academically respectable in work at the B.Ed. level".
89 Stanley Hewett, "Physical Education and the James Report", *B.J.P.E..*, vol.3, no.3, (May 1972).
90 *Report* (1978), p.8.
91 *Report* (1980), p.7.
92 The introduction to the 1978 submission refers to the work of David Best, Gordon Curl, Peter Renshaw and John Whiting.
93 LR 1982 Margaret Rosewarne-Jenkins.

Conclusion

1 Pauline Marks, "Femininity in the Classroom", in Juliet Mitchell and Ann Oakley eds., *The Rights and Wrongs of Women* (1976), p.188.
2 Dale Spender, *Invisible Women* (1982), p.1.
3 Anna Coote and Beatrix Campbell, *Sweet Freedom* (1982), p.184.
4 INT 1980 Freda Colwill (1913–15).
5 INT 1982 Irene Fardon (1940–3). Men were appointed as heads of human movement studies at Nonington and Lady Mabel in 1974, at Anstey and I.M. Marsh in 1975 and at Dartford in 1976. At present (1983) women are still in charge at Bedford, Chelsea and Dunfermline.
6 Fardon, op. cit.

Select Bibliography

Archive Material

The records of the former Bedford Physical Training College (at Bedford College of Higher Education) were consulted for this book, which also draws substantially on taped interviews with former students of the College. Papers relating to Madame Bergman-Österberg (including her own articles, "Physical Education", "Physical Training as a Profession", "The Training of Teachers in Methods of Physical Education" and "The Physical Education of Girls in England") were consulted in the library of the former Dartford Physical Training College, at Thames Polytechnic.

Books of Particular Interest

The Art of Movement Studio. *Studio 25*, 1971.

Bedford Physical Training College. *Margaret Stansfeld*. Privately printed, 1953.

Björkstén, E. *Principles of Gymnastics for Women and Girls: Part I*. English translation pub. J.&A. Churchill, 1937.

Boyd, M. *Lacrosse*. Kaye & Ward, 1969.

Caroll, J. and Lofthouse, P. *Creative Dance for Boys* Macdonald & Evans, 1969.

Crunden, C. *A History of Anstey College of Physical Education 1897–1972*. Anstey College, 1974.

Foster, J. *The influences of Rudolf Laban*. Lepus Books, 1977.

Ginner, R. *The Revived Greek Dance*. Methuen, 1933.

Godber, J. and Hutchins, I. *A Century of Challenge: Bedford High School 1882–1982*. Bedford High School, 1982.

James, J. Myrle, *Education and Physical Education*. G. Bell, 1967.

Laban, R. *Modern Educational Dance*. Macdonald & Evans, 1948.

Laban, R. *The Mastery of Movement*. Macdonald & Evans, 1950.

London County Council. *Educational Gymnastics* L.C.C., 1962.

McIntosh, P. *et al. Landmarks in the History of Physical Education*. RKP, 1957.

McIntosh, P. *Physical Education in England since 1800*. G. Bell, 1968.

McIntosh, P. *Sport in Society*. Watts, 1963.

Mason, M.C. & Ventre, A.G.L. *Elements of Physical Education: Philosophical Aspects*. Thistle Books, 1965.

May, J. *Madame Bergman-Österberg*. George Harrap, 1969,

Morison, R. *Educational Gymnastics*. I.M. Marsh College, 1956.

Select Bibliography

Morison, R. *A Movement Approach to Educational Gymnastics*. Dent, 1969.

Morgan, R.E. & Adamson, G.T. *Circuit Training*. G. Bell, 1957.

Munrow, A. *Physical Education*. G. Bell, 1972.

Munrow, A. *Pure and Applied Gymnastics*. Edward Arnold, 1955.

North, M. *Introduction to movement study and teaching*. Macdonald & Evans, 1971.

Physical Education Association. *Nine Pioneers in Physical Education*. Physical Education Association, 1964.

Pollard, M. *Fifty Years of Women's Hockey*. All England Women's Hockey Association, 1946.

Posse, N. *The Special Kinesiology of Educational Gymnastics*. Lee & Shepard, Boston, 1903.

Preston-Dunlop, V. *A Handbook for Dance in Education*. Macdonald & Evans, 1980.

Randall, M. *Basic Movement*. G. Bell, 1961.

Russell, J. *Creative Dance in the Primary School*. Macdonald & Evans, 1965.

Russell, J. *Creative Dance in the Secondary School*. Macdonald & Evans, 1969.

Smart, R. *Bedford Training College 1882–1982: A History of a Froebel College and its Schools*. Bedford Training College Publication Committee, 1982.

Smith, W.D. *Stretching their bodies: the history of physical education*. David & Charles, 1974.

Tey, J. *Miss Pym Disposes* Penguin, 1957.

Thornton, S. *A Movement Perspective of Rudolf Laban*. Macdonald & Evans, 1971.

Books of General Interest

Beale, D. *et al. Work and Play in Girls' Schools* Longman, 1898.

Burstall, S. *English High Schools for Girls*, Longman, 1907.

Burstyn, J. *Victorian Education and the Ideal of Womanhood*. Croom Helm, 1980.

Delamont, S. and Duffin, L. *The Nineteenth Century Woman : Her Cultural and Physical World*. Croom Helm, 1978. (See especially ch. 4, "Fitness, Feminism and Schooling", by Paul Atkinson.)

Dent, H.C. *The Training of Teachers in England and Wales*, Hodder & Stoughton, 1977.

Dyhouse, C. *Girls Growing Up in Late Victorian and Edwardian England*. RKP, 1981.

Gosden, P. *The Evolution of a Profession*. OUP, 1972.

Haddon, C. *Great Days and Jolly Days: the story of girls' school songs*. Hodder & Stoughton, 1977.

Hencke, D. *Colleges in Crisis*. Penguin, 1980.

Kenealy, A. *Feminism and Sex Extinction*, T.F. Unwin, 1920.

Morley, E.J., ed. *Women Workers in Seven Professions*, R.K.P., 1913.
Partington, G. *Women Teachers in the Twentieth Century*. NFER, 1976.

Journals

The major source is the journal of the Ling (Physical Education) Association,
  which changed its title many times over the period:

1908 – 1922	*Journal of Scientific Physical Training*
1923 – 1932	*Journal of School Hygiene and Physical Education*
1933 – 1944	*Journal of Physical Education and School Hygiene*
1944 – 1954	*Journal of Physical Education*
1955 – 1970	*Physical Education*
1970 –	*British Journal of Physical Education*

See also the Ling Association's monthly *Leaflet* (1904-1970), its *Annual
Reports* and the *Physical Education Year Book*. From time to time this
professional literature carries useful historical articles, such as D.D.
Molyneux, "Early Excursions by Birmingham Women into Games and
Sports", *Physical Education* (July 1959) or Bryn Lloyd Jones, "A Century of
Physical Education in our State Schools", *Physical Education Year Book*
(1973–4).

Official Publications

Special Reports on Educational Subjects, vol. 2, HMSO, 1898
Annual Reports of the Chief Medical Officer of the Board of Education,
  HMSO. (After 1922 these were published under the title "The Health of
  the School Child".)
Board of Education. *Syllabus of Physical Training for Schools*. HMSO, 1933.
Ministry of Education. *Moving and Growing. HMSO*, 1952.
Ministry of Education. *Planning the Programme*. HMSO, 1953.
Teachers and Youth leaders (McNair Report). HMSO, 1944.
Reports 1949–60 of the National Advisory Council on the Training and
  Supply of Teachers. HMSO.
Report of the Committee on Higher Education (Robbins Report). Cmnd.
  2154, HMSO, 1963.
Report of the Study Group on the Government of Colleges of Education
  (Weaver Report). HMSO, 1966.
Teacher Education and Training (James Report). HMSO, 1972.
Education: A Framework for Expansion. Cmnd. 5174, HMSO, 1972.

Unpublished Theses

Pauline C. Bell.   "A History of Physical Education in Girls' Public Schools 1870–1920, with particular reference to the influence of Christianity". Manchester M.Ed. 1978.

Margaret Claydon.   "How Strong the Girls Grow". London M.Sc., 1982.

Jeanette Ferrier.   "The Development of Physical Education Training for Women with particular reference to the Bedford College of Physical Education". Special study submitted in the Cambridge Certificate of Education course, Bedford College, 1965.

J.S. Pederson.   "The Reform of Women's Secondary and Higher Education in Nineteenth-Century England: A Study in Elite Groups". Berkeley, California D. Phil, 1974.

Janet Schofield.   "A history of Bedford College of Physical Education 1903–1981, with particular reference to the Human Movement Studies course". Dissertation submitted in the B.Ed. degree course, Bedford College of Higher Education, 1981.

I.M. Webb.   "Women's Physical Education in Great Britain 1800–1965". Leicester M.Ed., 1967.

I.M. Webb.   "The History of Chelsea College of Physical Education". Leicester Ph.D. 1977.

Index

Index